# BARACK OBAMA AND THE NEW AMERICA

# BARACK OBAMA AND THE NEW AMERICA

## The 2012 Election and the Changing Face of Politics

*Edited by Larry J. Sabato*

ROWMAN & LITTLEFIELD PUBLISHERS, INC.
*Lanham • Boulder • New York • Toronto • Plymouth, UK*

Published by Rowman & Littlefield Publishers, Inc.
A wholly owned subsidary of The Rowman & Littlefield Publishing Group, Inc.
4501 Forbes Boulevard, Suite 200, Lanham, Maryland 20706
www.rowman.com

10 Thornbury Road, Plymouth PL6 7PP, United Kingdom

British Library Cataloguing in Publication Information Available

**Library of Congress Cataloging-in-Publication Data**

Barack Obama and the new America : the 2012 election and the changing face
of politics / edited by Larry J. Sabato.
    pages cm
  ISBN 978-1-4422-2263-2 (cloth : alk. paper)—ISBN 978-1-4422-2264-9
(pbk. : alk. paper)—ISBN 978-1-4422-2265-6 (electronic)
  1. Presidents—United States—Election—2012. 2. Obama, Barack.
3. Political planning—United States. 4. United States—Politics and
government. I. Sabato, Larry.
JK5262012 .B37 2012
324.973'0932—dc23                                                    2012050783

∞™ The paper used in this publication meets the minimum requirements of
American National Standard for Information Sciences—Permanence of Paper for
Printed Library Materials, ANSI/NISO Z39.48-1992.

Printed in the United States of America

# CONTENTS

# PREFACE

Think back over the past twenty years. Americans have endured three recessions, the last one being the worst since the Great Depression; the devastating, life-changing attacks on September 11, 2001; two major wars in Afghanistan and Iraq, the former having become the longest conflict in U.S. history; and many disturbing acts of domestic terrorism, from the Oklahoma City bombing to mass killings at high schools, colleges, churches, theaters, and even a congressional town meeting. The national debt has grown massive and our spending obligations are crushing, yet the gap between rich and poor has grown, and the future for the nation's middle class as well as young people seeking educational and employment opportunities appears dimmer.

Yet the country has just reelected its third consecutive president, Barack Obama, after the two-term presidencies of Bill Clinton and George W. Bush. That hasn't happened since the White House tenures of Thomas Jefferson, James Madison, and James Monroe between 1801 and 1825.

It may be that Americans recognize the world's sole superpower will face great challenges regardless of who is in power. Voters also understand that in most cases presidents can't prevent bad things from happening and should be held accountable mainly for how they confront their tests and trials.

That helps to explain the reelection of President Obama in difficult economic times. While there has been disappointment, even among some of Obama's most fervent supporters, that more progress has not been made in returning the nation to prosperity, people understood that he inherited a mess and four years was a short time. Voters also judged his opponent, Republican Mitt Romney, wanting in critical respects.

The 2012 election was a highly competitive and hard-fought one, but the result was decisive, especially in the Electoral College. This book is a first look at this remarkable election—how it happened, what the voting patterns were, and why the electorate made the choices it did.

Some of the country's best academics and political analysts have come together to offer their viewpoints in this volume:

- After another closely contested presidential race, Americans are perhaps more divided than ever; Professor Alan Abramowitz of Emory University looks at these widening gaps in American life, partisan and otherwise, and how they manifested themselves this cycle.
- Professor James E. Campbell of the University at Buffalo–SUNY examines the fundamentals of this election—the economy, the president's approval rating, and other factors—and how they helped determine the outcome.
- Rhodes Cook, publisher of the widely respected *Rhodes Cook Letter* on politics and former writer for *Congressional Quarterly*, breaks down the presidential nominating process and ponders the future of the American political convention.
- Former Federal Elections Commission chairman Michael Toner and his colleague Karen Trainer write on the impact of the federal elections laws on this election, with a particular focus on outside group spending.
- Through mediums old (television) and new (social media), voters were inundated with political messaging throughout the election cycle. Media expert Diana Owen of Georgetown University looks at how the press covered the race.
- My superb colleagues at the University of Virginia Center for Politics, Geoffrey Skelley and Kyle Kondik, analyze 2012's down-ticket contests for the Senate and governorships (Skelley) and the House of Representatives (Kondik).
- We are pleased to feature three of the brightest new stars in political journalism in this volume: Nate Cohn of *The New Republic*, Jamelle Bouie of *The American Prospect*, and Robert Costa of *National Review*. Cohn does a deep dive into the exit polls to examine the demographics of Election 2012, while Bouie and Costa look forward to the futures of, respectively, the Democratic and Republican parties.
- After every presidential election, some are quick to say that the election signals a major change in American politics. Sean Trende, an analyst at RealClearPolitics, examines 2012's significance and what, if anything, its results might tell us about upcoming contests.

- Finally, Professor Susan MacManus of the University of South Florida finishes with some concluding thoughts about the future of the permanent American political campaign.

This volume could not have readied so quickly after the election without the hard work of the contributors, but also the professional staff of the University of Virginia Center for Politics. Those who helped keep the book on track include Center staffers Kondik and Skelley as well as Tim Robinson, Ken Stroupe, and Mary D. Brown.

We'd also like to thank Rowman and Littlefield for joining us in this endeavor; Senior Executive Editor Jonathan Sisk, Assistant Editor Benjamin Verdi, Marketing Manager Deborah Orgel Hudson, and Senior Production Editor Julia Loy were all invaluable in producing and polishing the book.

We hope our readers find the book helpful as they put the 2012 election into perspective. The contributors make clear how the face of American politics is changing, but in the end politics is shaped by the people who care to participate. The most useful participants are those who have taken the time to understand why we have arrived at our current juncture as a nation—and this volume may assist you on that path.

Larry J. Sabato
Director, University of Virginia Center for Politics
Charlottesville, Virginia
January 2013

# 1

# THE OBAMA ENCORE THAT
# BROKE SOME RULES

## Larry J. Sabato

We haven't had enough presidential elections—just fifty-seven in all—to draw many hard and fast rules. And what rules we are said to have are broken with regularity. No president could successfully seek a third term, until FDR did it in 1940. No president after FDR remade the office would willingly decline to seek reelection when eligible, but Harry Truman in 1952 and Lyndon Johnson in 1968 did so.[1] No presidential candidate who loses the New Hampshire primary could be elected in November, until Bill Clinton did so in 1992 and Barack Obama proved it was no fluke with his 2008 defeat in the Granite State primary. Presidents, it is often asserted, either win handy reelections or lose. But George W. Bush in 2004, with his narrow triumph for a second term, put the lie to that axiom.[2]

Coming into 2012 "everyone knew" that if the economy didn't come back strongly, President Obama would be done for. Another rule told us so: Since FDR, no president with unemployment above 7.4 percent had won. Yet with the jobless rate near 8 percent (it ticked up to 7.9 percent just before the November 2012 election[3]), Obama won a decent-sized victory in the popular vote and a healthy triumph in the Electoral College. So much for the unemployment maxim.

Prior to 2012, it was also considered impossible for a Republican to lose the White House when he approached 60 percent of the white vote; that was the level achieved by Ronald Reagan and George H. W. Bush in their clear triumphs in the 1980s. Mitt Romney secured 59 percent of whites yet fell well short of taking possession of the Oval Office. It isn't the 1980s anymore and the nation's demographics are changing rapidly.

Even old standbys misled in 2012. Take the Gallup Poll, with a reputation as the nation's gold standard in the survey industry. In an ominous sign for Democrats, Romney led Gallup's daily tracking fairly consistently in October, in majority territory and by margins that ranged up to 7 percent. The GOP understandably touted the fact that no candidate had been above 50 percent in Gallup so soon before the election and gone on to lose. With the Obama-Romney polls somewhat reminiscent of its miscalled 1948 Truman-Dewey election, Gallup emerged from 2012 badly tarnished.

It was that kind of year. Old truisms fell, some polls were highly inaccurate, and the two major parties lived in parallel universes. Rarely have both sides been so certain as Election Day approached that they were going to win. But only one side could.

## THE VOTERS' JUDGMENT

On November 6, 2012, the American electorate ratified the decision they had first made in 2008. President Obama received 65,582,643 votes, or 51 percent, to Mitt Romney's 60,840,191 votes, or 47.3 percent. Libertarian candidate Gary Johnson secured about 1 percent (1,273,814), and other candidates garnered a total of 958,409 (0.74 percent). While the national popular vote is compiled more out of curiosity—it is the Electoral College total that matters—it has some political impact. The news was mixed for Obama. He once again achieved an outright majority of all votes cast, with a plurality margin of 3.7 percent over Romney. This was greater than the reelection percentage of the previous president, George W. Bush in 2004 (2.4 percent). On the other hand, Obama lost about 2 percent of the vote percentage he compiled in 2008 (52.9 percent as a national average), and his edge over Romney was a little more than half the seven percentage points by which he defeated McCain.[4]

Obama also slipped a bit in the Electoral College, losing Indiana, North Carolina and the second district of Nebraska—all of which he had carried in 2008. Still, his 332 electoral votes (62 percent of the 538 total) constituted an impressive showing, not far off a rerun of the 365 electoral votes he posted four years earlier. Obama captured almost all of the competitive swing states for a second time, including Colorado and Nevada in the West, Iowa and Ohio in the Midwest, New Hampshire in the Northeast, and Virginia and Florida in the South. The latter turned out to be the closest state in the nation, with Obama edging Romney by less than a percentage point. The state considered by pre-election analysts to be most crucial, Ohio, was decided by 3 percent. Obama's victory there increased the state's win-loss record to twenty-eight of the last thirty presidential contests; that is, the Buckeye State has picked the White House winner in every contest since 1896 save for 1944 and 1960.[5] Nonetheless, Obama could easily have done without Ohio's eighteen electoral votes, as it turned out.

Most of the nine swing states weren't terribly competitive in the end, and Obama handily won all but a few. In fact, Obama's margin of victory in the states he carried was above 5 percent except in three states: Florida, Ohio, and Virginia. The only swing state Romney won, North Carolina, was his by 2 percent; all of his other states fell into the Republican column by wide margins. As for the other forty-one states and the District of Columbia, they could have safely been placed in the Republican Red or Democratic Blue column over the summer. By and large, the margins were predictable for Obama and Romney based on the Obama-McCain contest in 2008, with a few exceptions. For example, Utah backed its fellow Mormon Mitt Romney by 72.8 percent—fully 10 percent more than John McCain's total. Yet Alaska gave Romney 54.8 percent—a five-point drop from McCain in 2008, no doubt due to the absence from the Republican ticket of vice presidential candidate Sarah Palin of Alaska. The electoral map and various iterations of the popular vote totals are contained in the

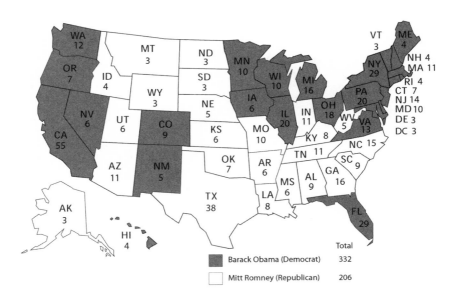

**Figure 1.1.  2012 Electoral College Map**

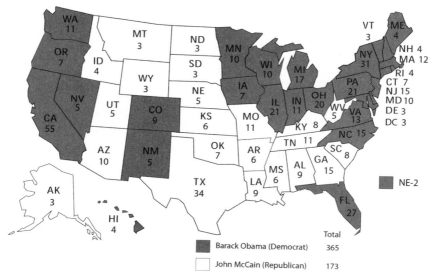

**Figure 1.2.    2008 Electoral College Map**

accompanying tables and figures, so you can compare and contrast the state returns for yourself.

Regionally, the 2012 election also stuck to the script. While President Obama won states across the map, his greatest strength was in the Democratic strongholds of the Northeast and the Pacific West. In both cases, he swept to a decisive landslide of about 59 percent (see table 1.1). The industrial Midwest was closer, but the president won by about five percentage points overall. For Romney, the Plains states produced his highest vote proportion (almost 60 percent), followed by the South (54 percent) and Mountain West (53 percent). Meanwhile, Romney captured the Inner West and Plains states (54.5 percent) and the Greater South (54.4 percent) by similar margins.

These regional divisions have become the norm for presidential politics, though the partisan changes over time are stark in most areas. Take, as one example, Appalachia—the parts of thirteen states classified as part of the mountain chain of the same name.[6] Democrats fared well there for generations. In 1976 Jimmy Carter captured 68 percent of the 428 counties and cities in Appalachia, and Bill Clinton 47 percent of them in 1996. But Barack Obama has hit rock bottom, with just 13 percent of these localities won in 2008 and a mere 7 percent in 2012. At the same time as Mitt Romney was sweeping Appalachia, he was doing exceptionally badly in the nation's fifty largest counties.[7] While George H. W. Bush secured a plurality

**Table 1.1. 2012 Presidential Vote by Region**

| Region | Electoral Vote Dem. | Rep. | Total Vote | Obama (Dem.) | Romney (Rep.) | Other | Rep.-Dem. Plurality | | Percentage of Total Vote Obama (Dem.) | Romney (Rep.) | Other |
|---|---|---|---|---|---|---|---|---|---|---|---|
| Northeast | 112 | 0 | 26,371,034 | 15,536,155 | 10,414,357 | 420,522 | 5,121,798 | D | 58.9% | 39.5% | 1.6% |
| Industrial Midwest | 80 | 11 | 25,768,506 | 13,554,285 | 11,794,230 | 419,991 | 1,760,055 | D | 52.6% | 45.8% | 1.6% |
| Pacific West | 78 | 3 | 18,688,525 | 11,009,467 | 7,170,494 | 508,564 | 3,838,973 | D | 58.9% | 38.4% | 2.7% |
| Greater South | 42 | 148 | 46,125,900 | 20,440,796 | 25,080,486 | 604,618 | 4,639,690 | R | 44.3% | 54.4% | 1.3% |
| Inner West & Plains | 20 | 44 | 11,718,146 | 5,043,395 | 6,384,944 | 289,807 | 1,341,549 | R | 43.0% | 54.5% | 2.5% |
| **National Total** | **332** | **206** | **128,672,111** | **65,584,098** | **60,844,511** | **2,243,502** | **4,739,587** | **D** | **51.0%** | **47.3%** | **1.7%** |

Source: Dave Leip's Atlas of American Elections, http://uselectionatlas.org/.
Note:
**States in each region:**
**Northeast**: Connecticut, Delaware, the District of Columbia, Maine, Maryland, Massachusetts, New Hampshire, New Jersey, New York, Pennsylvania, Rhode Island, Vermont
**Industrial Midwest**: Illinois, Indiana, Iowa, Michigan, Minnesota, Ohio, Wisconsin
**Pacific West**: Alaska, California, Hawaii, Oregon, Washington
**Greater South**: Alabama, Arkansas, Florida, Georgia, Kentucky, Louisiana, Mississippi, Missouri, North Carolina, Oklahoma, South Carolina, Tennessee, Texas, Virginia, West Virginia
**Inner West & Plains**: Arizona, Colorado, Idaho, Kansas, Montana, Nebraska, Nevada, New Mexico, North Dakota, South Dakota, Utah, Wyoming

in twenty-nine of these places in 1988, and George W. Bush did the same in sixteen of them in 2004, Romney was able to prevail in only six. Which is more important electorally? It's obvious: The party building its majorities in the most heavily populated places is going to win many more elections than the party doing better in shrinking rural America.

In history's context, Obama turned in a reelection performance that, under the economic circumstances, can be termed impressive. Since the Civil War, among all Democratic presidential nominees, only Samuel Tilden in 1876, FDR in his four elections, Lyndon Johnson in 1964, and Obama in 2008 amassed a larger majority than Obama did in 2012.[8] The other winning Democratic candidates—Grover Cleveland, Woodrow Wilson, Harry Truman, John F. Kennedy, Jimmy Carter, and Bill Clinton—secured 50.1 percent or less of the popular vote. In the Electoral College, among post–World War II presidents, Obama won a larger majority than Truman, Kennedy, Nixon (in 1968), Carter, and George W. Bush in either of his elections.

## A CAMPAIGN OF POLAR OPPOSITES

It is frequently true that the political party out of power in the White House misinterprets its midterm election successes. Democrats did so in 1982 and 1986—Democratic triumphs that preceded big GOP presidential wins in 1984 and 1988—and Republicans followed suit in 1994, incorrectly assuming that their takeover of Congress presaged a 1996 victory for president that never happened.

The GOP made the same error after its midterm coup in 2010, the year of "Tea Party" conservative conquests in elections around the nation. The negative public reaction to Obamacare (the president's health care reform program), and more important, to a continuing weak economy enabled a Republican takeover of the U.S. House of Representatives as well as sizable gains in many statehouses.[9] Yet a midterm election is always a preliminary reading of public opinion on a presidency, and it occurs in a low-turnout environment with voter participation a full fifteen to twenty percentage points below that of a presidential election. The missing voters in the 2010 midterm were mainly minority and Democratic-leaning; they would be back at the polls in 2012.

Because of 2010, though, Republicans took a hard turn to the right, and their 2012 presidential primary process was an exercise in alienating many individuals and groups critical to a general election victory. For example, GOP frontrunner Mitt Romney took a strong conservative position on illegal immigration, arguing for "self-deportation" and providing few options to citizenship for the millions of Hispanics already living and working in the United States. As we will see later on, Romney fared exceptionally poorly among Hispanic citizens in November; they sensed Romney's hostility (whether real or not), and returned the favor. Similarly, on the issue of abortion, Romney adopted a very conservative position on the topic, despite having been pro-choice in the 1990s. His efforts to win over more women in the fall were hampered. Romney also described his Massachusetts governorship as "severely conservative" when he had been a relative moderate in his party. These contortions were, in his view, necessary to secure the nomination, and his advisers planned an "Etch-a-Sketch" makeover in the general election. The old moderate Romney would reappear, except as the Romney team discovered, the conservatives running the Tea Party and the GOP in most states would have none of it.

What plays in GOP primaries and caucuses among right-wing activists often falls flat in the much more diverse electorate in November. Still, Romney probably had little choice if he wanted to win the party nomination. Even though he faced a weak field of challengers, almost all were more conservative than Romney, and thus they had substantial built-in support among Republican activists and groups. Former House Speaker Newt Gingrich of Georgia and former senator Rick Santorum of Pennsylvania capitalized on conservative doubts about Romney, a candidate who had clearly changed positions on social issues such as abortion, immigration, and gay rights. Santorum was the closest challenger, and he won eleven states to Romney's thirty-seven. Gingrich won two states, South Carolina and Georgia. Romney ended the primary season with 10 million votes (52.1 percent), while Santorum had 3.9 million votes (20.4 percent). Gingrich accumulated 2.7 million votes (14.2 percent), Texas Congressman Ron Paul had 2.1 million (10.9 percent), and a scattering of other candidates attracted the remaining 2.4 percent of the total votes.[10]

Meanwhile, President Obama was unopposed for renomination—no minor advantage since every president defeated for reelection in the twentieth century had been seriously opposed by one or more candidates in the party primaries.[11] Such intra-party fights divide the base, and steal volunteer energy and campaign funds from the bigger battle to come in the fall.

Moreover, Obama smartly sought to make the election a choice between himself and a "flawed" Republican nominee, rather than a simple referendum on his handling of the economy—the latter the obvious goal of the Republican campaign. Throughout the summer, Obama's team

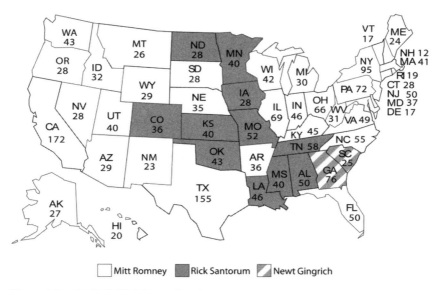

Mitt Romney     Rick Santorum     Newt Gingrich

**Figure 1.3.   2012 GOP Primary Results**

pounded Romney for his enormous wealth and some holdings in the Cayman Islands, Swiss bank accounts, and elsewhere, as well as the actions in his private equity firm, Bain Capital. The stories of those who were put out of work when Bain closed various financial deals were highlighted. In a major miscalculation, the Romney campaign chose not to respond in paid advertising to the tens of millions of dollars of anti-Romney ads aired by the Obama campaign. The image of Romney as a "rich guy" who didn't care about the average American lingered all the way to Election Day.

Compounding Romney's problem was his ineffective national convention. A hurricane threatening the East Coast cut a day off the late August GOP gathering, and the remaining three days became something of a mix-and-match jumble of rescheduling. While the key speeches by Romney and his wife Ann were presentable enough, the public did not appear to connect well with them and the nominee received none of the traditional polling "bounce"—a blip upwards often created by the good feelings generated by convention activities. Romney's speech was marred by the man chosen to introduce him, aging Hollywood actor Clint Eastwood, whose bizarre unscripted conversation on stage with an empty chair (supposedly representing President Obama) overshadowed everything Romney said.

By contrast, President Obama had a reasonably successful convention by most measures. The most memorable speech was given not by Obama, whose own effort fell flat, but by his Democratic predecessor, Bill Clinton. Despite his rivalry with Obama, and his on-again, off-again friendship with the incumbent who had defeated his wife, Hillary, for the Democratic nomination in 2008, Clinton made a powerful case for Obama's reelection, blaming the slow economy on George W. Bush and claiming that no president could have dealt with the aftermath of the 2008 economic collapse quickly. Unlike Romney, Obama got a modest bounce from his convention, and it lasted throughout September and suggested for a while that the president might win a sizable reelection.

Then came the first presidential debate on October 3 in Denver. In the entire history of televised face-offs for the White House, which began in 1960, there was not a more one-sided result. By a margin of about three-to-one, debate viewers said Romney had defeated Obama.[12] Overnight, the Romney campaign seemed to surge, from crowd sizes to polling numbers. As figure 1.4 shows, Romney achieved his first lead in the general election in the days following the Denver debate.

To judge by the polling averages contained in this figure, nothing much changed afterward—until the final days. While the second and third presidential debates featured a reinvigorated Obama, and he probably "won" them on points, the contest remained tight. This assumes that national polls were not flawed, but some clearly were. As noted earlier, Gallup defined a "likely voter" electorate that, had it been real, would have elected Romney. But Gallup and other polling groups screened out too many minorities and young people, who were disproportionately for Obama. It may well be that Romney was never as close as the line in figure 1.4 suggests; that is the contention of the Obama pollsters, whose model for likely voters was proven correct.[13] It is also possible that the superior Obama voter contact program, which stressed early voting as well as the identification of never-registered and less-likely-to-vote Americans, was able to "bank" many thousands of extra Obama voters in the swing states who were not included in the polling screens. More research is needed over the next months and years to determine the full truth. But already we know that many polling organizations missed a sizable chunk of potential voters, and need to expand their reliance on cell phones since an ever-growing proportion of voters do not have landlines. And we also know for sure that the Obama campaign was leaps and bounds better than Romney's team at voter identification and get-out-the-vote.[14]

To judge by the polls, though, Obama did get something of a small last-minute lift from Hurricane Sandy and its aftermath. The so-called Frankenstorm, a hurricane that turned into a nor'easter, was devastating to the

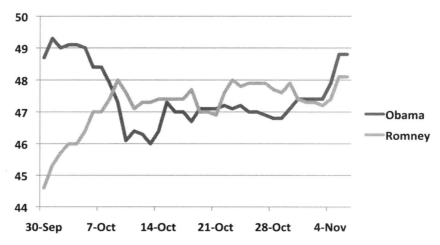

**Figure 1.4. The Obama-Romney Polling Average in the General Election's Last Month**
*Source*: RealClearPolitics, www.realclearpolitics.com/epolls/2012/president/us/general_election_romney_vs_obama-1171.html.

New York–New Jersey area, and it shoved Romney off the public stage at a critical moment. Obama assumed his designated nonpartisan role as presidential comforter-in-chief, with an assist from Republican governor Chris Christie of New Jersey, who effusively praised Obama for his recovery efforts. Ironically, Christie had been Romney's keynote speaker at the GOP convention, and was criticized then for saying a great deal about himself and little about Romney. Yet the hurricane was not the crucial factor in Obama's victory, if only because there were so few real undecided voters left by that time. The storm's lingering effects probably cost Obama hundreds of thousands of net votes in the Northeast, where power had not been restored by Election Day in many areas and people were overwhelmed with cleanup. No Electoral College shifts resulted, of course, but the hurricane helps to explain a bit of the lower turnout we saw in 2012 (discussed below).

Before leaving the campaign, it is vital to stress that the underlying electoral conditions favored the incumbent—not by a wide margin, but just enough. There was no major scandal that engaged the whole American public—the death of the U.S. ambassador to Libya and others in a September debacle at the Benghazi consulate stirred mainly Republicans. There was no unpopular foreign war eroding support for Obama; Iraq was essentially over and Afghanistan appeared to be winding down. Most of all, the economy was slow but seemed to most Americans to be gradually improving. Unemployment had drifted down from a high of 10.1 percent in October 2009 to 7.9 percent on election eve.[15] Consumer confidence had moved up modestly. The gross domestic product was growing slightly. While Obama's second quarter 2012 GDP increase was an unimpressive 1.3 percent, compare this to Jimmy Carter's disastrous economic *contraction* of almost 8 percent in the second quarter of 1980. There is a reason why Carter was the only twentieth-century president who lost the White House after his party held it for just one term. Conditions were so bad—recession, sky-high interest rates, inflation in double digits, the Iranian hostage crisis—that Americans were unwilling to accept excuses. In Obama's case, there was just enough good economic news to generate modest optimism. Just as important, Obama's predecessor, George W. Bush, was still deeply unpopular. Since the economic collapse had occurred on Bush's watch, voters blamed him more than Obama for the continuing problems. This is a hidden advantage that most first-term presidents have when their predecessor was disliked. (This advantage is explored later in this book.)

Some things don't change. Once again, and as usual, the vice presidential candidates had little discernible impact on the 2012 election outcome. Vice President Joe Biden had mixed ratings, due to the frequency of his verbal gaffes. Romney's choice for the second slot, forty-two-year-old U.S. Representative Paul Ryan of Wisconsin, may have galvanized conservatives but Romney would have won them anyway. Ryan was unable to carry the Badger State for Romney.

To judge by turnout, interest in this election was down from 2008 and even 2004. The total vote of 129 million was 58.7 percent of the voting-eligible population, down from 60.1 percent in 2004 and 61.6 percent in 2008.[16] Even in absolute terms, voter participation fell, despite substantial population growth. The 2012 presidential election had about 2.5 million fewer votes cast than the 131.3 million cast in 2008.[17]

Why did the decline occur? The answer isn't obvious. With record spending and a campaign that by any measure was exciting, one might have thought raw turnout would have been at least on par with 2008. Could the hundreds of millions of dollars spent on negative advertising have depressed turnout? Studies differ in this field; some suggest negative ads can depress turnout, while others argue negative ads actually increase participation.[18] But in swing states in 2012, negative ads from the campaigns and Super PACs were at near-saturation levels, an almost unprecedented volume that might have had unusual effects. Were some Democrats less enthralled with President Obama because of his first-term record, choosing not to vote rather than voting for Romney? Were some Republicans unimpressed with

**Table 1.2  The 2008 and 2012 Presidential Votes**

| State | 2-Party Vote %—2008 Obama Votes | Obama Percent | McCain Votes | McCain Percent | 2-Party Vote %—2012 Obama Votes | Obama Percent | Romney Votes | Romney Percent | Obama change from 2008 |
|---|---|---|---|---|---|---|---|---|---|
| Alabama | 813,479 | 39.1% | 1,266,546 | 60.9% | 795,696 | 38.8% | 1,255,925 | 61.2% | -0.3% |
| Alaska | 123,594 | 38.9% | 193,841 | 61.1% | 122,640 | 42.7% | 164,676 | 57.3% | 3.7% |
| Arizona | 1,034,707 | 45.7% | 1,230,111 | 54.3% | 1,025,232 | 45.4% | 1,233,654 | 54.6% | -0.3% |
| Arkansas | 422,310 | 39.8% | 638,017 | 60.2% | 394,409 | 37.8% | 647,744 | 62.2% | -2.0% |
| California | 8,274,473 | 62.3% | 5,011,781 | 37.7% | 7,854,285 | 61.9% | 4,839,958 | 38.1% | -0.4% |
| Colorado | 1,288,633 | 54.6% | 1,073,629 | 45.4% | 1,322,998 | 52.8% | 1,185,050 | 47.2% | -1.8% |
| Connecticut | 997,773 | 61.3% | 629,428 | 38.7% | 905,083 | 58.8% | 634,892 | 41.2% | -2.5% |
| Delaware | 255,459 | 62.6% | 152,374 | 37.4% | 242,584 | 59.4% | 165,484 | 40.6% | -3.2% |
| Florida | 4,282,367 | 51.4% | 4,046,219 | 48.6% | 4,237,756 | 50.4% | 4,163,447 | 49.6% | -1.0% |
| Georgia | 1,844,123 | 47.4% | 2,048,759 | 52.6% | 1,773,827 | 46.0% | 2,078,688 | 54.0% | -1.3% |
| Hawaii | 325,871 | 73.0% | 120,566 | 27.0% | 306,658 | 71.7% | 121,015 | 28.3% | -1.3% |
| Idaho | 236,440 | 37.0% | 403,012 | 63.0% | 212,787 | 33.6% | 420,911 | 66.4% | -3.4% |
| Illinois | 3,419,348 | 62.7% | 2,031,179 | 37.3% | 3,019,512 | 58.6% | 2,135,216 | 41.4% | -4.2% |
| Indiana | 1,374,039 | 50.5% | 1,345,648 | 49.5% | 1,152,887 | 44.8% | 1,420,543 | 55.2% | -5.7% |
| Iowa | 828,940 | 54.8% | 682,379 | 45.2% | 822,544 | 53.0% | 730,617 | 47.0% | -1.9% |
| Kansas | 514,765 | 42.4% | 699,655 | 57.6% | 440,726 | 38.9% | 692,634 | 61.1% | -3.5% |
| Kentucky | 751,985 | 41.8% | 1,048,462 | 58.2% | 679,370 | 38.5% | 1,087,190 | 61.5% | -3.3% |
| Louisiana | 782,985 | 42.8% | 1,048,462 | 57.2% | 809,141 | 41.3% | 1,152,262 | 58.7% | -1.5% |
| Maine | 421,923 | 58.8% | 295,273 | 41.2% | 401,306 | 57.9% | 292,276 | 42.1% | -1.0% |
| Maryland | 1,629,467 | 62.9% | 959,862 | 37.1% | 1,677,844 | 63.3% | 971,869 | 36.7% | 0.4% |
| Massachusetts | 1,904,098 | 63.2% | 1,108,854 | 36.8% | 1,921,290 | 61.8% | 1,188,314 | 38.2% | -1.4% |
| Michigan | 2,872,579 | 58.4% | 2,048,639 | 41.6% | 2,564,569 | 54.8% | 2,115,256 | 45.2% | -3.6% |
| Minnesota | 1,573,354 | 55.2% | 1,275,409 | 44.8% | 1,546,167 | 53.9% | 1,320,225 | 46.1% | -1.3% |
| Mississippi | 554,662 | 43.4% | 724,597 | 56.6% | 562,949 | 44.2% | 710,746 | 55.8% | 0.8% |

| State | 2008 Votes | 2008 % | 2008 Votes | 2008 % | 2012 Votes | 2012 % | 2012 Votes | 2012 % | Change |
|---|---|---|---|---|---|---|---|---|---|
| Missouri | 1,441,911 | 49.9% | 1,445,814 | 50.1% | 1,223,796 | 45.2% | 1,482,440 | 54.8% | -4.7% |
| Montana | 232,159 | 48.8% | 243,882 | 51.2% | 201,839 | 43.0% | 267,928 | 57.0% | -5.8% |
| Nebraska | 333,319 | 42.4% | 452,979 | 57.6% | 302,081 | 38.9% | 475,064 | 61.1% | -3.5% |
| Nevada | 533,736 | 56.4% | 412,827 | 43.6% | 531,373 | 53.4% | 463,567 | 46.6% | -3.0% |
| New Hampshire | 384,826 | 54.9% | 316,534 | 45.1% | 369,561 | 52.8% | 329,918 | 47.2% | -2.0% |
| New Jersey | 2,215,422 | 57.9% | 1,613,207 | 42.1% | 2,122,786 | 59.0% | 1,478,088 | 41.0% | 1.1% |
| New Mexico | 472,422 | 57.7% | 346,832 | 42.3% | 415,255 | 55.3% | 335,644 | 44.7% | -2.4% |
| New York | 4,804,945 | 63.6% | 2,752,771 | 36.4% | 4,159,441 | 63.4% | 2,401,799 | 36.6% | -0.2% |
| North Carolina | 2,142,651 | 50.2% | 2,128,474 | 49.8% | 2,178,391 | 49.0% | 2,270,395 | 51.0% | -1.2% |
| North Dakota | 141,403 | 45.6% | 168,887 | 54.4% | 124,966 | 39.9% | 188,320 | 60.1% | -5.7% |
| Ohio | 2,940,044 | 52.3% | 2,677,820 | 47.7% | 2,827,621 | 51.5% | 2,661,407 | 48.5% | -0.8% |
| Oklahoma | 502,496 | 34.4% | 960,165 | 65.6% | 443,547 | 33.2% | 891,325 | 66.8% | -1.1% |
| Oregon | 1,037,291 | 58.4% | 738,475 | 41.6% | 970,488 | 56.3% | 754,175 | 43.7% | -2.1% |
| Pennsylvania | 3,276,363 | 55.2% | 2,655,885 | 44.8% | 2,990,274 | 52.7% | 2,680,434 | 47.3% | -2.5% |
| Rhode Island | 296,571 | 64.2% | 165,391 | 35.8% | 279,677 | 64.0% | 157,204 | 36.0% | -0.2% |
| South Carolina | 862,449 | 45.5% | 1,034,896 | 54.5% | 865,941 | 44.7% | 1,071,645 | 55.3% | -0.8% |
| South Dakota | 170,924 | 45.7% | 203,054 | 54.3% | 145,039 | 40.8% | 210,610 | 59.2% | -4.9% |
| Tennessee | 1,087,437 | 42.4% | 1,479,178 | 57.6% | 960,709 | 39.6% | 1,462,330 | 60.4% | -2.7% |
| Texas | 3,528,633 | 44.1% | 4,479,328 | 55.9% | 3,305,242 | 42.0% | 4,566,172 | 58.0% | -2.1% |
| Utah | 327,670 | 35.5% | 596,030 | 64.5% | 251,813 | 25.4% | 740,600 | 74.6% | -10.1% |
| Vermont | 219,262 | 68.9% | 98,974 | 31.1% | 199,239 | 68.2% | 92,698 | 31.8% | -0.7% |
| Virginia | 1,959,532 | 53.2% | 1,725,005 | 46.8% | 1,971,820 | 52.0% | 1,822,522 | 48.0% | -1.2% |
| Washington | 1,750,848 | 58.8% | 1,229,216 | 41.2% | 1,755,396 | 57.6% | 1,290,670 | 42.4% | -1.1% |
| West Virginia | 303,857 | 43.3% | 397,466 | 56.7% | 238,202 | 36.3% | 417,655 | 63.7% | -7.0% |
| Wisconsin | 1,677,211 | 57.1% | 1,262,393 | 42.9% | 1,620,985 | 53.5% | 1,410,966 | 46.5% | -3.6% |
| Wyoming | 82,868 | 33.4% | 164,958 | 66.6% | 69,286 | 28.8% | 170,962 | 71.2% | -4.6% |
| Dist. of Col. | 245,800 | 93.4% | 17,367 | 6.6% | 267,070 | 92.6% | 21,381 | 7.4% | -0.8% |
| Total | 69,499,424 | 53.7% | 59,850,510 | 46.3% | 65,584,098 | 51.9% | 60,844,511 | 48.1% | -1.9% |

*Sources:*
2008 Data: Dave Leip's Atlas of U.S. Presidential Elections, http://uselectionatlas.org/RESULTS/.
2012 Data: Crystal Ball running spreadsheet, Dave Leip.

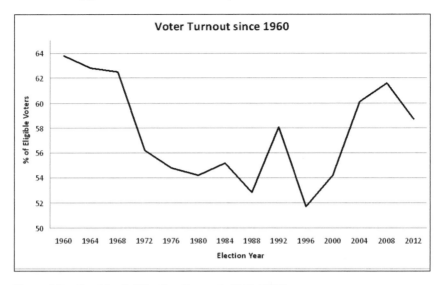

**Figure 1.5.   Presidential Election Turnout, 1960–2012**

their candidate, or turned off because of elements of his background or religion? Then, too, we know that Hurricane Sandy may have subtracted up to a million East Coast voters from the likely total. The reality of 2012's turnout drop is a subject that requires further study.

## THE POLITICAL MAP OF AMERICA

Twelve years ago in my book *Overtime: The Election 2000 Thriller* I introduced the concept of the "Political Map of America," ably executed by Joshua J. Scott of the University of Virginia Center for Politics.[19] As noted there, this exercise in cartography is based on the essential notion that "people vote, not trees or rocks or acres." The Electoral College has a certain small-state bias, for sure, driven by the two senatorial bonus votes added to every state, whether a lightly populated state such as Wyoming or a behemoth such as California. Yet the electoral vote result is driven by the *popular vote* in each state; the candidate who wins one more popular vote than the other in each state gets all the electoral votes that state has to offer (except in Maine and Nebraska, where one electoral vote is awarded to the winner of each congressional district, with the two senatorial votes given to the candidate who wins statewide).

Therefore, the Political Map, based on the population figures in the 2010 Census, is what politicians, their staffs, and political consultants actually see when they look at our nation. The Northeast has lost millions of residents in recent decades, but notice how large politically the geographically compact region still looms (see figure 1.6). The Northeast is more than matched by the South, whose volume on this map has more than *doubled* since the 1950s, led by Florida and Texas. California is the ultimate mega-state, more than twice its geographical size in the Political Map. The large, midwestern swing states are, like the Northeast, considerably reduced in size from what they were just a half-century ago, but their importance is still clear on the Political Map. Finally, many of our readers will be distressed to see their states shrunk to a volume so small that a postage stamp could cover most of them. These are the states that should be very grateful for the Electoral College and its bonus votes. As consolation, it should be stressed that many of these states are growing by leaps and bounds, and the next Political Map of America, to be drawn in 2021, will show progress. In any event, when it comes to the Political Map, as in so many other areas of life, size matters, and there is just no getting around that. Poor Alaska: It is a massive piece of territory, but in the Political Map, it is *smaller than Rhode Island*!

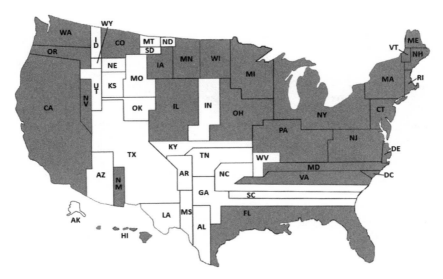

**Figure 1.6.  The 2012 Political Map of the United States (Shaded states were won by the Democratic candidate, states without shading were won by the Republican candidate.)**

So what does the 2012 political map add to our understanding of the presidential election? Just compare it to the 2004 Bush-Kerry map (figure 1.7), which shows the close division of that election, with Republican and Democratic territory fairly even and regionally polarized and Ohio as the stand-out, decisive state. By contrast, in 2012 (much like 2008) a blue Obama ocean has flooded much of the red GOP land. Romney's ground is restricted to the South and Rocky Mountain part of the continent, with islands of backing in Arizona and the Plains states.

It is possible to construct the American political map in a manner far more favorable to Republicans. Election Data Services did just this in its revealing popular-vote map that breaks down the results county by county across the United States (printed in color on the back of this book).

A visitor from Mars without access to the news would assume that Mitt Romney won the election, so vast is the mass of red from coast to coast. This map reflects the GOP's remaining demographic strength among rural voters. The lower the density of population, in general, the better Republicans seem to do politically—which is why Romney could win 2,455 counties to Obama's 698 and still lose the election.[20] Most territory is still sparsely settled in much of the United States, so a relative handful of voters casting GOP ballots can turn the nation red. Yet the blue dots on the map contain a large majority of the country's voters. These central cities,

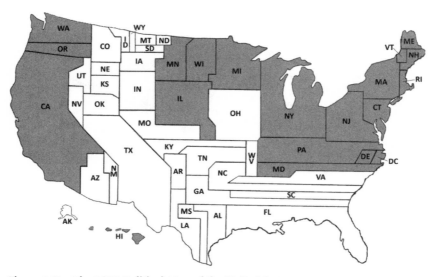

**Figure 1.7.   The 2004 Political Map of the United States**

suburbs, and gradually urbanizing "exurbs" powered Obama to victory in two elections. Also, the rural counties that are blue on election night are primarily majority-minority, that is, African Americans and/or Hispanics and Asian Americans constitute majorities. These voters (in the South, Southwest, California, and so on) have formed much of Obama's base and twice delivered massive backing for his candidacy.

## THE CHANGING FACE OF THE AMERICAN ELECTORATE: CRITICAL KEY TO THE 2012 RESULTS

Some election analysts thought the 2008 election was a fluke, that large turnout from various minority groups was a one-time phenomenon produced by the prospect of the historic election of an African American. The 2012 results have disabused them of that notion.

America has changed permanently, and the evolution continues with each passing year. In the 1980s, whites consistently comprised more than 80 percent of the national electorate. In 2008 whites were 74 percent, and in 2012, 72 percent. By mid-century whites will be a minority of the U.S. population, though still probably a majority of the actual voter turnout. But eventually, the voting populace will reflect the reality that the United States will be a nation of minorities, with no ethnic or racial group in the majority. This matters because there is a partisan coloration to skin color. Whites are by far the most Republican of racial groupings.

As we'll see, race is a key component of the presidential vote, though not the only one by any means and not always the most important. Our best source for slicing and dicing the electorate is the "exit poll"—the system of interviewing voters as they leave the polls, supplemented by calls to voters who cast a ballot early, in order to project election winners and break down the electorate into its constituent parts (gender, race, age, etc.). Once all the adjusting and weighting has been done, the exit poll gives us invaluable clues to the voting behavior of Americans. Any student of politics will want to study table 1.5 at the end of the chapter at length. Fully 26,565 voters were interviewed at polling places scattered across the United States for this national profile of the electorate, a far larger sample than public opinion polls provide prior to Election Day.[21] In this analysis, we are looking at a mosaic created by citizens who cast a ballot in all American jurisdictions combined.[22] Let's review some of the highlights and see what they can tell us about how we voted in 2012.

**Table 1.3.   Gender Gap in Presidential Elections, 1972–2012**

| Election | Men | | Women | |
|---|---|---|---|---|
| | *Dem %* | *GOP %* | *Dem %* | *GOP %* |
| 1972 | 36% | **62%** | 37% | 61% |
| 1976 | **50%** | 48% | **50%** | 48% |
| 1980 | 36% | **55%** | 45% | **47%** |
| 1984 | 37% | **62%** | 44% | **56%** |
| 1988 | 41% | **57%** | 49% | **50%** |
| 1992 | **41%** | 38% | **45%** | 37% |
| 1996 | 43% | **44%** | 54% | 38% |
| 2000 | 42% | **53%** | 54% | 43% |
| 2004 | 44% | **55%** | 51% | 48% |
| 2008 | **49%** | 48% | **56%** | 43% |
| 2012 | 45% | **52%** | 55% | 44% |

*Source*: Exit poll data in each presidential election.

### Gender Wars and Racial Divisions

In the 1970s men and women voted very much alike for president. But since 1980, there has been a "gender gap" in every presidential election, and men and women have tended to diverge in their political choices. Women are more likely to vote Democratic than men. (See table 1.3, below.) The reverse is also true: men are more likely to vote Republican. Some of the gender gap is explained by income, marital status, and the relative economic security of men and women. Specialized issues also come into play, such as abortion and contraception. Since women are a larger voter bloc than men—in 2012, for instance, women comprised 53 percent of the electorate—winning them over can be politically potent.

The gender gap usually ranges from five to ten points. In the 2000 Bush–Gore contest, for instance, it was ten points: Bush received 53 percent of the male vote but only 43 percent of the female vote. The gender gap narrowed a bit to 7 percent in 2004, with Bush garnering 55 percent of the male vote and 48 percent of the female vote. John Kerry garnered just 44 percent of men but won women with 51 percent.

In 2008 Barack Obama managed to perform a very difficult feat by carrying both men and women. Granted, Obama won men by just a single percentage point, 49 percent to John McCain's 48 percent (with 3 percent cast for other candidates). At the same time, Obama won women in a landslide, 56 percent to 43 percent. Even Bill Clinton had been unable to win men in his sizable defeat of Bob Dole in 1996. Clinton lost men by a percentage point, but he won women by a massive 16 percent.

The gender gap reverted to form in 2012, that is, the Republican was backed by men and the Democrat by women. Mitt Romney won men by 7 percent and Barack Obama won women by 11 percent.

Even greater polarization could be seen in the racial breakdown. As mentioned earlier, whites (both men and women, taken together) constituted 72 percent of the entire electorate (down from 74 percent in 2008), and they chose Romney by 59 percent to 39 percent for Obama. Obama fell four full percentage points among whites; he had received 43 percent of the white vote in 2008.

Again, there is quite a difference between the votes of men and women. White men favored Romney by a whopping 27 percent, but white women chose Romney by 14 percent. And while Obama had won a majority of the white vote in eighteen states in 2008, whites in just eight states (Connecticut, Iowa, Maine, Massachusetts, New Hampshire, Oregon, Vermont, and Washington) gave majorities to Obama in 2012. Further, Obama's white percentage fell below 20 percent in Mississippi (10 percent) and Alabama (15 percent) and barely topped 30 percent in North Carolina (31 percent), Arizona (32 percent), and Missouri (32 percent).

By contrast, there was relatively little distinction among African American men and women, though women were still inclined a bit more toward Obama. Both genders chose Barack Obama overwhelmingly, approaching unanimity (87 percent among men and 96 percent among women). Overall, Obama garnered 93 percent of African Americans, down a bit from his 95 percent in 2008 but higher than the 88–90 percent average for modern Democratic presidential nominees. African American turnout remained high, relative to past performance. Blacks comprised 13 percent of the overall electorate in both 2008 and 2012. In 2004 blacks had comprised just 11 percent of the national total.

Something truly amazing happened with respect to Latinos and Hispanics. They had favored Obama in 2008 by 67 percent to just 31 percent for McCain—a dramatic change from the approximately 40 percent who voted Republican in 2004. Many analysts wondered whether Obama could sustain this level of backing in 2012 under difficult economic conditions. In fact, Obama *increased* his Hispanic/Latino proportion, all the way to 71 percent. Romney's 27 percent was the worst for a presidential Republican since Bob Dole's 21 percent in 1996. Not only that, but Latinos increased their proportion of the overall turnout from four years earlier, moving from 9 percent to 10 percent of the electorate. Even here, the gender gap was apparent. Hispanic women were eleven percentage points more likely to favor Obama than Hispanic men.

The anti-illegal immigration policies of the national Republican Party, and of Mitt Romney in particular, backfired spectacularly. Look, for example, at the four states listed in table 1.4 below. The Hispanic vote grew substantially over eight years in each state, and combined with the overwhelming Latino backing for Obama, it made New Mexico uncompetitive and pushed the swing states of Colorado, Florida, and Nevada into the Democratic column.

The 3 percent of the voters who called themselves Asian Americans picked Obama by 73 percent to 26 percent—a considerable increase over the 62 percent that voted for Obama in 2008. Further, the 2 percent who self-identified as belonging to some other race (such as Native American, Pacific Islander, or multiracial) were pro-Obama by 58 percent to 38 percent.

Notice that Republicans are winning a majority only of the white vote. Now that nonwhites are 28 percent of the total vote (and growing every four years), and they are casting about 80 percent of their votes for the Democratic nominee, it is no longer enough for a GOP nominee to attract whites by a wide margin. In order to win presidential elections in the future, Republicans will have to broaden their appeal among nonwhites in at least a racial category or two.

**Table 1.4.  Hispanic Proportions of the Vote in Key States, 2004 and 2012**

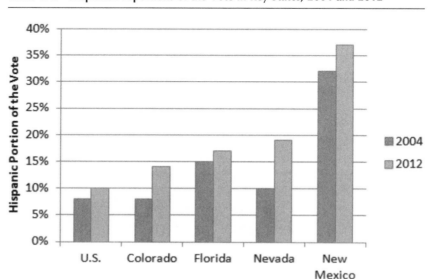

California is a prime example of the GOP's dilemma. Republicans were once highly competitive in this West Coast nation-state, with its unrivalled prize of fifty-five electoral votes. From 1948 to 1988, the Republican presidential nominee carried the Golden State in nine of eleven elections. But from 1992 to 2012, Democrats have won six of six times, usually with gargantuan majorities. In 2012 President Obama won California by 23 percent with virtually no effort. Mitt Romney carried California whites by 8 percent, but Obama swept the 40 percent of the voters who belong to a racial minority group.[23] California probably won't be the place where the GOP revival starts, or even finishes, but the trends that have transformed this state are affecting many others. Republicans need to be concerned that their Golden State fate is Christmas future in much of the rest of the country.

## The Youth Vote Stays Engaged

One of the most exciting developments in 2008 was the awakening of the youth vote, especially on college campuses across America. Perhaps it is more accurate to say "reawakening," since young people had driven American politics in the tumultuous late 1960s and early 1970s, as they embraced various causes from civil rights to opposition to the Vietnam War. It is no accident that the passage of the Twenty-Sixth Amendment to the Constitution, lowering the voting age from twenty-one to eighteen, occurred in July 1971. Unfortunately, after a burst of youth activity during the 1972 election, voter turnout among the young drifted much lower over the next several decades.

As we noted eight years ago in a similar book on the 2004 election, a ray of hope for the Democrats was observed even in the midst of John Kerry's defeat. The Massachusetts Democrat won voters aged eighteen to twenty-nine, 54 percent to 45 percent; it was the only age group he captured, in fact. The war in Iraq already appeared unpopular among the young, and their views on social issues such as abortion and gay rights were far more closely aligned with the Democrats than the Republicans.

In 2008 the political dam burst among the young. Attracted by Obama's style and multiracial background, as well as his positions on the economy, Iraq, environmentalism, and social issues, eighteen- to twenty-nine-year-old voters delivered a massive landslide to the Democrat, 66 percent to 32 percent for McCain. Their turnout was up slightly over 2004 as well. This was another ominous development for Republicans, in part because the young often keep their first party label for most or all of their lives, especially when the party identification was acquired in a memorable, intense election like 2008.

Conditions were different in 2012, and analysts were watching to see if young people would rejoin Obama's campaign despite a weak economy that had produced high unemployment for students just out of college. Republicans actually made progress among the eighteen- to twenty-nine-year-olds, but not nearly enough. Obama carried young voters again, but by 60 percent instead of 2008's 66 percent. Romney's 37 percent was still well below George W. Bush's 45 percent in 2004. And turnout among the young actually increased, to 19 percent of the overall electorate (from 17 percent in 2008). The employment problem cost Obama votes here, but conservative GOP positions on social issues probably minimized the Democratic loss. Younger voters are also much more racially diverse than older voters.

Obama did far less well with older Americans. He won those in their thirties by thirteen points (55 percent to 42 percent), but lost voters in their forties by 2 percent and ages fifty to sixty-four by 5 percent. Just as in 2008, Obama did worst with Romney's fellow senior citizens. Those aged sixty-five and older picked Romney by 56 percent to 44 percent.

Combining the characteristics of race and age produces some variation. Barack Obama did not win any age cohort among white voters, but he lost those aged eighteen to twenty-nine by just 7 percent. (In 2008 young whites voted for Obama by 10 percent.) Young Latinos were also slightly more inclined than their elders to back Obama. The Democrat gathered 74 percent of eighteen- to twenty-nine-year-olds in this racial group, compared to 65 percent of those over age sixty-five. Once again, there was no generation gap among African Americans. Over ninety of one hundred blacks in every age group supported Obama.

### The Effect of Income and Education on the Vote

To a certain degree, at least politically, you are what you earn. The Obama campaign stressed the president's desire for higher taxes among those making over $200,000 a year ($250,000 for couples), and this may have had some impact on the clear division in the income categories. Barack Obama won 60 percent among those with incomes under $50,000 annually, while Romney garnered 53 percent among those who make more than that. Another way to look at incomes is to see $100,000 as the key break point. Obama received the votes of 54 percent of those making less than that amount, and Romney won 54 percent of those making $100k or more. Of course, 72 percent of Americans make less than $100k, so the advantage was Obama's.

Income is strongly correlated with education. In earlier generations, Republican support tended to go up the income and education scale—the more years of formal education you had and the more you earned, the more likely it was that you would vote for the GOP candidate. This has changed at the top of the scale in recent times. Those with the most education (postgraduate training or degrees) tilt Democratic. In 2012 Obama captured 55 percent of the votes of the 18 percent of Americans in the postgraduate category, down slightly from his 58 percent in 2008. Four years earlier, John Kerry had also won 55 percent of postgraduates.

By contrast, Obama and Romney were effectively tied among those who had attended college without a degree or got a college degree with no postgrad education. Americans with just a high school degree leaned to Obama by 3 percent. It was those without even a high school diploma—disproportionately composed of minorities and only 3 percent of the voters—that favored Obama by the widest margin (64 percent).

Why have postgraduates been moving to the Democrats? There are many explanations, but Republican association with the religious right and, again, GOP positions on lifestyle and social issues such as abortion and gay rights appear to be especially relevant factors.

### Decision Time

Presidential races involving incumbents make the voting decision easy for most voters: They are either for reenlisting the incumbent or they aren't. Almost seven out of ten voters knew *before September* for whom they were going to vote, and Obama already had a 53 percent to 46 percent lead among them.

Among the approximately 30 percent who reported deciding their vote during the general election, a third said it happened in September, a third in October, and a third during the last few days or on the day of the election. Romney's best month was September, when 53 percent picked him, and October was essentially a tie—something of a surprise, given Romney's strong debate performance. But the truly late deciders leaned to Obama by six percentage points. Was this a result of President Obama's handling of Hurricane Sandy? Or is it an artifact of the late deciders' party identification, or something else entirely? It is impossible to say, but the exit poll data contradict the pre-election prediction by some TV pundits that late deciders would break heavily against the incumbent. It is also worth noting that among the 42 percent of voters who claimed Obama's hurricane actions were important to them, 68 percent voted for the president.

Notice that 3 percent of voters said they finally made up their minds on Election Day itself. While it's possible that most or all of these voters were already leaning strongly in the direction they chose, the number reminds campaigns that Election Day contact and persuasion is not wasted effort. Some contests are decided by a handful of votes, after all.

### Old Time and New Style Religion

Election watchers have learned that Catholics are the religious denomination to follow—a key swing group of about a quarter of the national electorate that usually ends up in the winner's circle. George W. Bush won them by a few percentage points in 2004. Barack Obama did even better in 2008, attracting 54 percent of Catholics. This time, Obama won Catholics much more narrowly, by 2 percent, reflecting the tighter battle.

As usual, Protestants voted Republican, choosing Romney by a wide 57 percent to 42 percent margin, a 3 percent better showing than John McCain achieved and only slightly off George W. Bush's 59 percent in 2004. Romney also out-performed McCain among Jewish voters (2 percent of the electorate), but he still lost to Obama by 69 percent to 30 percent. The criticism Obama received from more conservative supporters of Israel helped to shave nine percentage points off the Democrat's 2008 performance.

The 7 percent of Americans who identified with a religion other than Protestant, Catholic, and Jewish went overwhelmingly for Obama (74 percent), as did the 12 percent who said they had no religion (70 percent for Obama).

Notice that there is no separate category for Mormons, who comprise about 2 percent of the country's population. All pre-election polling suggested that Romney, the first member of the Church of Jesus Christ of Latter-day Saints (Mormon) to be a major-party presidential nominee, would win overwhelming backing from his own religious group. The returns in Mormon-heavy parts of the nation suggest that this did occur on Election Day.

When race and religion are combined, we see that Romney won white Protestants by 69 percent to 30 percent and white Catholics with 59 percent. The probability is that the key factor in this combination is race, not religion.

The frequency of church attendance has also been a tell-tale indicator of partisan allegiance in recent elections. Those who attend religious services weekly gave Romney 59 percent; the "occasional" attendees were Obama's with 55 percent, and those who never show up at church were the most likely to vote for Obama (62 percent)—a pattern we saw in 2008.

During the campaign there had been much speculation that white evangelical Christians would be put off by Romney's Mormonism, which is regarded as a cult by some Christian denominations. The exit poll data proves that allegation to be false, since Romney won 78 percent of this quarter of the electorate, the same as Bush in 2004 and 4 percent better than McCain. Whatever doubts evangelicals may have had about Romney in the primaries were more than balanced by their distaste for President Obama.

### Love, Marriage, and Sexual Orientation

Republicans usually fare better with voters who are married, and 2008 was no exception. Romney garnered 56 percent among the three-fifths of Americans who said they were married, whereas Obama won the normal Democratic landslide among the two-fifths that aren't married (62 percent). Also, as usual, Democrats swept the nearly quarter of the population who are unmarried women, 67 percent to 31 percent. (Married women voted for Romney, 53 percent to 46 percent.) Unmarried men also voted for Obama, but by a lesser 56 percent to 40 percent margin.

Among the 5 percent of all voters who said they were gay, lesbian, or bisexual, Obama won 76 percent, a jump of 6 percent since 2008. This makes sense given Obama's first-ever presidential endorsement of gay marriage and his abolition of "don't ask, don't tell" in the military. Among the 95 percent of the electorate that said they were not "gay, lesbian, or bisexual," Obama and Romney split the vote evenly, 49 percent to 49 percent.

### Issues Matter and Voters Are Logical

Every exit poll can be mined for precious stones, but few gems are worth excavating as much as the questions about the issues driving voters to their candidate. "Voters are not fools," wrote the great political scientist V. O. Key and as one studies the voters' responses in the 2012 exit poll, Key's wisdom is validated.[24] Americans who agreed with Obama or Romney on their platform could be found in the candidate's corner at the ballot box. It all makes sense.

Almost six in ten voters picked the economy as the most important issue facing the country, far more than any other topic, and Romney won them narrowly, 51 percent to 47 percent. The Republican also attracted two-thirds of the 15 percent who cared most about the budget deficit and national debt. Obama garnered 75 percent backing from those concerned about health care (18 percent of all voters) and 56 percent support from those picking foreign policy as the top issue.

If taxes were on the mind of a voter, there was a two-to-one chance he or she would be voting for Romney. Seventy percent of the voters who wanted taxes increased on those making more than $250,000 voted for

Obama. Seventy-five percent of those who were opposed to tax increases chose Romney.

On health care, the 44 percent who wanted Obamacare kept or expanded were for Obama by 85 percent to 11 percent. But the 49 percent who wanted Obamacare repealed in part or whole picked Romney, 83 percent to 16 percent.

Voters who wanted illegal immigrants working in the United States to be offered legal status chose Obama by 61 percent to 37 percent, and those who thought they should be deported were in Romney's corner by 73 percent to 24 percent.

Obama won close to three-quarters of voters who wanted same-sex marriage legal in their state; Romney won a similar margin among those who were opposed. Among the 59 percent of Americans who want abortion to be always or mostly legal, Obama secured 67 percent, while Romney got 77 percent among the 36 percent who want abortion to be mostly or totally illegal.

The role of government divided people into one camp or the other. Those who said "government should do more" voted for Obama by 81 percent to 17 percent; those who believed government was doing too much were for Romney, 74 percent to 24 percent.

Obama voters were very likely to say the economy was getting better and their family's financial situation was improving; those more pessimistic about the economy generally as well as their own family's condition moved to Romney.

The voters who blamed Obama for the nation's economic problems went for Romney by 94 percent to 5 percent, but those who blamed George W. Bush were Obama's by 85 percent to 12 percent. Luckily for Obama, voters blamed Bush over Obama by 53 percent to 38 percent.

The "right-track/wrong-track" question that pollsters love was also useful. Ninety-three percent of those who thought the nation was basically on the right track sided with Obama. Eighty-four percent of those who believed the country was on the wrong track were Romney's. Even better was the division over Obama's performance as president: 89 percent of those who approved of Obama's job performance voted for him, and 94 percent of those who disapproved were for Romney. President Obama's attacks on Mitt Romney may have deflected some of the heat, but this referendum on the incumbent's job performance is an inevitable part of any reelection contest.

An election is also the voters' comparative judgment on the two candidates' personal qualities. Obama arguably won the most vital comparison:

"Who is more in touch with people like you?" By 53 percent to 43 percent, people said Obama—and the president attracted 91 percent backing from this majority.

Therefore, voters mainly supported the presidential nominee with whom they agreed on the big issues of the day. This is precisely what we would expect rational voters to do, whether they are choosing their candidate on the basis of long-held views or adapting their views to conform to their personal identification with a political party and their candidate's platform. Partisan affiliation is as important as any factor discussed in this chapter, and this will be analyzed in some detail by Professor Alan Abramowitz in the next chapter.

## A CONFIRMING ELECTION IN PERSPECTIVE

If the 2008 election can be said to have set the nation's political course, then the 2012 election confirmed it. The demographics of the American electorate have changed significantly, and they will continue to shift in the same direction for the foreseeable future. The growth of minority populations, especially Hispanics, is a large part of this. But so is the galvanization of the young and certain portions of the female majority, such as single women.

It is more than demographics, of course. Specific issue clusters have had a large impact on critical segments of the electorate. For women, economic security and reproductive health concerns are prominent. For Hispanics, immigration has been central, along with the economy. For young people, concern about gay marriage and environmental matters complement economic issues such as student loans and job prospects.

Democrats have benefitted from these trends in the 2008 and 2012 presidential elections, and the underlying tide has assisted the party at all levels. Unexpectedly, Democrats added two Senate seats in 2012, creating a solid fifty-five-seat majority. Even though the House of Representatives stayed Republican, Democrats added eight seats—and actually won the popular vote for the House despite not winning the chamber. That last happened in 1996.[25] In the state legislatures, Democrats gained seven houses to the Republicans' five.[26]

For all the good news for Democrats, though, modifications by the Republicans can adjust the political outlook. A constructive approach on immigration, a muting of out-of-the-mainstream positions on abortion and gay rights, and an embrace of scientific fact on climate change and other matters can combine well with traditional Republican fiscal conservatism, which still appeals to many of every race, gender, and age group. A GOP platform stressing financial prudence, federalism, and personal freedom (borrowed from libertarianism) could fit the American people well in some election years. This transformation isn't just in the GOP's interests. Every democracy needs at least two strong parties, lest overconfidence and corruption become the norm when one side is guaranteed the victories.

Four years ago in this space, after Barack Obama's first election, I suggested that the demographic signs were bright for Democrats, but that governing results would also matter:

> Every election is a discrete event. Most do not signal a durable change in voter alignments. A few do, and these are called realigning elections. It is impossible to know yet into which category Obama's victory will fall. There are some positive signs for Democrats that encourage them to think of realignment. . . . As rosy as the picture seems to be for Democrats, real events and actual performance in office will determine the future. Campaigns are grueling, but they are actually the easy part. Governing is the ultimate test for any president, legislature, and party coalition.[27]

It is possible that 2008 was a realigning election, not because it caused millions to change party allegiance but because it activated and energized a new demographic majority in the electorate. The 2012 results endorse that view, and as such we have just had a confirmation election, proving that what we saw in 2008 was not a freakish event of political nature. This appears especially true since the economic conditions prevailing in 2012, while not calamitous, were also not especially favorable to the reelection of a president.

There is no question that the demographic transformation of America is real and will continue apace. That alone would argue for some permanence to the new political realities we've witnessed twice. But again, what actually happens in President Obama's second term—whether he is able to deliver for the people who elected him and the country as a whole, and avoid second-term gridlock, the arrogance of reaffirmed power, paralyzing scandals, and unpopular wars—will matter as much as demographics. So too will reform efforts within the Republican Party. Will the GOP's leadership, working with its ideologically driven activist base, be able to make the needed changes in policy and presentation to attract a much larger slice of the young and minorities? Republican leaders already see the handwriting on the Electoral College's walls, but the GOP base is less inclined to do what is needed to become competitive.

Politics offers no guarantees to either party. Performance will shape the nation's politics in 2016 and beyond.

**Table 1.5   U.S. President Election Results—National Exit Poll**

**Vote by Gender**

| Total | Obama 2012 | Change from 2008 | Romney 2012 |
|---|---|---|---|
| Male (47%) | 45% | -4% | 52% |
| Female (53%) | 55% | -1% | 44% |

**Vote by Age**

| Total | Obama 2012 | Change from 2008 | Romney 2012 |
|---|---|---|---|
| 18–29 (19%) | 60% | -6% | 37% |
| 30–44 (27%) | 52% | 0% | 45% |
| 45–64 (38%) | 47% | -3% | 51% |
| 65 and older (16%) | 44% | -1% | 56% |

**Vote by Age**

| Total | Obama 2012 | Change from 2008 | Romney 2012 |
|---|---|---|---|
| 18–24 (11%) | 60% | -6% | 36% |
| 25–29 (8%) | 60% | -6% | 38% |
| 30–39 (17%) | 55% | +1% | 42% |
| 40–49 (20%) | 48% | -1% | 50% |
| 50–64 (28%) | 47% | -3% | 52% |
| 65 and older (16%) | 44% | -1% | 56% |

**Vote by Race**

| Total | Obama 2012 | Change from 2008 | Romney 2012 |
|---|---|---|---|
| White (72%) | 39% | -4% | 59% |
| African American (13%) | 93% | -2% | 6% |
| Latino (10%) | 71% | +4% | 27% |
| Asian (3%) | 73% | +11% | 26% |
| Other (2%) | 58% | -8% | 38% |

**Vote by Age and Race**

| Total | Obama 2012 | Change from 2008 | Romney 2012 |
|---|---|---|---|
| White 18–29 (11%) | 44% | -10% | 51% |
| White 30–44 (18%) | 38% | -3% | 59% |
| White 45–64 (29%) | 38% | -4% | 61% |
| White over 65 (14%) | 39% | -1% | 61% |
| Black 18–29 (3%) | 91% | -4% | 8% |
| Black 30–44 (4%) | 94% | -2% | 5% |
| Black 45–64 (4%) | 93% | -3% | 7% |
| Black over 65 (1%) | 93% | -1% | 6% |
| Latino 18–29 (4%) | 74% | -2% | 23% |
| Latino 30–44 (3%) | 71% | +8% | 28% |
| Latino 45–64 (3%) | 68% | +10% | 31% |
| Latino over 65 (1%) | 65% | -3% | 35% |
| All others (5%) | 67% | +3% | 31% |

*(Continued)*

**Table 1.5   Continued**

### Vote by Gender and Race

| Total | Obama 2012 | Change from 2008 | Romney 2012 |
|---|---|---|---|
| White men (34%) | 35% | -6% | 62% |
| White women (38%) | 42% | -4% | 56% |
| Black men (5%) | 87% | -8% | 11% |
| Black women (8%) | 96% | 0% | 3% |
| Latino men (5%) | 65% | +1% | 33% |
| Latino women (6%) | 76% | +8% | 23% |
| All others (5%) | 66% | +2% | 31% |

### Vote by Ideology

| Total | Obama 2012 | Change from 2008 | Romney 2012 |
|---|---|---|---|
| Liberal (25%) | 86% | -3% | 11% |
| Moderate (41%) | 56% | -4% | 41% |
| Conservative (35%) | 17% | -3% | 82% |

### Vote by Party ID

| Total | Obama 2012 | Change from 2008 | Romney 2012 |
|---|---|---|---|
| Democratic (38%) | 92% | +3% | 7% |
| Republican (32%) | 6% | -3% | 93% |
| Independent (29%) | 45% | -7% | 50% |

### Vote by Education

| Total | Obama 2012 | Change from 2008 | Romney 2012 |
|---|---|---|---|
| No high school (3%) | 64% | +1% | 35% |
| High school graduate (21%) | 51% | -1% | 48% |
| Some college (29%) | 49% | -2% | 48% |
| College graduate (29%) | 47% | -3% | 51% |
| Postgraduate (18%) | 55% | -3% | 42% |

### Are You a College Graduate?

| Total | Obama 2012 | Change from 2008 | Romney 2012 |
|---|---|---|---|
| Yes (47%) | 50% | -3% | 48% |
| No (53%) | 51% | -2% | 47% |

### Did You Attend College?

| Total | Obama 2012 | Change from 2008 | Romney 2012 |
|---|---|---|---|
| Yes (76%) | 50% | -2% | 48% |
| No (24%) | 52% | -2% | 46% |

**Vote by Income**

| | Obama 2012 | Change from 2008 | Romney 2012 |
|---|---|---|---|
| Total | | | |
| Less than $50K (41%) | 60% | 0% | 38% |
| $50–100K (31%) | 46% | -3% | 52% |
| $100K or more (28%) | 44% | -5% | 54% |

**Vote by Income**

| | Obama 2012 | Change from 2008 | Romney 2012 |
|---|---|---|---|
| Total | | | |
| Less than $50K (41%) | 60% | 0% | 38% |
| $50K or more (59%) | 45% | -4% | 53% |

**Vote by Income**

| | Obama 2012 | Change from 2008 | Romney 2012 |
|---|---|---|---|
| Total | | | |
| Less than $100K (72%) | 54% | -1% | 44% |
| $100K or more (28%) | 44% | -5% | 54% |

**How Often Do You Attend Religious Services?**

| | Obama 2012 | Change from 2008 | Romney 2012 |
|---|---|---|---|
| Total | | | |
| More than weekly (14%) | 36% | -7% | 63% |
| Weekly (28%) | 41% | -2% | 58% |
| Monthly (13%) | 55% | +2% | 44% |
| Few times a year (27%) | 56% | -3% | 42% |
| Never (17%) | 62% | -5% | 34% |

**How Often Do You Attend Religious Services?**

| | Obama 2012 | Change from 2008 | Romney 2012 |
|---|---|---|---|
| Total | | | |
| Weekly (42%) | 39% | -4% | 59% |
| Occasionally (40%) | 55% | -2% | 43% |
| Never (17%) | 62% | -5% | 34% |

**Vote by Religion**

| | Obama 2012 | Change from 2008 | Romney 2012 |
|---|---|---|---|
| Total | | | |
| Protestant (53%) | 42% | -3% | 57% |
| Catholic (25%) | 50% | -4% | 48% |
| Jewish (2%) | 69% | -9% | 30% |
| Other (7%) | 74% | +1% | 23% |
| None (12%) | 70% | -5% | 26% |

*(Continued)*

**Table 1.5   Continued**

### Vote by Religion and Race

| Total | Obama 2012 | Change from 2008 | Romney 2012 |
|---|---|---|---|
| White Protestant (39%) | 30% | -4% | 69% |
| White Catholic (18%) | 40% | -7% | 59% |
| White Jewish (2%) | 71% | -12% | 29% |
| White/other religion (4%) | 61% | -6% | 35% |
| White/no religion (9%) | 63% | -8% | 31% |
| Nonwhite (28%) | 80% | +1% | 18% |

### Vote by Religion and Church Attendance

| Total | Obama 2012 | Change from 2008 | Romney 2012 |
|---|---|---|---|
| Protestant/attend weekly (15%) | 29% | -3% | 70% |
| Protestant/not weekly (14%) | 44% | -1% | 55% |
| Catholic/attend weekly (11%) | 42% | -7% | 57% |
| Catholic/not weekly (13%) | 56% | -2% | 42% |
| All others (46%) | 58% | -5% | 39% |

### Are You White Born-Again Christian?

| Total | Obama 2012 | Change from 2008 | Romney 2012 |
|---|---|---|---|
| Yes (26%) | 21% | -3% | 78% |
| No (74%) | 60% | -2% | 37% |

### Abortion Should Be . . .

| Total | Obama 2012 | Change from 2008 | Romney 2012 |
|---|---|---|---|
| Always legal (29%) | 76% | N/A | 22% |
| Mostly legal (30%) | 58% | N/A | 40% |
| Mostly illegal (23%) | 22% | N/A | 76% |
| Always illegal (13%) | 19% | N/A | 79% |

### Abortion Should Be . . .

| Total | Obama 2012 | Change from 2008 | Romney 2012 |
|---|---|---|---|
| Legal (59%) | 67% | N/A | 31% |
| Illegal (36%) | 21% | N/A | 77% |

### Opinion of Tea Party Movement

| Total | Obama 2012 | Change from 2008 | Romney 2012 |
|---|---|---|---|
| Support (21%) | 11% | N/A | 87% |
| Neutral (42%) | 42% | N/A | 57% |
| Oppose (30%) | 89% | N/A | 9% |

**Most Important Issue Facing Country**

| Total | Obama 2012 | Change from 2008 | Romney 2012 |
|---|---|---|---|
| Foreign policy (5%) | 56% | N/A | 33% |
| Deficit (15%) | 32% | N/A | 66% |
| Economy (59%) | 47% | N/A | 51% |
| Health care (18%) | 75% | N/A | 24% |

**Most Important Candidate Quality**

| Total | Obama 2012 | Change from 2008 | Romney 2012 |
|---|---|---|---|
| Shares my values (27%) | 42% | N/A | 55% |
| Strong leader (18%) | 38% | N/A | 61% |
| Cares about people (21%) | 81% | N/A | 18% |
| Vision for future (29%) | 45% | N/A | 54% |

**Biggest Economic Problem Facing People Like You**

| Total | Obama 2012 | Change from 2008 | Romney 2012 |
|---|---|---|---|
| Housing market (8%) | 63% | N/A | 32% |
| Unemployment (38%) | 54% | N/A | 44% |
| Taxes (14%) | 32% | N/A | 66% |
| Rising prices (37%) | 49% | N/A | 49% |

**2010 Health Care Law Should Be . . .**

| Total | Obama 2012 | Change from 2008 | Romney 2012 |
|---|---|---|---|
| Expanded (26%) | 92% | N/A | 5% |
| Kept as it is (18%) | 80% | N/A | 19% |
| Repealed in part (24%) | 27% | N/A | 72% |
| Repealed completely (25%) | 3% | N/A | 93% |

**Should 2010 Health Care Law Be Repealed?**

| Total | Obama 2012 | Change from 2008 | Romney 2012 |
|---|---|---|---|
| Yes (49%) | 15% | N/A | 83% |
| No (44%) | 87% | N/A | 11% |

**Income Tax Rates Should Be . . .**

| Total | Obama 2012 | Change from 2008 | Romney 2012 |
|---|---|---|---|
| Increased for $250K+ (47%) | 70% | N/A | 29% |
| Not increased (35%) | 23% | N/A | 75% |

*(Continued)*

**Table 1.5    Continued**

**Most Illegal Immigrants
Working in the U.S. Should
Be . . .**

|  | Obama 2012 | Change from 2008 | Romney 2012 |
|---|---|---|---|
| Total |  |  |  |
| Offered legal status (65%) | 61% | N/A | 37% |
| Deported (28%) | 24% | N/A | 73% |

**Who Is More In Touch with
People Like You?**

|  | Obama 2012 | Change from 2008 | Romney 2012 |
|---|---|---|---|
| Total |  |  |  |
| Obama (53%) | 91% | N/A | 7% |
| Romney (43%) | 1% | N/A | 98% |

**Who Would Better Handle
Economy?**

|  | Obama 2012 | Change from 2008 | Romney 2012 |
|---|---|---|---|
| Total |  |  |  |
| Obama (48%) | 98% | N/A | 1% |
| Romney (49%) | 4% | N/A | 94% |

**Who Would Better Handle
Medicare?**

|  | Obama 2012 | Change from 2008 | Romney 2012 |
|---|---|---|---|
| Total |  |  |  |
| Obama (52%) | 92% | N/A | 6% |
| Romney (44%) | 2% | N/A | 96% |

**Who Would Better Handle
Deficit?**

|  | Obama 2012 | Change from 2008 | Romney 2012 |
|---|---|---|---|
| Total |  |  |  |
| Obama (47%) | 98% | N/A | 1% |
| Romney (49%) | 3% | N/A | 95% |

**Opinion of Government**

|  | Obama 2012 | Change from 2008 | Romney 2012 |
|---|---|---|---|
| Total |  |  |  |
| Government should do more (43%) | 81% | +5% | 17% |
| Government doing too much (51%) | 24% | -3% | 74% |

**National Economic Conditions**

| Total | Obama 2012 | Change from 2008 | Romney 2012 |
|---|---|---|---|
| Excellent (2%) | N/A | N/A | N/A |
| Good (21%) | 90% | +67% | 9% |
| Not so good (45%) | 55% | +15% | 42% |
| Poor (31%) | 12% | -54% | 85% |

**National Economic Conditions**

| Total | Obama 2012 | Change from 2008 | Romney 2012 |
|---|---|---|---|
| Excellent/good (23%) | 90% | +64% | 9% |
| Not so good/poor (77%) | 38% | -16% | 60% |

**U.S. Economic Conditions Are . . .**

| Total | Obama 2012 | Change from 2008 | Romney 2012 |
|---|---|---|---|
| Getting better (39%) | 88% | +27% | 9% |
| Getting worse (30%) | 9% | -34% | 90% |
| Staying about the same (29%) | 40% | -12% | 57% |

**U.S. Economic Conditions Are . . .**

| Total | Obama 2012 | Change from 2008 | Romney 2012 |
|---|---|---|---|
| Getting better (39%) | 88% | N/A | 9% |
| Good and staying the same (4%) | 71% | N/A | 27% |
| Poor and staying the same (25%) | 35% | N/A | 62% |
| Getting worse (30%) | 9% | N/A | 90% |

**Your Family's Financial Situation**

| Total | Obama 2012 | Change from 2008 | Romney 2012 |
|---|---|---|---|
| Better (25%) | 84% | +47% | 15% |
| Worse (33%) | 18% | -53% | 80% |
| Same (41%) | 58% | +13% | 40% |

**Country is Going In . . .**

| Total | Obama 2012 | Change from 2008 | Romney 2012 |
|---|---|---|---|
| Right direction (46%) | 93% | +66% | 6% |
| Wrong track (52%) | 13% | -49% | 84% |

(Continued)

**Table 1.5    Continued**

### More to Blame for Economic Problems?

| | Obama 2012 | Change from 2008 | Romney 2012 |
|---|---|---|---|
| *Total* | | | |
| Barack Obama (38%) | 5% | N/A | 94% |
| George W. Bush (53%) | 85% | N/A | 12% |

### U.S. Economic System Generally . . .

| | Obama 2012 | Change from 2008 | Romney 2012 |
|---|---|---|---|
| *Total* | | | |
| Favors the wealthy (55%) | 71% | N/A | 26% |
| Is fair to most Americans (39%) | 22% | N/A | 77% |

### Should Taxes Be Raised to Help Cut Deficit?

| | Obama 2012 | Change from 2008 | Romney 2012 |
|---|---|---|---|
| *Total* | | | |
| Yes (33%) | 73% | N/A | 24% |
| No (63%) | 37% | N/A | 61% |

### Opinion of Obama Administration

| | Obama 2012 | Change from 2008 | Romney 2012 |
|---|---|---|---|
| *Total* | | | |
| Enthusiastic (25%) | 98% | N/A | 2% |
| Satisfied (24%) | 87% | N/A | 11% |
| Dissatisfied (30%) | 9% | N/A | 86% |
| Angry (19%) | 1% | N/A | 97% |

### Opinion of Obama Administration

| | Obama 2012 | Change from 2008 | Romney 2012 |
|---|---|---|---|
| *Total* | | | |
| Enthusiastic/satisfied (49%) | 93% | N/A | 6% |
| Dissatisfied/angry (49%) | 6% | N/A | 91% |

### How Obama Is Handling His Job as President

| | Obama 2012 | Change from 2008 | Romney 2012 |
|---|---|---|---|
| *Total* | | | |
| Strongly approve (29%) | 97% | N/A | 2% |
| Somewhat approve (24%) | 80% | N/A | 18% |
| Somewhat disapprove (13%) | 9% | N/A | 88% |
| Strongly disapprove (33%) | 1% | N/A | 96% |

## How Obama Is Handling His Job as President

| | Obama 2012 | Change from 2008 | Romney 2012 |
|---|---|---|---|
| *Total* | | | |
| Approve (54%) | 89% | N/A | 9% |
| Disapprove (45%) | 3% | N/A | 94% |

## Opinion of Barack Obama

| | Obama 2012 | Change from 2008 | Romney 2012 |
|---|---|---|---|
| *Total* | | | |
| Favorable (53%) | 93% | N/A | 6% |
| Unfavorable (46%) | 3% | N/A | 94% |

## Opinion of Mitt Romney

| | Obama 2012 | Change from 2008 | Romney 2012 |
|---|---|---|---|
| *Total* | | | |
| Favorable (47%) | 6% | N/A | 93% |
| Unfavorable (50%) | 92% | N/A | 5% |

## Do Obama Policies Generally Favor . . .

| | Obama 2012 | Change from 2008 | Romney 2012 |
|---|---|---|---|
| *Total* | | | |
| Rich (10%) | 9% | N/A | 89% |
| Middle class (44%) | 86% | N/A | 12% |
| Poor (31%) | 25% | N/A | 74% |

## Would Romney Policies Generally Favor . . .

| | Obama 2012 | Change from 2008 | Romney 2012 |
|---|---|---|---|
| *Total* | | | |
| Rich (53%) | 87% | N/A | 10% |
| Middle class (34%) | 6% | N/A | 93% |
| Poor (2%) | N/A | N/A | N/A |

## Trust Obama to Handle International Crisis?

| | Obama 2012 | Change from 2008 | Romney 2012 |
|---|---|---|---|
| *Total* | | | |
| Yes (57%) | 85% | N/A | 13% |
| No (42%) | 2% | N/A | 96% |

## Trust Romney to Handle International Crisis?

| | Obama 2012 | Change from 2008 | Romney 2012 |
|---|---|---|---|
| *Total* | | | |
| Yes (50%) | 13% | N/A | 86% |
| No (46%) | 90% | N/A | 7% |

*(Continued)*

**Table 1.5    Continued**

### Who Do You Trust to Handle International Crisis?

| Total | Obama 2012 | Change from 2008 | Romney 2012 |
|---|---|---|---|
| Only Obama (42%) | 97% | N/A | 1% |
| Only Romney (36%) | 1% | N/A | 98% |
| Both (13%) | 46% | N/A | 51% |
| Neither (4%) | 13% | N/A | 72% |

### Opinion of Presidential Candidate You Voted For

| Total | Obama 2012 | Change from 2008 | Romney 2012 |
|---|---|---|---|
| Strongly favor (65%) | 54% | N/A | 45% |
| Have reservations (23%) | 42% | N/A | 57% |
| Dislike opponent (10%) | 41% | N/A | 51% |

### When Did You Decide Presidential Vote?

| Total | Obama 2012 | Change from 2008 | Romney 2012 |
|---|---|---|---|
| Just today (3%) | 51% | +1% | 44% |
| Last few days (6%) | 50% | +3% | 45% |
| In October (11%) | 49% | -5% | 48% |
| In September (9%) | 45% | -9% | 53% |
| Before that (69%) | 53% | +1% | 46% |

### When Did You Decide Presidential Vote?

| Total | Obama 2012 | Change from 2008 | Romney 2012 |
|---|---|---|---|
| Today/last few days (9%) | 50% | +1% | 44% |
| Before that (89%) | 51% | -2% | 47% |

### When Did You Decide Presidential Vote?

| Total | Obama 2012 | Change from 2008 | Romney 2012 |
|---|---|---|---|
| In October or November (21%) | 50% | N/A | 46% |
| Before that (78%) | 52% | -2% | 47% |

### Vote by Marital Status

| Total | Obama 2012 | Change from 2008 | Romney 2012 |
|---|---|---|---|
| Married (60%) | 42% | -5% | 56% |
| Unmarried (40%) | 62% | -3% | 35% |

## Vote by Gender and Marital Status

| | Obama 2012 | Change from 2008 | Romney 2012 |
|---|---|---|---|
| Total | | | |
| Married men (29%) | 38% | N/A | 60% |
| Married women (31%) | 46% | N/A | 53% |
| Unmarried men (18%) | 56% | N/A | 40% |
| Unmarried women (23%) | 67% | N/A | 31% |

## Any Children Under 18 Living in Your Home?

| | Obama 2012 | Change from 2008 | Romney 2012 |
|---|---|---|---|
| Total | | | |
| Yes (36%) | 51% | -2% | 47% |
| No (64%) | 50% | -3% | 47% |

## Vote by Marital Status and Children

| | Obama 2012 | Change from 2008 | Romney 2012 |
|---|---|---|---|
| Total | | | |
| Married with children (27%) | 45% | -3% | 54% |
| All others (73%) | 53% | -3% | 45% |

## Vote by Gender and Children in Household

| | Obama 2012 | Change from 2008 | Romney 2012 |
|---|---|---|---|
| Total | | | |
| Fathers (16%) | 45% | N/A | 53% |
| Mothers (20%) | 56% | N/A | 43% |
| Men with no children (30%) | 47% | N/A | 50% |
| Women with no children (34%) | 54% | N/A | 45% |

## Is Anyone in Household a Union Member?

| | Obama 2012 | Change from 2008 | Romney 2012 |
|---|---|---|---|
| Total | | | |
| Yes (18%) | 58% | -1% | 40% |
| No (82%) | 49% | -2% | 48% |

## Do You Work Full-Time for Pay?

| | Obama 2012 | Change from 2008 | Romney 2012 |
|---|---|---|---|
| Total | | | |
| Yes (60%) | 49% | -6% | 49% |
| No (40%) | 53% | +3% | 45% |

(Continued)

**Table 1.5    Continued**

**Should Same-Sex Marriages Be Legal in Your State?**

| Total | Obama 2012 | Change from 2008 | Romney 2012 |
|---|---|---|---|
| Yes (49%) | 73% | N/A | 25% |
| No (46%) | 25% | N/A | 74% |

**Are You Gay, Lesbian, Bisexual?**

| Total | Obama 2012 | Change from 2008 | Romney 2012 |
|---|---|---|---|
| Yes (5%) | 76% | +6% | 22% |
| No (95%) | 49% | -4% | 49% |

**Importance of Obama's Response to Hurricane**

| Total | Obama 2012 | Change from 2008 | Romney 2012 |
|---|---|---|---|
| Most important factor (15%) | 73% | N/A | 26% |
| An important factor (27%) | 65% | N/A | 33% |
| Minor factor (22%) | 51% | N/A | 46% |
| Not a factor at all (31%) | 28% | N/A | 70% |

**Obama's Hurricane Response Important to You?**

| Total | Obama 2012 | Change from 2008 | Romney 2012 |
|---|---|---|---|
| Yes (42%) | 68% | N/A | 31% |
| No (54%) | 37% | N/A | 60% |

**Obama's Hurricane Response a Factor in Your Vote?**

| Total | Obama 2012 | Change from 2008 | Romney 2012 |
|---|---|---|---|
| Yes (64%) | 62% | N/A | 36% |
| No (31%) | 28% | N/A | 70% |

**Vote for U.S. House**

| Total | Obama 2012 | Change from 2008 | Romney 2012 |
|---|---|---|---|
| Democrat (50%) | 93% | +5 | 6% |
| Republican (48%) | 7% | -2% | 92% |

*Source*: CNN, www.cnn.com/election/2012/results/race/president#exit-polls.

# NOTES

1. Both chief executives might have been defeated for renomination or in the general election, but maybe not. Truman's upset in 1948 makes an analyst wary of closed-door prognostications.

2. Actually, Bush followed Woodrow Wilson's path, when Wilson won a second term in 1916 by 3 percent of the popular vote and a tight 277–254 vote in the Electoral College.

3. Political scientist John Wright argues that even when unemployment is high, the Democratic candidate for president is positioned well to benefit since Democrats "own" the issue. John R. Wright, "Unemployment and the Democratic Electoral Advantage," *American Political Science Review* 106 (November 2012): 685–702.

4. Election results used in this book were the most up-to-date available at time of publication; forty-nine of fifty states (all except New York) had certified their election results as of this writing.

5. Ohio narrowly voted for Thomas E. Dewey (R) over FDR in 1944, and Richard Nixon (R) over JFK in 1960.

6. Larry J. Sabato, Kyle Kondik, and Geoffrey Skelley, "12 from '12: Some Takeaways from a Wild Election," Sabato's Crystal Ball, November 15, 2012, accessed November 26, 2012, www.centerforpolitics.org/crystalball/articles/12-from-12-some-takeaways-from-a-wild-election/.

7. Sabato, Kondik, and Skelley, "12 from '12."

8. Of course, Tilden never became president, as all the disputed and decisive electoral votes were awarded to Republican nominee Rutherford B. Hayes.

9. Larry J. Sabato, *Pendulum Swing* (New York: Pearson Education, Inc., 2011).

10. Mitt Romney won the popular vote in the following U.S. territories: American Samoa, Guam, Northern Mariana Islands, Puerto Rico, and the U.S. Virgin Islands. Ron Paul won a plurality of delegates in Iowa, Louisiana, Maine, and Minnesota. Rick Santorum won the popular vote in Iowa, Louisiana, and Minnesota, while Mitt Romney won the popular vote in Maine.

11. In 1912, William Howard Taft was challenged for renomination by former president Theodore Roosevelt. In 1932, Herbert Hoover was challenged for renomination by Senator John J. Blaine of Wisconsin, former senator Joseph I. France of Maryland, and former senator James Wolcott Wadsworth Jr. of New York. In 1980, Jimmy Carter was challenged for renomination by Senator Ted Kennedy of Massachusetts and Governor Jerry Brown of California. In 1992, George H. W. Bush was challenged for renomination by conservative commentator Pat Buchanan.

12. In a CNN/ORC poll taken after the debate on October 3, 2012, 67 percent of respondents thought Romney had won the debate, while only 25 percent thought Obama won. CNN/ORC Poll, "CNN/ORC Poll—October 3—Debate," CNN.com, accessed November 26, 2012, http://i2.cdn.turner.com/cnn/2012/images/10/03/top12.pdf.

13. In a post-election article, Obama pollster Joel Benenson said, "The American electorate does not bounce around as if it's on a pogo stick. If you look at the exit polls, 70 percent of voters had made up their mind before September . . . Mitt Romney would have had to have a phenomenal two months . . . he would have had to won that 30 percent of voters, to make up a five point difference, by 17 points." Maggie Haberman, "Obama Pollster: Gallup, Public Polling Needs a Retooling," Politico.com, November 16, 2012, accessed November 26, 2012, www.politico .com/blogs/burns-haberman/2012/11/obama-pollster-gallup-public-polling-needs -a-retooling-149807.html.

14. How much the Obama voter contact program really meant to his vote total is unknown. Obama did not "over-perform" in swing states compared to non-swing states, where there was much less effort expended on organized voter contact, so one has to question how much difference the high-tech Obama GOTV campaign really made. As for Romney, his much-touted internal voter monitoring system broke down early on Election Day and never delivered as advertised. See Kimberley A. Strassel, "The GOP Turnout Myth," *Wall Street Journal*, November 22, 2012, accessed November 26, 2012, http://online.wsj .com/article/SB10001424127887324352004578133120431803606.html, and Michael Kranish, "ORCA, Mitt Romney's High-Tech Get-Out-the-Vote Program, Crashed on Election Day," *Boston Globe*, November 9, 2012, accessed December 3, 2012, www.boston.com/news/politics/2012/president/candidates/ romney/2012/11/10/orca-mitt-romney-high-tech-get-out-the-vote-program -crashed-election-day/gflS8VkzDcJcXCrHoV0nsI/story.html.

15. See note 3, above.

16. Michael McDonald, "United States Elections Project: 2004 General Election Turnout Rates," United States Elections Project, accessed November 26, 2012, http:// elections.gmu.edu/Turnout_2004G.html; Michael McDonald, "United States Elections Project: 2008 General Election Turnout Rates," United States Elections Project, accessed November 26, 2012, http://elections.gmu.edu/Turnout_2008G.html.

17. McDonald, "United States Elections Project: 2008 General Election Turnout Rates."

18. University of Virginia politics professor Paul Freedman has assembled some of the relevant research on the effects of negative advertising at the following link: www.centerforpolitics.org/crystalball/wp-content/uploads/2012/12/Political -Ads-and-Voter-Turnout.pdf.

19. Larry J. Sabato, *Overtime: The 2000 Election Thriller* (New York: Pearson Education, 2002), 103–5.

20. County-level data provided by Election Data Services.

21. Edison Research conducted the exit poll; more information is available here: www.edisonresearch.com/home/archives/2012/11/edison-successfully-conducts -the-2012-national-election-exit-polls.php.

22. To save on costs, the 2012 exit poll did not include sample precincts from some states, including Alaska, Arkansas, Delaware, District of Columbia, Georgia,

Hawaii, Idaho, Kentucky, Louisiana, Nebraska, North Dakota, Oklahoma, Rhode Island, South Carolina, South Dakota, Tennessee, Texas, Utah, West Virginia, and Wyoming. This is to be regretted, of course, but the national adjusted sample is still statistically valid.

23. Mark DiCamillo, "Post-Election Analysis: The Growing Political Might of Ethnic Voters in the 2012 California Elections," The Field Poll of California, Release #2435, November 19, 2012, accessed November 27, 2012, www.field.com/fieldpollonline/subscribers/Rls2435.pdf.

24. V. O. Key and Milton C. Cummings, *The Responsible Electorate: Rationality in Presidential Voting* (Cambridge, MA: Belknap Press, 1966), 7.

25. A study by the clerk of the House of Representatives in July 1997 showed that Democrats won the House by a popular vote margin of 272,708. Robin H. Carles, "Statistics of the Presidential and Congressional Election of November 5, 1996," Office of the Clerk of the U.S. House of Representatives, accessed November 27, 2012, http://clerk.house.gov/member_info/electionInfo/1996election.pdf.

26. In state legislatures, the Democrats took control of the Colorado House; the Maine House and Senate; the Minnesota House and Senate; the New Hampshire House; and the Oregon House. In New York, Republicans and a group of independent Democrats formed a controlling coalition in the state senate, even though Democrats appeared to capture the chamber on Election Night. In Washington, Democrats lost control of the state senate via two maverick Democrats joining with the Republican caucus to form a one-seat majority. The Republicans took outright control of the Arkansas House and Senate, the Alaska Senate, and the Wisconsin Senate.

27. Larry J. Sabato, *The Year of Obama: How Barack Obama Won the White House* (New York: Longman, 2010), 53.

## *2*

# VOTING IN A TIME OF POLARIZATION

## Why Obama Won and What It Means

### *Alan Abramowitz*

It was the most expensive presidential campaign in American history as well as one of the longest. More than $2 billion was spent by the candidates, the political parties and outside groups, including hundreds of millions by mostly pro-Republican Super PACs created in the aftermath of the Supreme Court's 2010 *Citizens United* decision. The general election campaign really began in the spring, as soon as Mitt Romney had clinched the Republican nomination, and long before the national party conventions. Yet after all of the months of campaigning and all of the money spent in a handful of battleground states, the outcome of the 2012 election closely reflected certain fundamental factors that were largely set long before Election Day. In this chapter I will examine those fundamental factors and explain how they shaped the 2012 presidential campaign and ultimately produced a fairly close but decisive victory for Barack Obama. I will also discuss some of the longer-term implications of the 2012 results for the future of electoral competition in the United States.

## THE POPULAR VOTE AND THE ELECTORAL MAP

With nearly all votes tabulated, Barack Obama had received 65.6 million votes, or 51 percent of the total vote, to 60.8 million votes or 47.3 percent of the total vote for Mitt Romney. Obama's margin of 4.8 million votes or 3.7 percentage points was about half the size of his seven-point margin in 2008. Nevertheless, it was larger than the popular vote margin in two of the previous three presidential elections. In terms of the national popular vote, the 2012 results continued the recent trend of relatively close presidential elections. No presidential candidate has won the popular vote by a margin of more than ten percentage points since Ronald Reagan in 1984.

But while the president's popular vote margin was relatively narrow, his electoral vote margin was quite impressive. Obama ended up carrying 26 states and the District of Columbia with a total of 332 electoral votes. Romney carried 24 states with a total of 206 electoral votes. Of the nine states that were generally seen as key battlegrounds in the final stages of the campaign, the president carried eight—all but North Carolina, which he lost by two points. Florida, Virginia, Colorado, Nevada, New Hampshire, Iowa, Ohio and Wisconsin all gave their electoral votes to Obama by margins ranging from one point in the case of Florida to seven points in the case of Wisconsin.

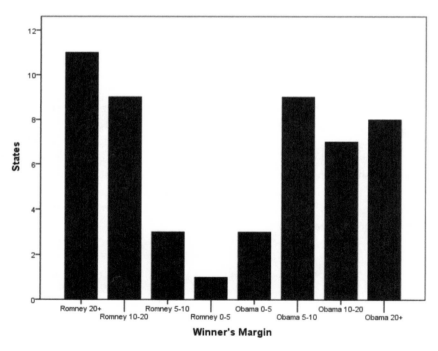

**Figure 2.1.   Winning Candidates' Margin in the States**

What is perhaps most striking about the results of the 2012 presidential election at the state level is that despite the closeness of the national popular vote, there were very few closely contested states. Figure 2.1 displays the distribution of the winning candidate's margin in the fifty states and the District of Columbia in 2012. Only four states were decided by a margin of less than five percentage points—Florida, Ohio, Virginia, and North Carolina. In 2008, six states were decided by that small a margin. On the other hand, twenty-seven states as well as the District of Columbia were decided by a margin of at least fifteen percentage points. In 2008, twenty-five states and the district were decided by such a decisive margin. Mitt Romney actually carried more states by landslide and near-landslide margins than Barack Obama, but the states that Obama carried had far more electoral votes than the ones that Romney carried.

The 2012 results continued the recent pattern of presidential elections that are decided by a narrow margin at the national level but by a landslide or near-landslide margin in many states. And that included some of the most populous and electoral vote-rich states in the country. Thus, President Obama carried California with its fifty-five electoral votes by a margin of twenty-three points, New York with its twenty-nine electoral votes by twenty-six points, and Illinois with its twenty electoral votes by seventeen points. Meanwhile, Romney won Texas's thirty-eight electoral votes by a margin of sixteen points.

This pattern of many deep red and blue states, including several of the nation's most populous states, represents a dramatic change from the pattern of electoral competition seen in close presidential elections during the 1960s and 1970s. In 1960 and 1976, when John F. Kennedy and Jimmy Carter won close, hard-fought battles for the White House, more than half of the states were battlegrounds. Moreover, in those elections every one of the nation's most populous states was closely contested, including California, Illinois, New York, and Texas.

Because there are so many deep red and blue states today, we can easily predict which party's candidate will carry the large majority of states long before Election Day. A year before the 2012 presidential election, there was very little doubt about which party at least thirty-five states would end up supporting. That is because there is a very high degree of consistency in voting patterns at the state level from election to election. In the end, forty-eight of fifty states along with the District of Columbia supported the same party in 2012 as in 2008. Only Indiana and North Carolina switched sides, with both going from the Democratic column to the Republican column.

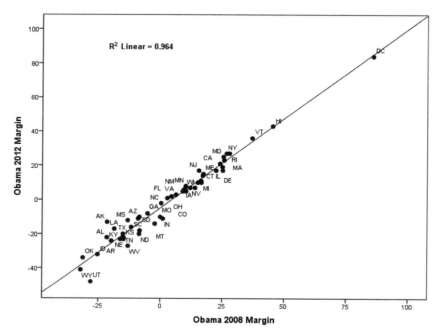

**Figure 2.2.   Obama 2012 State Margin by Obama 2008 State Margin**

The data displayed in figure 2.2 show that there was an extremely close relationship between Barack Obama's performance in 2012 and his performance in 2008 at the state level. In fact, the correlation between the results of the two elections was a remarkable .98, the strongest relationship between any two consecutive elections since World War II. Although Obama's share of the vote in 2012 was a few points less than his share of the vote in 2008 in almost every state, he did his best in the same states in 2012 as in 2008 and he did his worst in the same states in 2012 as in 2008.

Only two states deviated noticeably from this pattern. Obama did somewhat better than expected in Alaska, despite losing there by a wide margin, and he did somewhat worse than expected in Utah. In both cases, of course, there were obvious explanations for the results. The fact that Sarah Palin was no longer on the Republican ticket undoubtedly helped Obama to improve his performance in her home state of Alaska, and the fact that Mitt Romney was the first Mormon candidate for president clearly accounted for the sharp decline in the president's vote share in Utah.

## EXPLAINING THE RESULTS: A PARTISAN
## AND POLARIZED ELECTORATE

The remarkable consistency between the results of the 2008 and 2012 elections and the large numbers of deep blue and deep red states in these elections can both be explained by the fact that the American electorate today is sharply divided along party lines. This partisan divide was clearly evident in the results of the 2012 election at the individual level as well as at the state level. Thus, according to the national exit poll, 93 percent of Republican voters supported Mitt Romney while 92 percent of Democratic voters supported Barack Obama. This was the highest level of party loyalty in any presidential election since the advent of exit polls in 1972. Going back even farther, based on data from American National Election Study (ANES) surveys, this was the highest level of party loyalty in any presidential election since 1952.

Independents made up 29 percent of the electorate according to the national exit poll, and they divided their votes relatively evenly—50 percent for Romney to 45 percent for Obama. But that 29 percent figure undoubtedly exaggerates the size of the independent voting bloc because the exit poll does not ask independents whether they usually lean toward one party or the other. Based on data from ANES and other surveys, we know that the large majority of self-identified independents lean toward a party and that these leaning independents vote very similarly to regular partisans.

Another sign of the strength of party loyalties in the American electorate can be seen in the extraordinarily high level of straight ticket voting in 2012. According to the national exit poll, 92 percent of Obama voters supported a Democratic House candidate while 92 percent of Romney voters supported a Republican House candidate. Only 6 percent of Obama and Romney voters supported a House candidate from the opposite party as their presidential candidate. Similarly, state exit poll data showed that ticket splitting between presidential and Senate candidates was relatively rare with the exception of a few states such as Missouri and Indiana, where Democratic Senate candidates ran far ahead of President Obama. In most states with competitive Senate races, close to 90 percent of voters supported presidential and Senate candidates from the same party.

The high levels of party loyalty and straight ticket voting in 2012 extended a trend that has been evident in American elections for some time. Recent elections have seen consistently higher levels of party loyalty and straight ticket voting than elections from the 1970s and 1980s. Underlying this trend is the reality of an electorate in which the divide between supporters of the two major parties reflects the existence of deeper divisions in American society.

A close examination of the voting patterns in 2012 demonstrates the existence of three major divisions between Democrats and Republicans—a racial divide between a Democratic Party increasingly dependent on votes from nonwhites and an overwhelmingly white Republican Party, an ideological divide over the role and size of government, and a cultural divide over values, morality, and lifestyles.

## THE RACIAL DIVIDE

Perhaps the most important of the three major divides for the political system is the racial divide. It is so important because despite dramatic progress in race relations in recent decades, race and ethnicity continue to powerfully influence many aspects of American society including housing patterns, educational opportunities, economic opportunities, and health care. And the impact of the racial divide on the American party system and elections has been increasing due to the growing racial and ethnic diversity of American society.

The nonwhite share of the American population has increased dramatically since the end of World War II as a result of higher birth rates among nonwhites and high levels of immigration from Latin America and Asia. That demographic shift has also affected the racial composition of the American electorate although at a slower rate due to lower levels of citizenship, voter registration, and turnout among nonwhites. Nevertheless, between 1992 and 2008, according to data from national exit polls, the nonwhite share of the electorate doubled, going from 13 percent to 26 percent. And contrary to the expectations of some conservative pundits and Republican strategists, that trend continued in 2012 with nonwhites, including African Americans, Hispanics, Asian Americans, and other nonwhites making up 28 percent of the electorate according to the national exit poll.

As the nonwhite share of the American electorate has grown in recent decades, the racial divide between the Democratic and Republican electoral coalitions has also increased dramatically. In the 1950s, nonwhites (at that time almost exclusively African Americans) made up 7 percent of Democratic voters and 3 percent of Republican voters according to data from ANES surveys. In 2012, nonwhites made up 44 percent of

Democratic voters and 11 percent of Republican voters, according to data from the national exit poll.

The growing dependence of the Democratic Party on nonwhite voters has contributed to the flight of racially and economically conservative white voters to the GOP, thereby further increasing the size of the racial divide between the party coalitions. The effects of this trend were clearly evident in voting patterns in 2012.

The racial divide in voting in 2012 was one of the largest in the history of presidential elections. According to data from the national exit poll, and as mentioned in the previous chapter, Barack Obama lost the white vote by a margin of 20 percentage points, 59 percent to 39 percent. No Democratic candidate before Obama had ever won the presidency while losing the white vote by anything close to this large a margin. Yet despite this enormous deficit among white voters, Obama won the national popular vote by a margin of more than three percentage points by winning 80 percent of the nonwhite vote to only 18 percent for Mitt Romney.

## THE IDEOLOGICAL DIVIDE

The growing dependence of the Democratic Party on nonwhite voters and the resulting flight of conservative whites to the Republican Party have also contributed to a growing ideological divide between the parties. Since at least the New Deal era, Democrats and Republicans have differed on the question of the proper role and size of government. In recent years, however, that ideological divide has widened due mainly to a sharp turn to the right by the GOP. This division was clearly evident during the 2012 campaign with Republicans, including the party's presidential nominee, Mitt Romney, advocating cuts in taxes on upper income households and corporations, sharp reductions in spending on a variety of social programs, elimination of many health, safety and environmental regulations, and repeal of the health care reform law passed by Congress in 2010. On the other side, Democrats, including President Obama, were calling for tougher regulation of financial institutions and corporate polluters, increases in taxes on upper income Americans to ensure adequate funding of federal programs, and full implementation of the health care reform law.

The sharp partisan divide over the proper role and size of government was clearly evident in the American electorate as well. Thus, according to the national exit poll, 81 percent of those who wanted the government to do more to solve social problems voted for Barack Obama while 74 percent of those who felt that the government was doing too many things better left to individuals and private businesses voted for Mitt Romney. Along the same lines, 87 percent of those who wanted the health care law preserved or expanded voted for Obama while 83 percent of those who wanted the law partially or totally repealed voted for Romney.

## THE CULTURAL DIVIDE

Since the 1970s, a new set of issues have emerged in American politics alongside the older issues of spending, taxation and regulation—issues such as gay marriage and abortion that reflect deeply felt moral and religious values and lifestyle choices. Building on a growing alliance with religious conservatives of all faiths and evangelical Christians in particular, the Republican Party has become increasingly associated with policies supportive of traditional values and lifestyles including restrictions on access to abortion and opposition to same-sex marriage and other legal rights for homosexuals. Meanwhile, the Democratic Party has gradually shifted to the left on these issues.

Today, the vast majority of Democratic candidates and elected officials, including President Obama, support a woman's fundamental right to choose whether to terminate a pregnancy as well as access to contraceptives under the health care law. And an increasing number of prominent Democrats, including the president, now support the right of same-sex couples to marry along with protection from job discrimination and other legal rights for gays and lesbians. Certainly one of the most dramatic actions taken by President Obama during his first term was his decision to end the military's "Don't ask, don't tell" policy to allow gays and lesbians to serve openly in the armed forces. It was a decision that was strongly opposed by most Republican leaders, including the party's 2008 presidential candidate, John McCain, and its 2012 candidate, Mitt Romney.

The 2012 election was supposed to be all about jobs and the economy. And those certainly were the issues most on the minds of voters as they went to the polls. Nevertheless, cultural issues played a significant role in the 2012 elections. At least two Republican Senate candidates, Todd Akin in Missouri and Richard Mourdock in Indiana, lost their races as a direct result of controversial comments about rape and abortion. Meanwhile, voters in three states—Maine, Maryland, and Washington—passed referenda legalizing same-sex marriage. It was the first time that same-sex marriage had become law as a result of a vote of the people. And in Washington state and Colorado, voters for the first time passed referenda legalizing the sale and use of marijuana despite intense opposition by many conservative and religious groups.

The cultural divide was also clearly evident in the results of the 2012 presidential election. According to the national exit poll, white born-again or evangelical Christians made up 26 percent of the electorate and, despite any reservations they may have had about supporting a Mormon, they voted for Mitt Romney over Barack Obama by an overwhelming 78 percent to 21 percent margin. On the other hand, those who described their religious affiliation as "something else" or "none" made up 19 percent of the electorate, and they voted for Barack Obama over Mitt Romney by an almost equally overwhelming margin of 72 percent to 25 percent. And voters who identified themselves as gay, lesbian, or bisexual made up five percent of the electorate and supported Obama over Romney by 76 percent to 22 percent.

Cultural issues also contributed to two other striking voting patterns in 2012—the marriage gap and the generation gap. Unmarried voters and younger voters generally have more liberal views on cultural issues than married voters and older voters, as noted in the previous chapter. This helps to explain why there was a large gap in candidate preference between married and unmarried voters regardless of sex and a large gap between voters under the age of thirty and those sixty-five or older.

## WHY OBAMA WON

Based on a few fundamental factors that are known to influence the outcomes of presidential elections, by the summer of 2012 two things were fairly clear about this year's presidential race—it was likely to be a close contest and President Obama was likely to be the winner. In late August, before either national convention, I predicted the outcome of the national popular vote using my Time for Change forecasting model: Obama 50.6 percent, Romney 49.4 percent.

The Time for Change forecast was based on three variables that have correctly predicted the winner of the popular vote in every presidential election since 1988: the incumbent president's net approval rating in the Gallup Poll at the end of June (+2 percent), the estimated change in real GDP during the second quarter of the election year (+1.7 percent), and a first-term incumbency advantage, which I estimated at about 2.5 percent in the current era of partisan polarization.

In the end, the Time for Change model predicted the correct winner, President Obama, but underestimated his share of the major party vote by about one percentage point. However, this was well within the margin of error of the forecast and closer to the actual outcome than some national polls that were conducted immediately before the election including the Gallup and Rasmussen tracking polls, both of which predicted a victory for Mitt Romney. It was also a much more accurate forecast than those made on the eve of the election by a large number of prominent conservative pundits and political strategists. These pundits and strategists, including Dick Morris, Karl Rove, George Will, Michael Barone, Steve Lombardo, Jay Cost, and Fred Barnes, all confidently predicted that Mitt Romney would easily defeat Barack Obama.

Why did so many conservative pundits and strategists badly misread the mood of the electorate? In addition to wishful thinking, many of these individuals failed to recognize that despite a weak economic recovery and mediocre approval rating, President Obama had a significant advantage in 2012—the advantage of incumbency.

First-term incumbents like Barack Obama in 2012 rarely lose. Since 1900, there have been twelve presidential elections involving an incumbent whose party has held the White House for only four years, and only one of those incumbents, Jimmy Carter in 1980, was defeated. In the Time for Change forecasting model, first-term incumbents get an electoral boost beyond what would be expected based on their approval rating and economic conditions. Americans, it appears, are reluctant to throw an incumbent president out of office after his party has had only one term in the White House.

One indication of the advantage that being a first term incumbent gave to Barack Obama could be seen in voters' responses to a question on the national exit poll about who was more responsible for the country's economic problems in 2012—President Obama or his Republican predecessor George W. Bush. By a margin of 53 percent to 38 percent, voters blamed former president Bush more than President Obama for the country's economic problems. Fully 85 percent of those who believed that Bush was more to blame voted for Obama.

This incumbency advantage was almost certainly more politically significant than the impact of Hurricane Sandy, which struck the northeastern United States just a week before the election. Polls showed that Americans generally gave the president high marks for his handling of the disaster. However, contrary to the claims of some Republican strategists and commentators, there is no evidence that Hurricane Sandy altered the trajectory of the 2012 election.

Nor is there any evidence that Obama's victory was due to his campaign's superior performance in the swing states based on its use of highly sophisticated data mining and voter targeting techniques. In fact, an analysis of the results of the election at the state level shows that the president's performance in nine key swing states was almost exactly what one would have expected based on his performance in those states in 2008. In other words, Obama did no better and no worse in the swing states than he did in the other forty-one states where there was little campaigning.

The fact that Obama ended up winning the election by a somewhat greater margin than expected based on the Time for Change model may have reflected modest improvement in economic conditions between August and Election Day. As a result, while the large majority of voters still rated economic conditions in the nation as "not so good" or "poor," more voters felt that the economy was getting better than getting worse.

Declining unemployment, increasing consumer confidence, and an improving housing market may have also contributed to an uptick in the president's overall approval rating. In the national exit poll, Obama's net approval rating was +9 (54 percent approval versus 45 percent disapproval) compared with a net approval rating of +2 at the end of June. That increase in approval could easily account for the difference between a one-point margin of victory and a three-point margin.

## LONGER-TERM FORCES:
## A CHANGING ELECTORATE

Beyond the immediate causes of the president's reelection—a positive net approval rating, a gradually improving economy, and the advantage of being a first-term incumbent—there were also deeper forces at work in American society that helped to create the conditions that made his victory possible, especially changes in the racial and ethnic composition of the American electorate and in attitudes on social issues.

Between 1992 and 2012, the nonwhite share of the American electorate increased from 13 percent to 28 percent. Moreover, this trend is certain to continue for many years because nonwhites make up a much larger share of the youngest age cohorts in the population, those that will be entering the electorate over the next several election cycles, than of the oldest age cohorts, those that will be gradually leaving the electorate. As a result, the nonwhite share of the American population is expected to increase from about 37 percent now to about 53 percent in 2050, according to Census Bureau projections. It is very likely, therefore, that the nonwhite share of the electorate will continue to increase at an average rate of about two percentage points every four years for the next several decades.

But we do not have to wait thirty or forty years to see the impact of shifting demographics on American elections. We can see its effects clearly over the last few election cycles. The growing Hispanic vote has already had profound consequences for presidential elections. Since 2004, New Mexico, which has the largest proportion of Hispanics in its population of any state, has shifted from a swing state to a solidly Democratic state, while Colorado and Nevada have shifted from leaning Republican states to leaning Democratic states. And in Florida, the growing non-Cuban Hispanic vote was crucial to Barack Obama's narrow victory in 2012.

In addition to these demographic changes, the results of the 2012 elections clearly reflected another important trend in American society—the emergence of an increasingly secular and socially liberal electorate. Thus, when it comes to religious affiliation, the fastest growing group in the American electorate consists of voters who classify themselves as "something else" or "none." These two groups made up 19 percent of the electorate in 2012, according to the national exit poll. And according to the Gallup Poll, in 2012, for the first time, Americans who wanted the government to "promote traditional values" were outnumbered by those who thought the government "should not favor any particular set of values" by 52 percent to 40 percent. This represented a significant shift from eight years earlier, when those who wanted the government to promote traditional values outnumbered their opponents by 56 percent to 40 percent.

The decline in support for traditional values was reflected in changing attitudes on a variety of cultural issues. And on issues involving the rights of gay, lesbian, and bisexual Americans, the changes have been rapid and quite dramatic. According to Gallup, the percentage of American adults supporting legal recognition of same-sex marriage nearly doubled in five years, going from 27 percent in 2006 to 53 percent in 2011.

The success of referenda legalizing same-sex marriage in three states in 2012 was no fluke. According to the 2012 exit poll, 49 percent of voters across the nation supported legal recognition of same-sex marriage in their own state compared with 46 percent who were opposed. And the 2012 exit poll also found strong support among voters for preserving the right to legal abortion guaranteed by the Supreme Court's 1973 *Roe v. Wade* decision: 59 percent of voters favored keeping abortion legal either always or most of the time, up from 55 percent in the 2004 exit poll.

The growing cultural liberalism of the electorate was also evident on the issue of marijuana legalization. As with the passage of referenda legalizing same-sex marriage, the votes to legalize marijuana use in Colorado and Washington state appeared to reflect long-term shifts in national sentiment. According to Gallup, the percentage of American adults supporting legalization of marijuana use increased from only 12 percent in 1970 to 36 percent in 2006 and 50 percent in 2012.

One of the most striking patterns in public opinion on cultural issues is the tendency of younger Americans regardless of race or ethnicity to hold more liberal attitudes than older Americans. This is especially true when it comes to the issue of same-sex marriage. Thus, in a 2011 Gallup Poll, 70 percent of Americans under the age of thirty-five favored legal recognition of same-sex marriage compared with only 39 percent of Americans over the age of fifty-five. And younger Americans today are also much less likely to attend religious services regularly and much more likely to describe their religious affiliation as "something else" or "none." Based on these generational differences in attitudes and behavior, the trend toward a more secular and socially liberal electorate seems likely to continue for the foreseeable future.

## CONCLUSIONS: HAS THE EMERGING DEMOCRATIC MAJORITY FINALLY EMERGED?

In their 2002 book, *The Emerging Democratic Majority*, John Judis and Ruy Teixeira famously predicted that long-term demographic and economic trends in the United States were contributing to the emergence of a new Democratic electoral coalition that would dominate American politics for many years. Two years later, George W. Bush was reelected and Republicans solidified their control of both chambers of Congress. But based on the results of the 2012 election, can we now say that the Democratic majority envisioned by Judis and Teixeira has finally emerged?

Certainly there are good reasons for Republican leaders and strategists to be worried. Democratic candidates have now won the popular vote in five of the last six presidential elections and no Republican candidate since 1988 has won as many electoral votes as the 332 garnered by Barack Obama in 2012. It would be an exaggeration to say that the Democratic Party now has a lock on the Electoral College but Democrats clearly appear to have an advantage there. Barack Obama carried 24 states with 272 electoral votes by at least 5 percentage points. That is more than the 270 electoral votes needed for victory. And that Democratic advantage in the

Electoral College appears to be increasing. The growth of the Hispanic vote has shifted several states toward the Democratic Party since 2004, including New Mexico, Nevada, Colorado, and one of the biggest prizes of all—Florida. In another decade or two the growth of the Hispanic vote could even turn Texas into a swing state.

Of course all is not lost for the GOP. Despite its poor showing in the 2012 presidential and Senate elections, the party still retains a firm grip on the House of Representatives. But even the Republicans' House majority may not be as secure as it appears. Democratic candidates across the country actually won more votes than Republican candidates in the 2012 House elections. Republicans maintained control of the House due to the heavy concentration of Democratic voters in big metropolitan areas and clever redrawing of district lines by Republican state legislatures and governors after the 2010 midterm election. Eventually the advantages conferred by redistricting are likely to erode due to demographic trends and population movement. Unless Republicans can expand their party's appeal beyond its current base of older white conservatives, it is likely to experience a continued decline in its electoral fortunes in a nation that is becoming increasingly diverse and socially liberal.

# 3

# A FIRST PARTY-TERM INCUMBENT SURVIVES

## The Fundamentals of 2012

### *James E. Campbell*

On November 6, 2012, the American electorate reelected President Barack Obama to a second term. He defeated his Republican Party rival, former Massachusetts governor Mitt Romney, in a fairly close election: Obama won the national two-party vote by 3.8 percentage points.[1] As is normally the case, the electoral vote division was wider: 332 Obama to 206 Romney. The popular vote split, however, better characterized the election. As late as just a week before Election Day (October 30), Romney held a slight lead over Obama in the RealClearPolitics average of major national polls. In terms of the actual vote division, of the twenty-eight prior presidential elections since 1900, the winner had a larger share of the two-party popular vote in all but six elections (1916, 1960, 1968, 1976, 2000, and 2004). Nearly 80 percent of these elections were won more decisively and about 20 percent more closely than 2012.[2]

Why did Obama narrowly defeat Romney? The answer is that pre-campaign fundamental conditions set the stage for Obama's narrow victory. While I will elaborate shortly about what is included under the banner of fundamentals, they include considerations like incumbency, partisanship and the economy.[3] These and other fundamentals leading into the 2012 campaign established a political context that substantially shaped the course of the campaign and tipped the odds in favor of President Obama's reelection. While there are twists and turns in every campaign that are unanticipated, and these may make some difference, the general course of campaigns and the outcomes of elections depend to a large degree on the fundamentals. They certainly did in 2012.

The importance of the fundamentals may be appreciated through a metaphor. Without trivializing the seriousness of the choice, electoral politics in some respects may be compared to a card game. The fundamentals are the cards dealt to each player (the candidate). They are the raw materials each has to work with and the conditions that voters may take into account in reaching their decisions. The campaign is like playing the cards, and the same hand can be played more or less skillfully. Similarly, each candidate's campaign can make the most of what it has been dealt or fall short. But when you are dealing with players who are generally at the top of their games, candidates who have survived the rigors of winning their parties' nominations, the game (the election) will usually be won by the player who was dealt the stronger hand. The fundamentals usually tell the story of the election.

This analysis of the fundamentals in 2012 is presented in three sections. The first discusses five fundamentals and their impact on the election. The second summarizes these fundamentals and their incorporation into election forecasting models. The final section offers an explanation of the election's outcome based on the fundamentals. To preview the explanation, it claims that President Obama survived the terrible economic record of his first term because of his first party-term incumbency advantage. The key to his reelection was that as a first party-term incumbent, he could and did escape a good deal of accountability for the nation's economic problems. Voters placed more of the blame on President Obama's predecessor, President George W. Bush, than on President Obama. Unlike Harry Truman, the "buck" did not stop on President Obama's Oval Office desk—it was forwarded to President Bush.[4]

## THE FUNDAMENTALS

The fundamentals are the context in which the campaign and the election takes place. Some of the fundamentals involve the inclinations that voters bring into the election and others involve conditions that candidates and voters may take into account or might affect the thinking of voters during the campaign. While there are differences over what is included among the fundamentals, five are considered in this analysis. They are: (1) the long-term predispositions of the American electorate, (2) the general competitiveness of presidential campaigns, (3) the initial pre-campaign assessments by the electorate of the candidates, (4) the state of the economy, and (5) the advantages of presidential incumbency.

## PARTISANSHIP AND IDEOLOGY

Partisanship and ideology are two long-term voter predispositions crucial to a campaign's context. Party identification is the single most important political predisposition of American voters.[5] About 90 percent of voters identify to some degree as either a Democrat or a Republican and, in recent elections, 85 percent or more of partisans vote for their party's presidential candidate.[6] While the measurement of ideological orientations has been somewhat more elusive, there is little question that the values and general perspectives of voters on politics and government is crucial to their votes and, collectively, important to an election's outcome.

In the last several decades, the American electorate has become nearly equally balanced between Democrats and Republicans. Averaging party identifications of voters in the 2004 and 2008 (after correcting the data to the turnout and vote choice distributions), the electorate was about 48 percent Democratic and 46 percent Republican.[7] In terms of ideological orientations, the electorate is also less moderate than it had been. In the 1970s and 1980s, typically about 48 percent of voters were self-professed moderates or could not describe their ideological orientation. Since the 1990s, only about 41 percent of voters were centrists, a drop of seven percentage points.[8] Self-identified conservatives continue to significantly outnumber self-professed liberals, but the most important development is that both are growing while the center is shrinking.[9] Additionally, the two long-term predispositions of partisanship and ideology have become more closely entwined with one another.[10] Democrats generally lean to the political left and Republicans to the right. Conservative Democrats and liberal Republicans are now rare birds. The reinforcement of partisanship and ideology has fortified the political divide. American voters are intensely divided into two parties of nearly equal size.

The clearest consequence of this is that elections have become more closely decided than they had been. Table 3.1 presents the evidence from the last six elections (prior to 2012) compared to the preceding six. The average winning vote percentage since 1988 is less than half that of elections from 1964 to 1984. Polarized and evenly balanced parties are a fundamental force for closely pitched political battles. Based on partisanship and polarization, the conditions leading into the 2012 election augured a close race.

**Table 3.1.  Closeness of Presidential Elections, 1964–2008**

| | Years of Presidential Elections | |
|---|---|---|
| Election Outcome | 1964 to 1984 | 1988 to 2008 |
| Mean winning vote | 56.5 | 53.0 |
| Elections won with 55% or more | 4 of 6 | 0 of 6 |
| Largest winning vote | 61.8 (1972) | 54.7 (1996) |

Note: Votes are the percentage of the two-party popular vote.

## HYPER-COMPETITIVE PRESIDENTIAL CAMPAIGNS

A second fundamental is the perennial competitiveness of presidential campaigns. The presidency is the most highly prized and most intensely fought over political office in the nation. Each candidate's campaign receives extensive media coverage, has access to the best political strategists, and is well funded. Like the nearly even division of polarized partisans, the nearly equal strength of intense campaigns should produce more equal election results.

This perennial effect of the general election campaign may have become even more so in recent elections as the balance in long-term predispositions has ratcheted up the perceived stakes in the election, as media outlets and technologies have proliferated and diversified, and as campaign spending has skyrocketed with the collapse of the presidential public financing system and the emergence of Super PACs. When all the accounting is done, the Obama and Romney campaigns along with their parties and supportive PACs will each have spent about a billion dollars on their 2012 campaigns. A nearly equal amount of spending at such a high level should have the effect of producing a more equal vote division between the candidates.

## PRE-CAMPAIGN ASSESSMENTS OF THE CANDIDATES

The public's pre-campaign assessment of the candidates is the third fundamental that may influence how views might develop in the campaign. Partisanship and ideological orientations as well as the economy and incumbency may influence these early readings of the public's views, but factors beyond these other fundamentals also come into play. Voters have lots of opportunities to observe the candidates, to form impressions of their personal strengths and weaknesses, and to evaluate their positions and records on a wide range of issues.

With respect to President Obama, pre-campaign opinions were divided. While many Americans found him likable or even charismatic, many others found his policies to be too liberal compared to their own preferences. This was evidenced in the results of the 2010 midterm election in which Democrats sustained huge congressional losses, the largest in over sixty years. That defeat was widely interpreted as a dramatic repudiation of President Obama's liberal policies in general and Obamacare in particular.

With respect to Governor Romney, despite support from the Republican establishment, considerable financial backing, and an image as a competent manager with considerable private sector experience and success, there was great resistance to his nomination. Conservative Republicans regarded Romney as unreliably conservative with an unfortunate history of flip-flopping on the issues. As a result, he had to battle through a long line of nomination challengers. He failed to reach 40 percent in the polls among Republicans until mid-April, after thirty-six primaries and caucuses. While Romney fended off nomination rivals, Obama mounted an ad campaign defining Romney to voters as a callous corporate tycoon out of touch with the problems of average Americans.

While Romney's nomination disadvantages were considerable, they appeared to only offset disappointment with Obama's record. The electorate's pre-campaign assessments of the candidates were nearly neutral. President Obama's presidential approval rating in mid-July stood at 46 percent in Gallup. Of the ten incumbents who sought reelection since 1952, Obama ranked seventh. Each of the six presidents with higher ratings won. Each of the three presidents with lower ratings lost. Obama sat right on the cusp. Gallup's pre-convention preference polls painted the same picture. Obama stood at 49.5 percent of the two-party division in Gallup's preference poll before the first national party convention. Of the last ten presidents up for reelection, Obama again ranked seventh. Of the six incumbents with higher poll numbers, five won and one lost. Of the three with lower poll numbers, two lost and one won. In short, like partisan parity, ideological polarization and the campaign's hyper-competitiveness, the pre-campaign assessments of the candidates signaled that the election would be close.

## THE ECONOMY

The economy is the fourth fundamental. It was decidedly not neutral in 2012. It was potentially a devastating liability for Obama's reelection bid and provided a huge boost to Romney's prospects.

The economy is perennially a major consideration in presidential elections.[11] Presidents are expected by voters to foster the nation's economic prosperity. Few presidential responsibilities are more politically important. The economy is important to voters because it directly affects their standard of living from their jobs to the homes they live in, their schools and neighborhoods, their hospitals, and everything else that requires financing. It is also politically crucial because the economy affects the public's mood toward everything the candidates say and do.[12] When the economy is strong, the audience for the president is friendly and receptive. When it is weak, the electorate's trust in the president may waver, or worse.

The economy in 2012 had been sluggish since the early days of President George W. Bush's second term in 2005. The last two quarters of 2004 and the first quarter of 2005 were the last in which the economy (as measured by the change in the real gross domestic product, GDP) grew at 3 percent or more for three consecutive quarters.[13] In mid-September 2008, matters went from bad to far worse with the Wall Street meltdown of financial institutions. With the GDP shrinking at nearly nine percentage points in the fourth quarter of 2008, voters turned against the in-party Republicans and toward the Democrats and Barack Obama to get the economy back on track. That was Obama's mandate, the reason voters elected him.

Nearly four years later, and almost three and a half years after the Bush recession had ended in June 2009 according to the National Bureau of Economic Research (2010), the nonpartisan monitor of recessions and expansions, the economy under President Obama remained in bad shape. One sign of this was unemployment. Typically in the range of 5 percent to 6 percent, unemployment rates stubbornly remained over 9 percent throughout most of Obama's term, dipping only slightly below 8 percent as the election neared. No president since the Great Depression had been reelected with such high unemployment numbers.

The more broad-based GDP growth measure of economic conditions was equally grim. During the entirety of Obama's time in office, Americans had not experienced even two consecutive quarters of growth over 2.5 percent. Tables 3.2 and 3.3 provide more systematic historical comparisons of President Obama's economic record to those of other modern presidents. Table 3.2 takes the long-term view by examining economic growth rates from the beginning of the second year of a presidency (to set aside inherited economic conditions) through the second quarter of the president's reelection year since 1956. The correlation of the economic record in these cases and the two-party popular votes was very strong ($r = .84$). Table 3.3

**Table 3.2.   Economic Growth over a President's Term, 1956–2012**

| Rank | President and Reelection Year | GDP Growth over Term (%) | Election Outcome |
|------|------------------------------|--------------------------|------------------|
| 1. | Kennedy/Johnson, 1964 | 5.2 | Won |
| 2. | Ronald Reagan, 1984 | 4.1 | Won |
| 3. | Dwight Eisenhower, 1956 | 3.9 | Won |
| 4. | Bill Clinton, 1996 | 3.5 | Won |
| 4. | Richard Nixon, 1972 | 3.5 | Won |
| 6. | George W. Bush, 2004 | 2.9 | Won |
| 7. | Jimmy Carter, 1980 | 2.6 | Lost |
| **8.** | **Barack Obama, 2012** | **2.1** | **Won** |
| 9. | George H. W. Bush, 1992 | 1.5 | Lost |
| 9. | Nixon/Ford, 1976 | 1.5 | Lost |

*Source*: Bureau of Economic Analysis.
*Note*: Mean real GDP growth is based on the ten quarters from Q1 of year 2 to Q2 of year 4. The series starts with 1956 because of data availability.

**Table 3.3.   Economic Growth in the Second Quarter of Reelection Years, 1948–2012**

| Rank | President and Reelection Year | GDP Growth in 2nd Quarter (%) | Election Outcome |
|------|------------------------------|-------------------------------|------------------|
| 1. | Richard Nixon, 1972 | 9.8 | Won |
| 2. | Harry Truman, 1948 | 7.5 | Won |
| 3. | Ronald Reagan, 1984 | 7.1 | Won |
| 3. | Bill Clinton, 1996 | 7.1 | Won |
| 5. | Lyndon Johnson, 1964 | 4.7 | Won |
| 6. | George H. W. Bush, 1992 | 4.3 | Lost |
| 7. | Dwight Eisenhower, 1956 | 3.2 | Won |
| 8. | Gerald Ford, 1976 | 3.0 | Lost |
| 9. | George W. Bush, 2004 | 2.6 | Won |
| **10.** | **Barack Obama, 2012** | **1.3** | **Won** |
| 11. | Jimmy Carter, 1980 | -7.9 | Lost |

*Source*: Bureau of Economic Analysis.

compares economic growth rates just prior to the reelection bid. It compares presidential records in the second quarter (April to June) of reelection years since 1948. The correlation of the second quarter economy and the incumbents' popular vote was also strong ($r = .67$).

From either perspective, President Obama's economic record ranked near the bottom of the lists. He ranked eighth out of ten presidents in economic growth over their terms and tenth out of eleven for the economy leading into the fall campaign. Whether from a long-term or short-run time frame, each president with a weaker record lost his reelection bid. In both cases, there was also at least one president with a stronger record who also was defeated. President Obama's average economic growth rate was only 2.1 percent after the first year of his term, and only 1.3 percent in the second quarter of his reelection year. The average economic growth rate for modern reelected presidents has been about 3.8 percent, and it is even higher just before their fall campaigns. In short, by historical standards, President Obama's economic record was one that no incumbent would want to defend.[14]

It was hardly surprising that 77 percent of voters in the election's exit poll said that they thought that the economy was "not so good" or "poor," and that 55 percent thought that the economy was not getting better. In 2008 and 2010, 63 percent of voters in exit polls said that the economy was the most important problem. In 2012, it was virtually unchanged (59 percent). The question for 2012 was not whether the economy was good or bad—it was definitely bad, and voters clearly knew it. The question was whether President Obama could survive his economic record.

## PRESIDENTIAL INCUMBENCY

Last, but certainly not least, is the fundamental of presidential incumbency. Incumbents have many advantages. Sitting presidents benefit from the inertia or risk aversion of the voters. Familiarity with a candidate is generally comforting, and incumbent presidents are certainly familiar to voters. Perceptions of incumbents are enhanced by the halo effect of "the Rose Garden strategy," the elevated status and respect accorded the office of the presidency. President Obama's advantage in this regard was highlighted by his response to the Hurricane Sandy disaster a week before the election. Incumbents typically are unchallenged en route to their party's nomination and can use those pre-nomination months and resources to get an early start on the fall campaign. Incumbents stand a much better than fifty-fifty chance of being reelected. As table 3.4 shows, of the nineteen incumbents seeking reelection since 1900, fourteen (74 percent) were returned to office.

The electoral advantages are considerably greater for one type of incumbent, the first party-term incumbent. A first party-term incumbent is one who succeeds a president of the opposite party. First party-term incumbents are normally given more slack or the benefit of the doubt by the public. Their opposition may be less unified than it would be after several

**Table 3.4.   Incumbency and Presidential Election Outcomes, 1900–2008**

| Incumbency: Personal and Party | Won | Lost | Total |
|---|---|---|---|
| Incumbent presidents | 14 (74%) | 5 (26%) | 19 |
| First party-term | 10 (91%) | 1 (9%) | 11 |
| Second or more party-term | 4 (50%) | 4 (50%) | 8 |

terms out of office, and their own party may remain more unified with the memory of being the out-party still fresh. First party-term incumbents are also in the enviable position of being able to use the appeals to voters of both change and stability. As an incumbent, the stability theme is always available and useful if things are going well. If things are not going so well, first party-term incumbents can still claim to be the agent of change. In contrast, the change theme is not credible for incumbents whose party has been in office for two terms or longer. Relatedly, and importantly, a first party-term incumbent always has the option of blaming his opposite-party's predecessor for continuing problems. In contrast, other incumbents cannot very well blame their own party's predecessor for leaving them with a mess to clean up.

It is an understatement to say that the public is loathe to turn a first party-term president out of office.[15] The evidence is closer to indicating that first party-term incumbents may be almost unbeatable (unless they beat themselves).[16] The lower portion of table 3.4 breaks down the evidence. Ten of the eleven (91 percent) first party-term incumbents who sought reelection from 1900 to 2008 won: William McKinley in 1900, Woodrow Wilson in 1916, Calvin Coolidge in 1924, Franklin Roosevelt in 1936, Dwight Eisenhower in 1956, Lyndon Johnson in 1964, Richard Nixon in 1972, Ronald Reagan in 1984, Bill Clinton in 1996 and George W. Bush in 2004 won reelection as first party-term incumbents.

The only first party-term incumbent to lose since 1900 was President Jimmy Carter. Carter is the exception that proves the rule. His record leading into the fall 1980 campaign could hardly have been worse. In the months before the fall campaign, the economy was shrinking by nearly 8 percent (see table 3.3). This is a comparable to the devastating economic slide of 2008's Wall Street Meltdown (a nearly 9 percent drop in the fourth quarter). The misery index (unemployment plus inflation) reached its peak of nearly twenty-one points in 1980. Things were so bad that he barely survived a nomination battle with Senator Ted Kennedy. If this were not enough to derail Carter's reelection bid, fifty-two Americans were held hostage in Iran by Islamist militants, and the president appeared helpless. Even so, despite all of the catastrophes around him, President Carter led his Republican challenger, Ronald Reagan, in the polls even as late as late October.

In light of this history, Barack Obama's first party-term incumbency advantage going into the 2012 election was an enormous and possibly insurmountable advantage. A key question that confronted the Romney campaign from the outset was whether it could convince a majority of American voters to take the nearly unprecedented step of firing a first party-term incumbent.

## SUMMARY AND FORECASTS

The likely effects of the five fundamentals in 2012 are summarized in table 3.5. Three pushed the election toward an even division of the vote, one (the economy) clearly favored Romney, and one (incumbency) clearly favored Obama. The election hinged on whether the economy or incumbency weighed more heavily in voter deliberations, whether the economy was sufficiently bad enough for voters to set aside their predisposition to keep a first party-term incumbent in office, and whether the fundamentals collectively had set up the election to be so close that other considerations and the campaigns might be decisive.

As this summary suggests, translating the fundamentals, especially when they are in conflict, into expected specific election results is not a simple task. The fundamentals in 2012 might lead to a conclusion that the election would be a moderate-sized win based on incumbency for President Obama to a moderate-sized win based on the economy for Governor Romney. Resolving this vagueness is where election forecasting models come into play in statistically evaluating electoral history.

**Table 3.5.    The Fundamentals in 2012**

| The Fundamentals | Impact in 2012 Election | | |
| --- | --- | --- | --- |
|  | Obama | Close Election | Romney |
| Partisan parity and polarization |  | X |  |
| General campaign competition |  | X |  |
| Initial candidate assessment |  | X |  |
| The economy |  |  | X |
| Presidential incumbency | X |  |  |

In reviewing the twelve election forecasting models assembled for a meeting of the American Political Science Association in early September 2012 (and later published in the October issue of *PS: Political Science and Politics*[17]), each of the models tapped into at least three of the five fundamentals in one way or another, and six of the models could be interpreted as taking all five of the fundamentals into account to some degree. Often the models captured the effects of a fundamental indirectly, implicitly or partially (e.g., picking up some of the partisanship and polarization effects by using preference or approval polling) and the indicators and their timings varied considerably, but while the specifics varied, the common threads of the fundamentals generally kept them fairly accurate. Six of the twelve forecasts, each made between 299 to 57 days before the election, were impressively within one and a half percentage points of the actual vote. Drawing on the fundamentals, my convention bump and economy model predicted immediately after the Democratic National Convention that President Obama would receive 51.3 percent of the national two-party popular vote, just six-tenths of a percentage point off of the actual vote.[18] In general, the models that included more of the fundamentals, especially a pre-campaign public opinion variable, more accurately predicted a narrow Obama victory. To the question of whether economics benefitted Romney enough to overcome Obama's incumbency advantage, the more comprehensive successful models anticipated that they would not. They were correct.

## EXPLAINING 2012

### *What Did Not Decide the Election*

In explaining the 2012 election, it might be best to start with what most definitely did not affect the election. The election was decidedly not an endorsement of President Obama's liberal policy perspectives nor was it a repudiation of conservative Republican political philosophy. It also had little to do with the often discussed sociodemographics of the electorate—Democratic strength among women, Hispanic, Asian, and younger voters. These are groups whose votes Republicans need to compete for more effectively in the future, but this political sociology did not make the difference this time. Even the superior GOTV ("get out the vote") operation of Obama's campaign, while probably making some difference to the vote division, was not nearly large enough to decide the election.

Table 3.6 provides the evidence from the exit polls that, whatever its sociodemographic composition, the electorate did not elect President

**Table 3.6.  Ideological Division of 2012 Voters**

| | Voter Response (%) | |
|---|---|---|
| Exit Poll Question | Conservative | Liberal |
| Self-identification of ideological orientation | 35 | 25 |
| Shares my values (candidate choice) | 55 | 42 |
| Repeal some or all of Obamacare | 49 | 44 |
| Government doing too much or too little | 51 | 43 |
| Raise taxes to cut deficit | 63 | 33 |

Obama to a second term because it favored a liberal policy option over a conservative alternative. Responses to five separate questions on the national exit poll paint the same picture. The electorate that elected Barack Obama to a second term was, amazingly, substantially more conservative than liberal in its political orientations. President Obama was elected despite his liberal political perspectives, not because of them.

### What Did Decide the Election

So what did decide the election? Beyond pitting President Obama against former governor Romney and the Democrats against the Republicans, the 2012 election pitted first party-term incumbency against the economy as two powerful fundamentals pulling the election and the electorate in opposite directions. The protective powers of incumbency triumphed over the rejection that might have been expected to accompany the weak economic record.

With respect to the economy, there was no question that the economic numbers were very poor. No modern president had survived such a weak economy. A large majority of voters knew that economic conditions were weak (77 percent called them "not so good" or "poor"). A sizable majority also did not think that the economy was improving (55 percent said it was "poor and staying the same" or was "getting worse"). The logic of Clint Eastwood's memorable chat with an empty chair at the Republican National Convention seemed compelling: "and when somebody does not do the job, we got to let them go." It would appear that President Obama, as Clint suggested, did not do the job, he failed, but then voters for some reason did not let him go. Why?

The answer lies in a key advantage of a first party-term incumbent, the possibility of placing the blame on his predecessor. Instinctively, former president Bill Clinton raised the issue in his speech at the Democratic

National Convention. He told the convention and a national audience that "No president, no president—not me, not any of my predecessors—no one could have fully repaired all the damage that he [President Obama] found in just four years." In a different way, President Obama suggested the same in his response to a reporter's question about what grade he would assign himself for his handling of the economy. He responded that he would give himself "an incomplete." Presidents do not normally get an incomplete. The vote is a grade for their performance. First party-term presidents, however, are an exception.

A majority of voters were convinced that President Bush was more to blame for the nation's economic problems than President Obama. Table 3.7 presents the data. Conditions were awful, but most voters did not focus the blame on President Obama. As a result, when asked which candidate would do a better job handing the economy, Romney's lead over Obama in late campaign polls was only in single digits, and he was only up by one percentage point on that question in the exit polls. President Obama had presided over nearly four years of economic doldrums, yet voters gave him an incomplete.

The fact that incumbency tilted the election to President Obama does not mean that his reelection was inevitable. Obama's poor economic record tested the limits of his incumbency advantage. The Romney campaign could have done much more to make its case that the economic problems facing the nation were not a continuation of the Bush recession (that ended in June of 2009), but were instead the consequences of an anemic Obama recovery. He needed to make the case to voters that the nation's lethargic economy was the consequence of the failings of Obama's policies, that the administration's economic stimulus, energy, regulatory, tax, and Obamacare policies actually impaired economic recovery and growth.

He made headway on this score in the first presidential debate, but then grew cautious. Whether Romney could have convinced voters that Obama and not Bush was responsible for the economic record of the Obama presidency is an open question, but it was his best hope.

**Table 3.7.   Responsibility for Economic Problems**

| *Responsibility for the Economy* | *August Poll* | *Exit Poll* |
|---|---|---|
| President Obama | 32 | 38 |
| Former president Bush | 54 | 53 |
| Both/neither/unsure | 14 | 9 |

*Source*: ABC News/*Washington Post* poll, Aug. 22–25, 2012, N=1,002, and National Exit Poll.

The 2012 presidential election raises some potentially disturbing questions about accountability in the American electoral process. It suggests that the reelection of a first party-term incumbent is almost a foregone conclusion. Unless a first party-term incumbent's record is an unmitigated disaster (Carter), he can survive to serve a second term. Since 1900, the record of first party-term incumbents is eleven wins and one loss. The 92 percent victory rate (in 41 percent, or twelve of twenty-nine presidential elections since 1900) is not far removed from the often-lamented House incumbency reelection rate. It appears that first party-term presidents are elected to something tantamount to an eight-year term.

## NOTES

1. Dave Leip, "2012 Presidential General Election Results," Dave Leip's Atlas of U.S. Presidential Elections, accessed December 18, 2012, http://uselectionatlas .org/RESULTS/national.php?year=2012&off=0&elect=0&f=0.

2. Congressional Quarterly, *Guide to U.S. Elections*, 6th ed. (Washington, DC: Congressional Quarterly, 2009).

3. James E. Campbell, *The American Campaign: U.S. Presidential Elections and the National Vote*, 2nd ed. (College Station: Texas A&M University Press, 2008).

4. The irony of Obama's campaign slogan, "Forward," is duly noted.

5. Angus Campbell, Philip E. Converse, Warren E. Miller, and Donald E. Stokes, *The American Voter* (New York: Wiley, 1960).

6. Campbell, *American Campaign*.

7. James E. Campbell, "Explaining Politics, Not Polls: Examining Macropartisanship with Recalibrated NES Data," *Public Opinion Quarterly* 74 (2010): 616–42.

8. James E. Campbell, "Polarization Runs Deep, Even by Yesterday's Standards," in *Red and Blue Nation? Characteristics and Causes of America's Polarized Politics*, ed. Pietro S. Nivola and David W. Brady (Washington, DC: Brookings, 2007), 106–16.

9. Campbell, "Polarization Runs Deep"; Alan I. Abramowitz, *The Disappearing Center: Engaged Citizens, Polarization, and American Democracy* (New Haven, CT: Yale University Press, 2010); Alan I. Abramowitz, "Disconnected or Joined at the Hip?," in *Red and Blue Nation? Characteristics and Causes of America's Polarized Politics*, ed. Pietro S. Nivola and David W. Brady (Washington, DC: Brookings, 2007), 72–85.

10. Alan I. Abramowitz and Kyle L. Saunders, "Ideological Realignment in the U.S. Electorate," *Journal of Politics* 60 (1998): 634–52.

11. Morris P. Fiorina, *Retrospective Voting in American National Elections* (New Haven, CT: Yale University Press, 1981), and Robert S. Erikson, "Economic Conditions and the Presidential Vote," *American Political Science Review* 83 (1989): 567–73.

12. Campbell, *American Campaign*.

13. Real GDP growth data are from the Bureau of Economic Analysis "Gross Domestic Product: Percent Change from Preceding Period," accessed November 25, 2012, www.bea.gov/national/index.htm#gdp.

14. Voters need not know anything about actual growth rates of the economy in order to experience the effects of the economy and to hear bad economic news reflecting the growth numbers.

15. Ray C. Fair, "The Effects of Economic Events on Votes for President," *Review of Economics and Statistics* 60 (1978): 159–73; Alan I. Abramowitz, "An Improved Model for Predicting Presidential Outcomes," *PS: Political Science and Politics* 4 (1988): 843–47; Helmut Norpoth, "Is Clinton Doomed? An Early Forecast for 1996," *PS: Political Science and Politics* 28 (1995): 1–7; James E. Campbell, "The Science of Forecasting Presidential Elections," in *Before the Vote*, ed. James E. Campbell and James C. Garand (Thousand Oaks, CA: Sage, 2000); Campbell, *American Campaign*; Herbert F. Weisberg, "Partisanship and Incumbency in Presidential Elections," *Political Behavior* 24 (2002): 339–60; David R. Mayhew, "Incumbency Advantage in U.S. Presidential Elections: The Historical Record," *Political Science Quarterly* 123 (2008): 201–28.

16. One might suspect that some of the incumbency advantage, both personal and party, reflects the strength of a party. The majority party tends to win more elections and incumbents may win because they are candidates of the majority party and not because they are also incumbents. However, a number of minority party incumbents won despite being in the minority party (Wilson, Eisenhower, and Nixon) and first party-term incumbents continue to do well in an era with the parties near parity (Clinton, G. W. Bush, and now Obama).

17. James E. Campbell, "Forecasting the 2012 American National Elections: Editor's Introduction," *PS: Political Science and Politics* 45 (2012): 610–12.

18. Campbell, "Forecasting the 2012 American National Elections."

# 4

# UN-CONVENTIONAL WISDOM

## The 2012 Conventions and
## the Nominating Process

### *Rhodes Cook*

The presidential nominating process these days is long, expensive, and an ongoing source of controversy. It begins shortly after the mid-term elections and ends at the national party conventions, held barely two months before the November presidential election. All in all, that is a period of nearly two years.

The long preamble to the actual primary and caucus voting was once known as "the invisible primary." No more. Activity in the year before the election is now highly visible, replete with debates, straw polls, lots of fund-raisers, and frequent visits to the lead-off states of Iowa and New Hampshire.[1]

Primaries as a whole have grown over the years to their present total of forty, give or take a few dependent on the election year. Meanwhile, caucuses, such as the one in Iowa, have drawn criticism for the accuracy of their vote counts.

And the conventions, which once provided the determinative conclusion to the nominating process, are now little more than party pep rallies, as every presidential nomination since 1972 has essentially been decided during the primary season.

Meanwhile, spending for the primaries has soared as the system of public financing that was in vogue in the last quarter of the twentieth century has basically disappeared. None of the major candidates in 2012 took public funds, instead augmenting their own fund-raising by turning to the largesse of emerging cash cows called "Super PACs." With these new entities, a wealthy individual or two could pour millions of dollars into the race in support of the candidate of their choice, and not be bound by the individual contribution limit of several thousand dollars mandated by campaign finance law.

In short, the presidential nominating process is constantly changing and sometimes is barely recognizable from one generation to another. Or, in the case of 2008 and 2012, from one election to another.

The nominating process in recent years has drawn a lengthy chorus of critics. A frequent complaint was that too many primaries scheduled too close to the beginning of the election year had produced a rush to judgment that left the winner largely unvetted and too many voters without a meaningful voice in the nominating process.

After 2008, rules makers in both parties vowed to change that, and they created a process for 2012 that was dramatically different than those immediately before. Rather than having a "front-loaded" calendar that generally produced nominees by the ides of March, the schedule of primaries and caucuses was spread out in 2012, so nearly half the events occurred in the spring.

"Super Tuesday"—the one-day, multistate vote-fest—was moved back a month from early February 2008 to early March 2012. New nominating rules in both parties also called for the opening contests beginning in Iowa and New Hampshire to be moved back from January 2008 to February 2012. States that wanted to hold primaries before Super Tuesday were to be penalized with the loss of 50 percent of their delegates.[2]


## 2012: AN ASSESSMENT

How did it all work out? Well enough that Republican rules makers expressed satisfaction. But not so well that the always evolving nominating process will escape at least some tinkering before 2016.

In testing the new system in 2012, the Democrats did not really count because President Barack Obama was without major opposition for renomination. But the competitive part of the GOP nominating campaign did last a month longer in 2012 than it had in 2008. Then, the race essentially concluded in early March after the eventual nominee, John McCain, drove his last major rival from the field. In 2012, the Republican nominating contest ran until early April, when Mitt Romney sent his last major challenger to the sidelines.

But the new rules were still unable to stop a number of states from rushing to the front of the calendar. Iowa, New Hampshire, South Carolina, and Nevada were given special exemptions to hold their events in February 2012. But the GOP's warning that any other state would lose half their delegates if they voted before early March proved a weak deterrent.

By the time that the calendar was settled, four states (Iowa, New Hampshire, South Carolina, and Florida) had claimed spots in January. Three states (Colorado, Minnesota, and Missouri with a nonbinding primary) had established dates in early February. And two other states (Arizona and Michigan) scheduled primaries in late February. For good measure, Republicans in Washington state placed their caucuses on the eve of Super Tuesday in early March. The attention that many of the January and February states gained for their early events more than offset the loss of 50 percent of their delegates.

Nor did the "new look" Republican calendar provide a spike in voter turnout. In 2008, a record of more than 57 million voters cast ballots in the primaries. In 2012, the total was less than half that. It was no surprise that the Democratic primary turnout dropped from 37 million to barely 9 million, given that in 2012 Obama was essentially unopposed for renomination. Four years earlier, Senator Hillary Clinton of New York and Obama, then a senator from Illinois, were engaged in one of the closest and most historic primary contests ever. Clinton was bidding to become the first woman to win a major party nomination, while Obama was on course to be the first African American. Their competition extended across the nominating season from January to June.

But the Republican primary turnout also dropped, from 21 million in 2008 to roughly 19 million four years later, even though in 2012 it was the "only game in town."[3]

Part of the decline was due to the nature of the calendar both years. When McCain reached the "mop-up" stage of the 2008 Republican campaign in early March, the primary season was in reality already close to the end. Only a dozen primaries remained to be held. But when Romney reached a similar stage of the "back-loaded" 2012 GOP nominating process in early April, nineteen primaries remained with little on the presidential ballot to stir high turnout.

But voter turnout in the 2012 GOP primaries was also affected by the impression that the Republican presidential field was less than compelling. It featured a former one-term governor of Massachusetts, Mitt Romney; a former senator from Pennsylvania, Rick Santorum, who had been routed from office in 2006 by a margin of seventeen percentage points; former

House Speaker Newt Gingrich of Georgia, who had abruptly resigned his position in the wake of a poorer-than-expected showing by House Republicans in the 1998 elections; and Ron Paul, a septuagenarian Texas congressman who had emerged as leader of the party's libertarian wing. With the exception of Paul, none of the candidates began with an ardent corps of supporters.

Texas governor Rick Perry, former Utah governor Jon Huntsman, Representative Michele Bachmann of Minnesota, and Georgia businessman Herman Cain were also among the early field of candidates. But by the beginning of 2012, they were either fading forces, or in the case of Cain, already out of the race.

From the start, Romney was considered the favorite of the Republican establishment. He had strong credentials as a successful businessman and a political pedigree as the son of Michigan governor George Romney, plus he was coming off a runner-up finish in the 2008 Republican presidential primaries. The latter was an important credential in a party that has tended to nominate the next in line.

But Romney had trouble winning the support of a party base that was well to the right of where he had positioned himself in Massachusetts. Over the course of 2011, he was successively challenged for the lead in Republican presidential preference polls by Bachmann, Perry, Cain, and Gingrich, all seeking to establish themselves as the conservative alternative to Romney.[4]

Once the primaries began, Romney had trouble establishing much forward momentum. He lost Iowa on January 3 (although the unofficial caucus night tally showed him narrowly ahead) but won the New Hampshire primary January 10. He lost the South Carolina primary January 21 but won the high-stakes contest in Florida January 31. He lost caucuses in Colorado and Minnesota, plus a nonbinding primary in Missouri a week later, but won primaries in Arizona and Michigan on February 28.

Romney swept six states on Super Tuesday March 6, including the primary in the battleground state of Ohio. But he lost primaries across the South in Georgia, Oklahoma, and Tennessee. Romney carried the Hawaii caucuses on March 13, but lost primaries the same day in Alabama and Mississippi. He rebounded with a win in the Illinois primary March 20, but lost the primary in Louisiana March 24. On April 3, he scored a clean sweep of the primaries in Maryland, Wisconsin, and the District of Columbia.

That was enough for Santorum, Romney's main rival most of the primary season. The calendar of events in May looked favorable for the former Pennsylvania senator, an ardent social conservative, when a number of states in the American heartland were scheduled to vote. But getting there was a problem. Romney had built a wide lead in the delegate count, and a quintet of Northeastern states was slated to vote on April 24, including Santorum's home state of Pennsylvania. Short on cash, Santorum did not wish to run the risk of an embarrassing defeat there.

Gingrich made a last-gasp effort in Delaware in late April, but lost the primary there by a margin of better than two to one. Paul soldiered on, but with a low-key effort that tended to focus on picking off delegates at district and state conventions rather than an intensive public bid to win primary votes in late-balloting states such as California.

After April 3, Romney had the nomination in hand. But his performance as a vote-getter in the competitive stage of the Republican nominating process was at best mixed. He ran well in cities and suburbs, which carried him to critical victories in major states such as Florida, Illinois, Michigan, Ohio, and Wisconsin. But he fared less well in conservative rural and small-town terrain in the South and agrarian Midwest. Altogether, Romney won nineteen primary and caucus states in the competitive stage of the GOP primaries. Santorum took eleven and Gingrich two (South Carolina and his home state of Georgia). Romney's overall share of the GOP primary vote through April 3 was just 40 percent.

As Romney struggled to nail down the Republican nomination, Obama cruised to renomination. No Democrat of consequence filed to run against him, giving the president's campaign the opportunity to get the jump on Romney by organizing the fall swing states down to the grass roots level.

Nationwide, Obama ended up collecting more than 90 percent of the Democratic primary ballots. But in four socially conservative states from West Virginia to Oklahoma, he drew less than 60 percent. In addition, he lost dozens of counties in these states (a group that also included Arkansas and Kentucky) to an "uncommitted" line or array of political unknowns that essentially served as a "none of the above" option.

But in states pertinent to the general election—such as New Hampshire, Michigan, and Wisconsin—Obama did much better among Democratic voters, taking 80 percent or more of the party's primary ballots.[5]

In the end, Obama joined Ronald Reagan, Bill Clinton, and George W. Bush as recent presidents who won reelection after gliding to renomination with little or no opposition.

Meanwhile, Romney's full-throated bid to win the support of ardent conservatives in Republican primaries and caucuses left a "highlight reel" filled with what Democrats claimed were flip-flops from his past positions. They were employed with effect by the Obama team in the fall campaign.

# A BRIEF HISTORY OF AN
# EVOLUTIONARY PROCESS

The election of the president of the United States has two parts. First, each party goes through the process of nominating its presidential candidate. Then, the nation elects its chief executive from the choices that it is given.

The latter is short and sweet, with basically a two-month general election campaign that culminates with a one-day nationwide vote that often produces a winner within hours. Except for the rise in early voting, this electoral endgame has been largely unchanged for generations.

The former, by contrast, is drawn out and constantly evolving. Rather than measured in hours or days, the process of nominating a president is figured in months, even years.

It has already gone through four basic stages over the course of the nation's history. At first, presidential candidates were selected by their party's members in Congress in quickly held events that became known as "congressional caucuses."

As democracy began to flourish in the early nineteenth century, these "in house" caucuses were replaced by conventions, with state parties sending representatives to a national conclave to select their party nominee. Initially, conventions were held in cities centrally located between north and south, Baltimore being a prime choice before the Civil War. Afterward, as the country pushed west, Chicago emerged as a frequent convention host.[6]

Voters did not gain a direct voice in the nominating process until the early twentieth century, when presidential primaries came on the scene as a major innovation of the Progressive era. But for generations, the primaries were so few in number that they possessed no more than an advisory role in selecting nominees. The convention ruled supreme until the 1970s, when primaries began to multiply and assume the deciding role in the nominating process.

That is where we stand today. Primaries decide. Conventions are now merely coronations, an anticlimactic ending to a nominating process that for all practical purposes is over months earlier.

## CONVENTIONS AND THEIR FUTURE

Conventions of late are not what they used to be: determinative, unpredictable, and routinely watched by large numbers of the nation's voters. Before 1972, national conventions were the venue where nominations were settled. And they were usually midsummer extravaganzas, not the Labor Day events that have recently come into vogue.

In its heyday, each day of the convention had its significance. Mondays were typically devoted to settling credentials disputes and adopting the rules for the convention. Republicans also often adopted their rules for the next nominating process, an activity the Democrats have traditionally left to a post-election rules committee. Monday evening would end with the keynote address, often delivered by a rising star in the party.

Tuesdays were often devoted to consideration of the party's platform. Particularly controversial topics, such as the Vietnam War, might draw majority and minority reports that would necessitate lengthy debate and a roll-call vote.

Wednesdays were the centerpiece of the convention week, the day that the presidential nomination was decided. But not before an array of nominating speeches, long and loud demonstrations, and the roll-call vote for president. It was always an evening of color and drama, even though no presidential nominating fight since 1952 had gone beyond one ballot.

On Thursdays the newly minted presidential nominee would announce his pick for vice president. That evening, the two would give their acceptance speeches.

In contrast, the modern convention essentially features one speech after another from beginning to end. Many of these orations are tightly scripted, although actor Clint Eastwood provided a conspicuous exception on the final night of the 2012 Republican convention. Eastwood spoke to an empty chair that was supposed to represent President Obama. It was a rambling performance that left observers scratching their heads and no one eager to take credit for it.

Once worthy of gavel-to-gavel coverage on the major networks, conventions nowadays are fortunate to get an hour of network television coverage per night. Even the once awaited presidential roll call has become so anticlimactic that it has been shunted out of primetime to an off hour. At the 2012 Democratic convention in Charlotte, the roll call was held around midnight on Wednesday, after the major speeches of the evening had taken place. At the time of the roll call, the hall was virtually empty and live coverage of the tally was essentially limited to C-SPAN.

The 2012 Republican presidential roll call was also held well out of primetime near the beginning of the party's convention in Tampa. But it did produce some notes of interest. While rolls calls at recent conventions have produced nearly unanimous support for the nominee, more than 200 of the 2,286 GOP delegates cast their votes for candidates other than Romney. It was the largest number of delegate votes cast against the Republican nominee since President Gerald Ford barely beat back the challenge from former California governor Ronald Reagan in 1976.

The main recipient of non-Romney votes in Tampa was Ron Paul, who increased his share of delegates more than tenfold from an earlier run for the Republican nomination in 2008 (his total jumped from 17 to 190). Paul did not win any primary or first-round caucus votes in 2012. But his libertarian message drew an intense cadre of supporters who were particularly effective in relatively low-turnout caucus states. Paul won a majority of delegates in three such states—Iowa, Minnesota, and Nevada—by dominating the less public, later stages of the process where delegates are actually selected.[7]

Even though the modern convention is much less compelling than it once was, it still has some significance. The convention offers both parties an unobstructed block of time to make their case to the American people as well as to introduce their ticket on a national stage—a particularly important factor for the "out" party in years such as 2012 when an incumbent president is on the ballot.

A successful convention also brings together party leaders and activists from across the country in one place, and can energize them and the party faithful watching at home for the fall campaign. If an independent voter or two are converted in the process, all the better.

But few people believe anymore that a convention nowadays needs to be four days long. That has been the traditional length for generations. But Republicans showed in both 2008 and 2012 that three days is more than enough, because in both years the convention lost its opening day to weather concerns.

Some observers speculate, why even hold three-day conventions? One day might be enough, although the parties would probably be reluctant to give up the extra days of free air time.

Holding the conventions in the same city is another possibility, which would be of help to the media covering them.

There is also the question of whether the "in" party should always hold its convention last. This is an informal tradition that was not a concern a generation or so ago when both parties held their national gatherings earlier in the summer. But in recent years, conventions have tended to be held in back-to-back weeks around Labor Day.

With the conventions scheduled so close to the start of the fall campaign, an important ripple (if not a wave) of momentum has tended to go to the party that has gotten the last word. In 2012, that was the Democrats, and the convention bump they received helped to keep Obama in the lead in many electoral vote projections up to (and through) Election Day.

## WHAT'S NEXT?

The final set of ground rules for the 2016 presidential nominating process remains to be written. Democrats traditionally review their rules in the year or two after a presidential election. Republicans usually adopt theirs at the party convention four years in advance of their implementation. But this time, according to veteran GOP rules maker David A. Norcross, a Washington lawyer, the window is still open for the Republican National Committee to make changes in the 2016 rules if they muster support from at least 75 percent of the members.

The GOP has already relaxed the 2012 rule that required all states that voted before April 1 to use proportional representation in allocating their delegates. The language for 2016 has been changed, says Norcross, from "shall be proportional" to "*may* be proportional." That could allow many of the early voting states to return to some variation of winner-take-all in the distribution of their delegates. That in turn could shorten the length of the Republican nominating process in 2016 by helping the front-runner more quickly acquire delegates than was possible in 2012.[8]

This is not an issue for the Democrats, since they require all states— whenever they vote—to divide their pledged delegates to proportionally reflect the primary or caucus result. Instead, Democratic rules makers may continue post-2008 discussions on the role of "superdelegates" (who are automatic Democratic delegates by virtue of their position as party and elected officials). To the chagrin of the Clinton forces in 2008, many of the superdelegates broke for Obama at a critical point in the nominating process.

Democrats also may revisit the status of the early voting states, particularly the lead-off spots that Iowa and New Hampshire have held for a generation. For years, the privileged positions for Iowa and New Hampshire have been a flash-point for controversy within Democratic rules bodies. And Iowa Republicans did the state no favors in 2012 with a questionable tally.

On caucus night, the numbers from state GOP headquarters showed Romney with an eight-vote lead. The tentative results were treated as a Romney victory by the candidate and the media and swelled his momentum as the political caravan rolled off to New Hampshire. But when the final results from the Iowa caucuses were posted a fortnight later, Santorum had pulled ahead by thirty-four votes. Since results from several precincts could not be tracked down, the Iowa Republican Party declared that no true winner could be determined and congratulated candidates "on a hard-fought effort during the closest contest in caucus history." All in all, it was an embarrassment that did not reflect well on the Iowa caucuses in particular or the caucus process in general.[9]

In short, there is always something for rules makers of both parties to debate as they look ahead to next election cycle. The presidential nominating process is a work in progress that never gets completed. It is always under review and always subject to change. The shape of the nominating process in 2016 may not be markedly different from 2012. But it will be different. That is the way that the process works.

## NOTES

1. Arthur T. Hadley, *The Invisible Primary* (Englewood Cliffs, NJ: Prentice-Hall, Inc., 1976), xiii.

2. "The Rules of the Republican Party as Adopted by the 2008 Republican National Convention September 1, 2008 (Amended by the Republican National Committee on August 6, 2010)," 25, www.gop.com/images/legal/2008_RULES _Adopted.pdf.

3. Rhodes Cook, Alice V. McGillivray, and Richard Scammon, *America Votes 28: Election Returns by State 2007–2008* (Washington, DC: CQ Press, 2010), 50, 52; *The Rhodes Cook Letter*, June 2012, 6.

4. Gallup Polls on Republican presidential preferences taken throughout 2011.

5. *The Rhodes Cook Letter*, June 2012, 3, 10.

6. Congressional Quarterly, *Guide to U.S. Elections*, 6th ed., vol. 1 (Washington, DC: CQ Press, 2010), 490, 492.

7. Congressional Quarterly, *Guide to U.S. Elections*, 751; *The Rhodes Cook Letter*, August 2012, 12.

8. David A. Norcross, e-mail to author, November 19, 2012.

9. David A. Fahrenthold and Debbi Wilgoren, "Iowa's Final Count Puts Santorum 34 Votes Ahead of Romney," *Washington Post*, January 20, 2012.

# 5

# THE SIX-BILLION-
# DOLLAR ELECTION

## The Impact of Federal Election Laws

### *Michael E. Toner and Karen E. Trainer[1]*

The 2012 presidential election was the first contest since 1972 in which neither major party nominee accepted public funds for any portion of the campaign, which helped pave the way for President Obama's and Governor Romney's presidential campaigns to raise a record-breaking $1.2 billion combined for the 2012 presidential race.[2] In addition, in the aftermath of the U.S. Supreme Court's ruling in *Citizens United v. FEC* and recent lower federal court decisions, Super PACs and other outside groups raised and spent unprecedented sums of money in connection with the 2012 presidential election, including approximately $416 million on behalf of Romney and approximately $142 million on behalf of Obama.[3] Moreover, the Republican National Committee (RNC) and the Democratic National Committee (DNC), despite laboring under the hard-dollar fund-raising restrictions of the McCain-Feingold campaign finance law, raised a near record amount of money for the 2012 election cycle.

These extraordinary fund-raising forces, in tandem with the perceived closeness of the Obama-Romney presidential race, combined to create a perfect storm of fund-raising in which more than $6 billion was spent in connection with the 2012 election,[4] the most money ever spent on a single election cycle in American history. Given the dramatic increase in election-related spending that has taken place in the last dozen years since the 2000 Bush-Gore presidential campaign, we are likely to see even more money raised and spent in connection with the 2016 presidential election, particularly given that 2016 will be an open-seat race in which there will be contested primaries in both parties.

## THE OBAMA AND ROMNEY CAMPAIGNS COMBINED TO RAISE RECORD SUMS OF MONEY FOR THE 2012 PRESIDENTIAL RACE

We have witnessed a remarkable evolution of presidential campaign fund-raising during the last fifteen years, which has created a presidential fund-raising environment that would have been unimaginable from the 1970s through the 1990s when successful candidates operated within the confines of the presidential public financing system.

The presidential public financing system was created after the Watergate scandal and first went into effect for the 1976 presidential election. Under the system, presidential candidates have the option of accepting public funds for their primary election or general election campaigns, or both. For the primaries, presidential candidates can receive matching funds from the government of up to $250 for each individual contribution they receive. To be eligible to receive matching funds, candidates must raise at least $5,000 in twenty or more states from individuals in amounts of $250 or less. For the 2012 primaries, each presidential candidate could receive a maximum of approximately $22 million in matching funds.[5] However, candidates electing to receive matching funds for the 2012 presidential race were subject to a nationwide spending limit during the primaries of approximately $55 million, as well as state-by-state spending limits based upon the population of each state.[6] Under the federal election laws, the primary season runs from the time a person legally becomes a presidential candidate through the national nominating conventions, which can last eighteen months or even longer. The national and state-by-state spending limits apply throughout this period of time. By contrast, candidates who decline to take matching funds are not subject to any spending limits for the primaries and are free to raise as much money as they can, subject to the contribution limits.[7] For the general election, presidential candidates have the option of accepting a public grant to finance all of their political activities[8] and be subject to a nationwide spending limit, or candidates can turn down public funds and raise private contributions subject to the contribution limits and operate without any spending restriction. The public grant for the general election in 2012 was approximately $91 million, as was the corresponding national spending limit.[9]

The presidential public financing system has become obsolete during the last decade as presidential candidates have operated more and more of their campaigns outside of the system in order to free themselves of the spending limits that come with the acceptance of public funds. In the 2000 presidential race, George W. Bush raised $100 million for his campaign and became the first candidate to turn down matching funds for the primaries and be elected president. In 2004, both major-party nominees for the first time turned down matching funds for the primaries, as George W. Bush raised $270 million and John Kerry raised $235 million for the primary season. Significantly, both Bush and Kerry in 2004 accepted the $75 million public grant for the general election and joined every major-party nominee since 1976 in doing so. However, the historical practice of accepting public funds for the general election was shattered in 2008 when President Obama became the first presidential candidate to be elected president who turned down public funds for both the primaries and the general election, which helped clear the way for Obama to raise an astounding $750 million for his campaign, including $414 million for the primaries alone. By contrast, Senator John McCain in 2008 raised $221 million for the primaries but opted to accept the $85 million public grant for the general election, which provided McCain with a total of $306 million for his entire campaign, which was barely 40 percent of the total funds that the Obama campaign had at its disposal.[10]

Given the record-breaking $750 million that the Obama campaign raised for the 2008 election, it was certainly no surprise when Obama decided to turn down public funds once again for the 2012 primaries and general election. In light of the extraordinary resource advantage that the Obama campaign achieved over the McCain campaign in 2008 during the general election phase of the campaign, all of the top-tier Republican candidates announced during the 2012 primary season that they would join Obama in operating outside of the presidential public financing system for the primaries and the general election and thereby be free of any spending limits for the entire campaign.[11]

The Obama campaign raised a total of $741 million for the 2012 presidential race, including approximately $442 million for the primaries and $299 million for the general election.[12] Interestingly, although record amounts of money were raised and spent in connection with the 2012 election, the Obama campaign did not match the $750 million total that it had raised in 2008, which surprised some observers given that incumbent presidents typically raise more money for their reelection campaigns than they do for their initial presidential campaigns. The Romney campaign raised a total of $473 million for the 2012 presidential race, including approximately $253 million for the primaries and $220 million for the general election.[13] Romney's decision to join Obama in turning down public funds for the general election as well as for the primaries proved to be prescient, as the Romney campaign ended up having $167 million and 54 percent more funds to spend on the 2012 race than did McCain on the 2008 race.

Nonetheless, the Obama campaign still ended up raising $268 million more than the Romney campaign, including $101 million more during the September–November general election period. Obama also enjoyed a significant fund-raising advantage in the final weeks leading up to the election. In the first seventeen days of October, the Obama campaign raised $77 million, compared to the Romney campaign's $51 million.[14] Similarly, between October 18 and Election Day, the Obama campaign raised $85 million, compared to the Romney Campaign's $60 million.[15] Table 5.1 below summarizes the fund-raising totals of the major party nominees from 2000 to 2012.

Table 5.1 reveals the remarkable increase in presidential candidate fund-raising that has occurred during the last twelve years. In 2000, Bush and Gore conducted their campaigns with a combined total of $300 million. In 2008, the Obama and McCain campaigns had a combined $1.056 billion of campaign funds to spend, which was more than three times the amount of money that the Bush and Gore campaigns had spent collectively only eight

**Table 5.1.   Summary of Major Party Nominee Fund-Raising Totals (2000–2012)**

| Candidate | Primary Fund-Raising Total | General Fund-Raising Total | Total Campaign Funds |
|---|---|---|---|
| **2000** | | | |
| Bush | $100 million | $75 million* | $175 million |
| Gore | $50 million* | $75 million* | $125 million |
| **2004** | | | |
| Bush | $270 million | $80 million* | $350 million |
| Kerry | $235 million | $80 million* | $315 million |
| **2008** | | | |
| Obama | $414 million | $336 million | $750 million |
| McCain | $221 million | $85 million* | $306 million |
| **2012** | | | |
| Obama | $442 million | $299 million | $741 million |
| Romney | $253 million | $220 million | $473 million |

*Source*: Federal Election Commission data. The 2012 primary and general totals are estimates based upon analysis of FEC reports.

*Candidate Accepted Public Funds

years earlier. By 2012, the Obama and Romney campaigns had four times the amount of money that the Bush and Gore campaigns had to spend in 2000.[16]

The Obama campaign used its fund-raising advantage to finance a large advertising push in the final weeks leading up to Election Day. Published reports indicate that the Obama campaign spent $40 million on advertisements in the last three weeks of September compared to the Romney campaign's $19 million.[17] In addition, press reports indicate that the Obama campaign bought $24.2 million of advertising airtime for the final week of the campaign compared with only $21.2 million for the Romney campaign.[18] The Obama campaign's total spending of $775 million also far exceeded the Romney campaign's total spending of $460 million.[19]

As the amount of money raised by presidential candidates has increased significantly in recent years, so has the amount of time that presidential candidates have spent attending fund-raising events and participating in other fund-raising activities. A recent study of presidential campaigns by Professor Brendan J. Doherty of the U.S. Naval Academy found a marked increase during the last four decades in the number of fund-raising events that sitting presidents have attended for various political committees.[20] Table 5.2 lists the total number of fund-raising events for various political committees that were attended by each president.

Professor Doherty's study found that President Obama attended 121 fund-raising events for various political committees between the beginning of his term in January 2009 and June 2011.[21] By contrast, President Reagan attended only eighty fund-raising events during his entire first term.[22]

**Table 5.2.    Presidential Attendance at Fund-Raising Events (1977–2011)**

| President | Total Number of Fund-Raising Events |
| --- | --- |
| Jimmy Carter | 85 |
| Ronald Reagan (First Term) | 80 |
| Ronald Reagan (Second Term) | 100 |
| George H. W. Bush | 137 |
| Bill Clinton (First Term) | 167 |
| Bill Clinton (Second Term) | 471 |
| George W. Bush (First Term) | 173 |
| George W. Bush (Second Term) | 155 |
| Barack Obama | *121 |

*Source*: Brendan J. Doherty, *The Rise of the President's Permanent Campaign*. Figures include fund-raising events for each president's own campaign committee, other campaign committees, and political party committees.

*Data through June 2011.

Remarkably, the study found that Reagan "did not appear at *any* fund-raisers for the Reagan-Bush campaign committee in large part because the fund-raising efforts of the direct mail operation and those spearheaded by Vice President Bush were so successful that the campaign stopped soliciting funds in May 1984" (emphasis added).[23] The fact that President Reagan did not need to attend even a single fund-raising event for his 1984 reelection campaign was at least partly attributable to his campaign accepting public funds for the primaries and the general election. Nevertheless, such a development would be unthinkable for incumbents running for president in the twenty-first century.

## SUPER PACS AND OTHER OUTSIDE GROUPS SPENT EXTRAORDINARY AMOUNTS OF MONEY ON THE 2012 ELECTION

Passage of the McCain-Feingold campaign finance law, combined with recent court decisions permitting unlimited corporate, union, and individual contributions to finance independent expenditures sponsored by outside organizations such as Super PACs and 501(c) organizations, have led to a rapid proliferation of outside groups that are having a growing impact on federal elections. These outside groups, which have flourished on both the right and the left in recent years, are increasingly engaged in political activities that were once the province of political parties, such as voter registration drives, absentee ballot programs, GOTV, voter identification, and political advertising and issue advocacy efforts. In many ways, we witnessed the full flowering of outside group activities during the 2012 presidential campaign and it may be a harbinger for future presidential races.

The McCain-Feingold law, which took effect during the 2004 presidential election cycle, prohibits the RNC, DNC, and the other national political party committees from raising or spending soft-money funds for any purpose. "Soft money" is defined as funds raised outside of the prohibitions and limitations of federal law, including corporate and labor union general treasury funds and individual contributions in excess of federal limits. Funds raised in accordance with federal law come from individuals and from federally registered PACs and are harder to raise; hence, these funds are commonly referred to as "hard money." Prior to McCain-Feingold, the national political parties were legally permitted to accept unlimited corporate, union, and individual soft-money contributions and could use these funds to help underwrite a wide variety of political and electoral activities, including voter registration efforts, absentee ballot drives, GOTV activities, slate cards, and similar ticket-wide political activities. The national political parties prior to McCain–Feingold were also able to use soft-money contributions to help finance issue advertisements supporting and opposing presidential candidates. "Issue advertisements" are public communications that frequently attack or promote federal candidates and their records, but which refrain from expressly advocating the election or defeat of any candidate (which is referred to as "express advocacy"). Under federal law, the national political parties can accept individual contributions of up to $30,800 per year and this contribution limit is indexed for inflation each election cycle.

In *Citizens United v. FEC*, the U.S. Supreme Court struck down the long-standing prohibition on corporate independent expenditures in connection with federal elections. In *SpeechNow v. FEC*, a federal appeals court invalidated limits on contributions from individuals to political committees that fund only independent expenditures for or against federal candidates. In advisory opinions issued after the *SpeechNow* decision, the FEC concluded that political committees formed strictly to make independent expenditures supporting or opposing federal candidates could accept unlimited contributions from individuals, corporations, and labor organizations.[24] These new political committees, which are prohibited from making contributions to federal candidates and other federal political committees, are commonly referred to as "Super PACs."

501(c) organizations are entities that are organized and operate under Section 501(c) of the Internal Revenue Code, including social welfare organizations established under Section 501(c)(4) and trade associations and business leagues organized under Section 501(c)(6). Section 501(c)(4) and 501(c)(6) entities are permitted to accept unlimited corporate, union, and individual contributions and may engage in partisan political activities, provided that such political activities do not become their primary purpose. By contrast, Super PACs, as political committees registered with the FEC, are by definition partisan entities and may spend all of their funds on partisan political activities. Super PACs are required to publicly disclose their donors; 501(c) organizations are generally not required to disclose their donors to the public.

As a result of these changes to the legal landscape, outside groups spent an estimated $1 billion on advertising in connection with 2012 federal elections.[25] The three largest outside groups, American Crossroads, Crossroads GPS, and Restore Our Future, accounted for over a third of the total amount spent.[26] This outside spending contributed to a 40 percent increase in the total number of advertisements aired by the presidential campaigns, political parties, and outside groups in the final months of the 2012 election as compared with 2008.[27] The number of advertisements disseminated in connection with the 2012 election exceeded the 1 million mark nearly a week before Election Day, which broke all previous records.[28] Table 5.3 below identifies the top outside group spenders during the 2012 election cycle.

As a result of spending by pro-Republican outside groups such as American Crossroads, Crossroads GPS, and Restore Our Future, Republican-leaning entities outspent their Democratic counterparts by nearly two-to-one in the final days leading up to the 2012 election.[29] In total, Republican-leaning outside groups spent an estimated $440 million in connection with the presidential race, and their spending represented approximately 70 percent of the total spending by outside groups on the 2012 election.[30] Total spending by the Romney campaign and its allied organizations exceeded the collective spending of the Obama campaign and its outside group supporters despite the Obama campaign's fund-raising advantage over the Romney campaign. One published report estimated that the Romney campaign and its allied entities (including outside groups and national party committees) collectively spent $1.2 billion on the 2012 presidential race compared with $1 billion spent by the Obama campaign and its allies.[31]

Because Super PACs and 501(c) organizations may not make contributions to federal campaign committees, traditional PACs, which can

**Table 5.3.    Largest Non-party Outside Spenders (2012 Election Cycle)**

| Name | 2011–2012 Disclosed Spending | Entity Type |
|---|---|---|
| American Crossroads/ Crossroads GPS | $175,808,214 | Super PAC/501(c) |
| Restore Our Future | $142,655,220 | Super PAC |
| Priorities USA Action | $67,496,077 | Super PAC |
| Majority PAC | $37,409,074 | Super PAC |
| Americans for Prosperity | $36,637,591 | 501(c) |
| U.S. Chamber of Commerce | $36,177,667 | 501(c) |
| House Majority PAC | $30,735,096 | Super PAC |
| Service Employees International Union | $30,100,169 | Super PAC/501(c) |
| American Future Fund | $24,986,522 | 501(c) |
| FreedomWorks | $19,156,817 | Super PAC |

*Source*: Opensecrets.org/outsidespending.

only accept contributions subject to federal contribution limits and source prohibitions, remain an important vehicle for supporting federal candidates. Table 5.4 below lists the ten largest PACs based upon the total amounts contributed to candidates during the 2012 election cycle. Each of these PACs are "connected" PACs associated with corporations, trade associations, labor organizations, and membership organizations. A number of connected PACs disseminated advertisements supporting or opposing federal candidates in addition to making direct contributions to candidates.

## THE NATIONAL POLITICAL PARTIES RAISED A NEAR RECORD AMOUNT OF MONEY FOR THE 2012 ELECTION

As was noted above, when the McCain–Feingold law was passed a decade ago many political observers feared that national political party fund-raising would be severely curtailed and the national parties would be marginalized in American politics. However, as table 5.5 indicates below, both the RNC and the DNC have consistently raised more funds since McCain–Feingold became law than they did prior to the soft-money ban, which first went into effect for the 2004 presidential election.

During the 2000 election cycle—when it was still legal for the national political parties to raise and spend unlimited soft-money contributions—the RNC raised $316 million and the DNC raised $210 million. For the 2004 presidential election cycle, both the RNC and the DNC raised more hard-money funds than the two committees had raised in hard- and

**Table 5.4.   Largest PACs by Total Contributions (2012 Election Cycle)**

| PAC Name | 2011–2012 Total Contributions |
| --- | --- |
| National Assn of Realtors PAC | $3,779,471 |
| Operating Engineers Union PAC | $2,953,887 |
| Honeywell International PAC | $2,910,159 |
| National Beer Wholesalers Assn PAC | $2,721,000 |
| National Auto Dealers Assn PAC | $2,620,500 |
| American Bankers Assn PAC | $2,529,150 |
| Intl Brotherhood of Electrical Workers PAC | $2,488,000 |
| AT&T Inc PAC | $2,424,500 |
| American Assn for Justice PAC | $2,421,500 |
| Northrop Grumman PAC | $2,261,900 |

*Source*: OpenSecrets.org. Based on data released by the FEC on November 12, 2012.

**Table 5.5.    Fund-Raising Totals for the RNC and DNC (2000–2012 Election Cycles)**

|     | 2012 | 2008 | 2004 | 2000 |
| --- | --- | --- | --- | --- |
| RNC | $381 million | $417 million | $330 million | $316 million |
| DNC | $289 million | $255 million | $299 million | $210 million |

*Source*: Federal Election Commission data.

soft-money funds combined for the 2000 election cycle, with the RNC increasing its fund-raising total by $14 million and the DNC increasing its receipts by $89 million. These fund-raising trends largely continued during the 2008 presidential election cycle, with the RNC raising $87 million more than it had raised during the 2004 cycle and the DNC raising $45 million more than it had raised during the 2000 cycle. Table 5.5 compares RNC and DNC fund-raising totals for the past four presidential election cycles.

As table 5.5 indicates, both the RNC and the DNC raised near record amounts of money for the 2012 election cycle. The RNC and the DNC collectively raised $670 million during the 2012 election cycle, with the RNC raising $381 million and the DNC raising $289 million.

One technique that helped facilitate the RNC and DNC's fund-raising efforts for the 2012 election was the use of joint fund-raising committees involving the presidential campaigns, the national political party committees, and selected state political party committees. Under FEC regulations, candidates and political parties may simultaneously raise hard-money funds through joint fund-raising committees (JFCs) that permit them to combine the per-recipient contribution limits and solicit greater amounts of money from donors at any one time.[32]

Historically, joint fund-raising committees supporting presidential candidates have included as participants the presidential candidate's campaign committee, a national political party committee such as the RNC or the DNC, and state political party committees in select battleground states. In 2012, the Obama campaign followed this practice by including in the Obama JFC (known as the Obama Victory Fund 2012) the DNC and state Democratic Party committees in states such as Florida, Colorado, and Ohio. The Romney JFC (called Romney Victory) took a different approach by including state Republican Party committees in non-battleground states such as Vermont and Massachusetts. Romney Victory also included the RNC as well as the National Republican Senatorial Committee (NRSC) and the National Republican Congressional Committee (NRCC). By including additional party committee participants, Romney Victory was able to accept larger contributions from individuals and PACs than otherwise would have been possible and this helped fuel the Republican Party's fund-raising efforts during the 2012 campaign.

As was noted above, the national political parties have done an excellent job of adapting to the McCain-Feingold law's soft-money ban and have raised record amounts of money in recent election cycles. However, because outside groups do not labor under the hard-dollar fund-raising restrictions that apply to the national political parties, outside groups can raise large amounts of money from a small group of donors in a very short period of time. In addition, Super PACs, 501(c) organizations, and other types of outside groups are now spending more on independent expenditures and other election-related communications than are political party committees. As is detailed in figure 5.1 below, Super PACs reportedly made $631 million in independent expenditures and other election-related communications in the 2012 election cycle, whereas political parties spent only $252 million.

Given the fund-raising advantages that outside groups (including Super PACs) currently enjoy, this spending imbalance may become even more pronounced in the future unless the campaign finance laws are changed to allow the national political parties to raise and spend the same kinds of funds as outside groups are legally able to do.

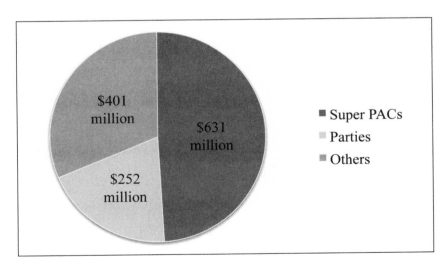

**Figure 5.1.  2012 Outside Spending by Entity Type**
*Source*: www.opensecrets.org/outsidespending/.  Data through November 6, 2012.

## ONLINE POLITICAL ACTIVITY CONTINUED TO PLAY AN IMPORTANT ROLE IN THE 2012 RACE AND REMAINED LARGELY UNREGULATED BY THE FEC

The Internet came of age politically in 2008 as the Obama campaign developed an unprecedented web-based strategy that involved millions of Americans in the presidential race through sophisticated and cutting-edge online technologies. During the 2012 election, federal candidates, PACs, and outside interest groups once again developed and implemented new Internet technologies to disseminate political information in real time to millions of voters and raised increasing amounts of campaign funds online. Fund-raising through text message was the latest online innovation that federal candidates and committees used to raise funds during the 2012 election cycle.

One key factor that has contributed to the rapid growth of the Internet in American politics in recent years has been the FEC's deregulatory approach to online activities. In 2006, the FEC adopted regulations, which remain in place today, concerning the use of the Internet in federal elections. The FEC's regulations exempt the Internet from the various prohibitions and restrictions of the McCain–Feingold law with only one exception: paid advertising placed on another person's website.[33] The practical effect of the FEC's regulations has been that individuals, volunteers, and anyone else with access to a computer can conduct a wide range of Internet activities on behalf of federal candidates—such as setting up and maintaining websites, blogging, e-mailing, linking, and posting videos on YouTube—without fear that the FEC will monitor or restrict their activities. Although it is difficult to measure or gauge precisely, there is no question that the FEC's hands-off regulatory approach to online political activities has helped the Internet play a growing and vital role in American politics in recent years.

The Obama campaign had a significant online advantage over the McCain campaign during the 2008 presidential race.[34] In somewhat of a surprise, Republican candidates made major strides during the 2010 mid-term election in using the Internet to advance their candidacies, and some Republican candidates even surpassed their Democratic opponents in several important online metrics in 2010.[35] Given the Internet gains that some prominent Republican candidates had made in 2010, it was unclear at the outset of the 2012 presidential race whether the Obama campaign would have as pronounced an online advantage over the Republican nominee as was the case in 2008. However, by any plausible metric, the Obama campaign dominated the Romney campaign online in 2012 and this may have helped fuel the Obama campaign's voter turnout advantage in the battleground states on Election Day. As table 5.6 demonstrates below, the Obama campaign far outpaced the Romney campaign in a wide variety of online indicators during the 2012 presidential race.

As was noted above, one legal development that had an impact on fund-raising in 2012 was an FEC decision allowing federal campaigns to accept contributions via text message for the first time. In an advisory opinion issued in June 2012, the FEC approved a proposal for federal campaigns to accept text message contributions, provided that certain safeguards are followed to ensure compliance with FEC regulations.[36] While the FEC was considering the advisory opinion, both the Obama and Romney campaigns urged the FEC to approve the proposal. Subsequent FEC advisory opinions provided additional clarity on the recordkeeping and legal compliance obligations of federal campaigns when they receive text message contributions. In the aftermath of these FEC advisory opinions, contributions to federal campaigns and other federal political committees can now be made by text message in the same way that text message contributions were accepted by the American Red Cross in the wake of recent natural disasters such as the 2010 earthquake in Haiti.

Both the Obama and Romney campaigns declined to publicly disclose the amount of funds that they raised from text messages during the 2012 presidential race. Since FEC reporting regulations do not require presidential campaigns to divulge such information, it is difficult to determine definitively the amount of funds that the Obama and Romney campaigns raised through text message programs. However, based upon the fees that the two campaigns paid to one of the entities involved in the FEC text

**Table 5.6.  Comparison of Obama and Romney Campaign Online Activity**

|  | *Obama* | *Romney* |
|---|---|---|
| Number of Twitter followers | 21,788,383 | 1,700,910 |
| Number of Facebook fans | 31,887,871 | 12,015,371 |
| Average number of tweets per day | 26 | 3 |
| Number of YouTube videos posted since 1/1/11 | 931 | 320 |
| Number of YouTube subscribers | 275,544 | 28,959 |
| Number of YouTube views | 270,997,865 | 33,015,075 |

*Sources*: www.campaignpop.com, www.youtube.com. Data through November 6, 2012.

message advisory opinions, one published report estimated that between late August and the end of September 2012 the Obama campaign raised approximately $836,550 in text message donations while the Romney campaign raised only $1,520.[37] If this estimate is accurate, the Obama campaign's online dominance of the Romney campaign extended to text message contributions in addition to the more traditional indicators of online political strength noted above.

Because the FEC's Advisory Opinions allowing federal campaigns to accept text message donations were issued relatively late in the 2012 election cycle, it is difficult to predict how prevalent text message contributions will be in future federal elections. However, it is likely that text message contributions will become a permanent part of the online fund-raising strategies of federal campaigns in the future, and we may witness a significant increase in the volume of text message contributions that are made to federal candidates and other federal political committees during the 2014 midterm election cycle and beyond.

## EARLY VOTING LAWS HAD A MAJOR IMPACT ON CAMPAIGN STRATEGY IN 2012

For many years, voters who expected to be absent from their home communities on Election Day could apply for an absentee ballot and could cast an absentee ballot prior to the election. However, in order to obtain an absentee ballot, many jurisdictions required voters to show cause or otherwise explain why they were not able to vote on Election Day in their local precincts, which reduced the number of people who voted absentee.[38] In 1980, California amended its laws to permit voters to cast ballots before Election Day without providing any excuse or showing any cause.[39] In recent years, many more states have permitted voters to vote prior to Election Day without cause, either in person or by mail. Some states allow voters to become permanent absentee voters and automatically receive absentee ballots for each election without having to submit a request.

As a result of these legal changes, the number of Americans voting prior to Election Day has grown steadily during the last two decades, reaching 16 percent of voters in 2000 and 22 percent of voters by 2004.[40] Approximately 39 million votes were cast early in the 2008 election, which constituted 30 percent of the total votes cast.[41] As of late September 2012, twenty-nine states had started sending absentee ballots or allowing early in-person voting for the 2012 election.[42] A total of thirty-two states and the District of Columbia allowed voters to vote early for the 2012 election without providing an excuse. Some analysts estimate that 30 million early votes were cast through the day before Election Day in 2012[43] and that 26.6 percent of the total votes cast in the 2012 election were cast early.[44] President Obama was among the millions of people who voted early in 2012, reportedly making him the first sitting president to do so.[45]

In a number of swing states in 2012, significantly more registered Democrats voted early than did registered Republicans. In the final days leading up to the election, Obama campaign advisers contended that Romney would need to win up to 60 percent of the votes cast on Election Day to overcome Obama's early vote margin in certain states.[46] Table 5.7 outlines early votes by party in several key states in 2012.

Data on early voting advantages in Virginia and Ohio is limited because neither state requires voters to register by party. However, the Obama campaign claimed in the final days of the campaign that it had a significant early vote lead in both Virginia and Ohio.[47] A *Time* magazine poll conducted in late October appeared to corroborate the Obama campaign's contention that it had an edge in early voting in Ohio.[48]

The extraordinary increase in early voting during the last three decades has had a profound impact on the strategies and tactics of modern presidential campaigns. For many years, the last seventy-two hours before Election Day were the primary focus for GOTV efforts, but now those campaign operations must be performed for a month or even longer in certain states. With some election analysts predicting that up to half the electorate will be voting early in the years ahead, there is no question that future presidential campaigns will closely track any changes in early voting laws and will continue to refine their GOTV and voter contact strategies accordingly. There is no longer a single Election Day in America but rather a multiweek

**Table 5.7.   Early Voting by Party Affiliation (2012 General Election)**

| State | Percentage of Early Votes Cast by Registered Democrats | Percentage of Early Votes Cast by Registered Republicans | Percentage of Early Votes Cast by Registered Other/ No Affiliation |
|---|---|---|---|
| North Carolina | 47.6% | 31.5% | 20.9% |
| Iowa | 41.9% | 32.0% | 26.1% |
| Nevada | 43.9% | 37.0% | 19.1% |
| Florida | 42.9% | 39.1% | 18.0% |
| Colorado | 34.3% | 36.1% | 29.6% |

*Source*: http://elections.gmu.edu/early_vote_2012.html. Data as of November 6.

election window, and maximizing early voting margins in battleground states will become a key strategic objective of future presidential campaigns.

## LOOKING AHEAD TO 2016

The 2012 presidential election was the first race since 1972 to be conducted entirely outside of the presidential public financing system, as both President Obama and Governor Romney turned down public funds for the primaries and the general election alike, raising well in excess of $1 billion combined for their campaigns. Unless Congress takes drastic steps to overhaul the presidential public financing system—which very few observers think is likely—the two major party nominees in 2016 will almost certainly follow Obama's and Romney's strategy of turning down public funds for the entire presidential race and raising as much money as they can for their campaigns without being subject to any spending limits.

Should Secretary of State Hillary Rodham Clinton decide to run for president in 2016, she would instantly become the frontrunner for the Democratic nomination and could end up raising between $750 million and $1 billion for her campaign and perhaps even more. Vice President Joseph Biden and New York governor Andrew Cuomo would also likely have significant fund-raising strength. The bench of potential Republican candidates for 2016 is deep and strong, and includes among others Florida senator Marco Rubio, New Jersey governor Chris Christie, Louisiana governor Bobby Jindal, and former Florida governor Jeb Bush. With Super PACs able to raise and spend unlimited sums of money, and likely to play an even broader role four years from now, the imperative for presidential campaigns to raise records amounts of money will never be greater. An open seat for president, strong top-tier candidates in both parties, a highly polarized electorate, higher contribution limits, and a favorable legal terrain—all of the ingredients are present to make the 2016 presidential race the most expensive in American history.

## NOTES

1. Michael E. Toner is former chairman of the Federal Election Commission and is co-chair of the Election Law and Government Ethics Practice Group at Wiley Rein LLP in Washington, DC. Karen E. Trainer is a senior reporting specialist at Wiley Rein LLP.

2. Federal Election Commission data.

3. "2012 Presidential Independent Expenditures," OpenSecrets.org, www
.opensecrets.org/pres12/indexp.php.

4. Matea Gold, "2012 Campaign Set to Cost a Record $6 Billion," *Los Angeles Times*, October 31, 2012.

5. Federal Election Commission, "Federal Election Commission Certifies Federal Matching Funds for Jill Stein for President," Federal Election Commission news release, August 28, 2012, www.fec.gov/press/press2012/20120828_SteinMatchFund .shtml.

6. The state spending limits in some of the most important early primary and caucus states were very low in 2012. For example, the spending limit in New Hampshire was only $912,400, which was the same spending limit as existed for American Samoa. Similarly, the spending limit for the Iowa caucuses was only $1,706,500. See Federal Election Commission, *Presidential Spending Limits for 2012*, www.fec.gov/pages/brochures/pubfund_limits_2012.shtml.

7. Individuals could contribute up to $2,500 per election to presidential candidates for the 2012 election and federal multicandidate PACs could contribute up to $5,000 per election, with the primary and general elections considered separate elections. The individual contribution limits are adjusted for inflation each election cycle.

8. The only exception is that publicly financed general-election presidential candidates are permitted to raise private contributions to defray legal and accounting costs incurred in complying with the federal election laws. These funds, which are known as general election legal and accounting compliance funds (GELAC funds), may accept individual and PAC contributions subject to the contribution limits. Senator John McCain's GELAC fund raised $48.3 million for the 2008 presidential race. (Federal Election Commission data.)

9. The public grant for the general election and the corresponding national spending limit are adjusted for inflation each election cycle. See Federal Election Commission, *Presidential Spending Limits for 2012*, www.fec.gov/pages/brochures/ pubfund_limits_2012.shtml.

10. The Obama campaign had a remarkable resource advantage over the McCain campaign in 2008, including a nearly four-to-one edge during the general election phase of the campaign. The Obama campaign's broad resource advantage was particularly pronounced in the final weeks of the 2008 campaign. In September 2008 alone the Obama campaign raised over $150 million, and between October 15 and November 24 the Obama campaign raised an additional $104 million and spent $136 million. To put these Obama campaign fund-raising and spending figures in perspective, the McCain campaign received only $85 million of public funds to finance all of its political activities during the entire general election campaign.

11. Jill Stein, Gary Johnson, and Buddy Roemer accepted matching funds for the 2012 presidential primaries. No presidential candidate accepted public funds for the 2012 general election. See FEC news releases regarding public funding at www.fec.gov/ press/press2004/PublicFundingReleases.shtml.

12. Federal Election Commission data. Primary and general election contribution totals are estimates based upon analysis of FEC reports. Under the federal election laws, presidential candidates may roll over and spend during the general election any unused campaign funds that remain from the primaries. This is a key legal advantage for incumbent presidents like Obama who are unopposed for their party's nomination.

13. Federal Election Commission data.

14. Federal Election Commission data.

15. Federal Election Commission data.

16. The 2012 Obama campaign spent an estimated $72 million on advertising in Ohio alone. Peter Bell and Reid Wilson, "Ad Spending in Presidential Battleground States," *National Journal* online, June 20, 2012, updated November 4, 2012, www.nationaljournal.com/hotline/ad-spending-in-presidential-battleground -states-20120620. This amount was nearly as much as the Gore and Bush campaigns each spent on their entire 2000 general election campaigns.

17. Laura Baum, "Obama Dominates Advertising in Key States," Kantar Media/ CMAG with analysis by the Wesleyan Media Project, October 3, 2012, http:// mediaproject.wesleyan.edu/2012/10/03/obama-dominates-ads-in-key-states/ #more-2014.

18. Kevin Bohn, "Candidates Buy $45 Million More in Ads in Record-Setting Campaign," CNN, October 31, 2012, www.cnn.com/2012/10/31/politics/ad-buys/ index.html.

19. Federal Election Commission data (campaign spending data through Election Day.)

20. Brendan J. Doherty, *The Rise of the President's Permanent Campaign* (Lawrence: University Press of Kansas, 2012), 81.

21. Doherty, *Rise of the President's Permanent Campaign*, 81.

22. Doherty, *Rise of the President's Permanent Campaign*, 57.

23. Doherty, *Rise of the President's Permanent Campaign*, 59.

24. FEC Advisory Opinions 2010-09 and 2010-11.

25. Michael Beckel, "Spending by Outside Groups Topped $1 Billion by Election Day," Center for Public Integrity, November 7, 2012, www.publicintegrity .org/2012/11/07/11789/spending-outside-groups-topped-1-billion-election-day.

26. Beckel, "Spending by Outside Groups Topped $1 Billion."

27. Laura Baum, "Presidential Ad War Tops 1M Airings," Kantar Media/ CMAG with analysis by the Wesleyan Media Project, November 2, 2012, http:// mediaproject.wesleyan.edu/2012/11/02/presidential-ad-war-tops-1m-airings/.

28. Baum, "Presidential Ad War Tops 1M Airings."

29. Jake Harper, "Republican Groups Swamping Democrats in Outside Spending," http://reporting.sunlightfoundation.com/2012/two-to-one/.

30. Beckel, "Spending by Outside Groups Topped $1 Billion."

31. Kenneth P. Vogel, "The Billion-Dollar Bust?," *Politico*, November 7, 2012.

32. For example, if a JFC included a presidential campaign, a national political party committee, and two state political party committees, individual donors could contribute up to $55,800 to the JFC—up to $5,000 to the presidential campaign ($2,500 for the primary and $2,500 for the general election), $30,800 to the national political party, and $10,000 each to the two state political parties. Any prior contributions that individual donors made to any of the entities participating in the JFC would count against what could be contributed to the JFC.

33. For example, if an individual spends money to take out an advertisement for a federal candidate that appears on the home page of Yahoo.com or CNN.com, the transaction will be subject to regulation in a fashion similar to television, radio, and other mass-media advertising. However, messages that individuals create on their own websites or post without charge on other websites such as YouTube are not subject to FEC regulation.

34. The Obama campaign far surpassed the McCain campaign in a number of key online indicators in 2008, particularly in the volume of Obama political activity that occurred on popular social networking websites such as Facebook, YouTube, and Twitter. For example, the Obama campaign in 2008 had nearly 2.4 million Facebook friends while the McCain campaign had under 625,000 (Andres Rasiehj and Micah Sifry, "The Web: 2008's Winning Ticket," *Politico*, November 12, 2008, 24). Similarly, the Obama campaign had more than 125,000 Twitter followers as compared with only 5,319 for the McCain campaign, and the Obama campaign posted more than 1,800 videos on YouTube whereas the McCain campaign posted only 330 such videos (Rasiehj and Sifry, "The Web," 24).

35. See HeadCount, "GOP Winning Social Media Battle by Wide Margin," *Exclusive Midterm Elections Report*, September 23, 2010, www.headcount.org/wp-content/uploads/2010/09/VIEW-REPORT1.pdf.

36. FEC Advisory Opinion 2012-17.

37. Janie Lorber, "Obama's Campaign Quick to Capitalize on Text-to-Donate Option," *Roll Call*, October 24, 2012.

38. For example, scholars estimate that only about 5 percent of the nation's voters cast absentee ballots in 1980. June Krunholz, "Forget Election Day—Early Voting for President Has Started," *Wall Street Journal*, September 23, 2008.

39. Michael P. McDonald, "Early Voting in 2012: What to Expect," *Huffington Post*, August 13, 2012, www.huffingtonpost.com/michael-p-mcdonald/early-voting-in-2012-what_b_1773768.html.

40. Stephen Ohlemacher and Julie Pace, "A Third of Electorate Could Vote Before Nov. 4," Associated Press, September 22, 2008.

41. Phillip Elliot and Jim Kuhnhenn, "Weeks Before Election Day, Early Voting Kicks Off," Associated Press, September 5, 2012.

42. "Polling News & Notes: Overlooked Recent Polling and Insights," Karl Rove & Co., September 27, 2012, www.rove.com/polling_notes/0000/0223/Polling_News_and_Notes_9_27_12.pdf.

43. Ann Gerhart, "Election 'Day'? With Early Voting, It's More Like Election Month," *Washington Post*, November 5, 2012.

44. The early voting percentage was calculated as of November 14, 2012 using popular vote data from http://elections.msnbc.msn.com/ns/politics/2012/all and early voting data from http://elections.gmu.edu/early_vote_2012.html. The final figures may change if additional votes are counted subsequent to the publication date for this book.

45. Gregory J. Krieg, "Obama Casts Early Vote and Reminds Dems of 2000 Recount," ABC News, October 25, 2012, http://abcnews.go.com/politics/OTUS/Obama-cast-early-vote-reminds-dems-2000-recount/story?id=17563272.

46. David Lauter, "Obama Appears to Have Early Vote Lead in Key States," *Chicago Tribune*, November 3, 2012.

47. Jeremy Herb, "Team Obama Says It Has the Advantage over Romney in Early Voting," *The Hill*, November 3, 2012.

48. Alex Altman, "TIME Poll: Obama Leads by 5 in Ohio," *Time Swampland*, October 24, 2012, http://swampland.time.com/2012/10/24/time-poll-obama-leads-by-5-in-ohio.

# 6

# VOTERS TO THE SIDELINES

## Old and New Media in the 2012 Election

### *Diana Owen*

Election 2012 was the most media-saturated campaign of all time in terms of the sheer volume of messages disseminated via a vast array of communications platforms. Voters experienced blanket election coverage in the news and on social media. They were bombarded by millions of campaign ads.[1] They were inundated with the results of thousands of often conflicting polls. They watched the candidates face off in a series of highly publicized debates, and endured incessant post-debate punditry. They withstood relentless "fact-checking"—the media gimmick du jour.

Despite the din, media in the 2012 presidential election did not break as much new ground as in 2008. Instead, trends established in previous campaigns were amplified. News coverage focused heavily on the election game, especially the horse race, fund-raising drives and campaign strategies. As was the case in 2008, the small number of journalists "on the bus" with candidates meant that more news stories were based on secondhand information, polls, and now, fact-checks. Press coverage of the candidates was more negative overall than it had been four years earlier.

Voters experienced advertising overload as candidates, political parties, and independent organizations engaged in exceptionally hostile ad wars. The proliferation of advertising was facilitated by easier and cheaper production methods, more platforms for presentation, and better techniques for distribution. More sophisticated microtargeting strategies employing data on individuals' political orientations and consumer behavior improved candidates' ability to tailor specific messages to individual voters.

The campaigns and media organizations ramped up their social media presence. However, social media efforts were aimed more at controlling messages than actively engaging voters. This trend was a step back from the more populist social media campaign of 2008. The content of social media was especially mean-spirited, as the campaigns used these platforms to launch attacks on their opponents in the hopes that they would generate viral coverage and mainstream media attention.

This chapter will begin with an examination of news coverage of the election. It will then explore the nature and extent of political advertising in the campaign followed by a discussion of the role of social media. The final section will consider the media preferences of the electorate over time.

## NEWS COVERAGE

The manner in which election news is imparted can influence voters' perceptions about candidates. News frames portray events and issues in a particular way, and simplify political reality. They determine what type of information will be reported or excluded as well as the tone and character of coverage.[2] The news media long have treated American presidential elections like an elaborate game between competing teams. The game frame privileges the poll-driven horse race between candidates, the campaign tactics, and the battle to gain the upper hand in made-for-media campaign events, like debates. The strategic aspects of campaigns are highlighted at the expense of issue and policy coverage.[3] The tone of this type of coverage tends to be more critical than positive, as the press seeks to expose campaign organizations' failings and candidates' missteps.[4] Since the 1990s, a majority of newspaper and television news stories have focused on the election game, compared to 45 percent in 1960.[5] The game frame now carries over to new forms of media, such as blogs and Twitter feeds.

The game frame has become more prevalent in recent elections for reasons associated with journalistic norms and practices. The never-ending campaign makes it necessary for journalists to develop new story lines to keep the public engaged. Making the election into a competition—especially a close one—is one way of maintaining citizens' interest. In addition, the number of journalists on the campaign trail covering candidates firsthand has been on the decline since the 2004 presidential contest. It has become common practice for journalists who have fewer resources for news gathering to manufacture stories from data. Poll results have become such a prominent source of news that when Hurricane Sandy made landfall, journalists expressed concerns that it would disrupt polling operations and they would not have much to report on about the campaign. Instead, they turned to speculation about how the storm might influence the outcome of the election.[6] Journalists also have come to rely heavily on information gleaned from digital media, especially material generated by commentators, like conservative Bill O'Reilly and liberal Rachel Maddow; election analysts, like the *New York Times'* Nate Silver; and citizen content posters.

Horse-race coverage was prominent in the 2012 election, as poll-driven stories were a daily staple of the election. This type of coverage was rampant during the Republican presidential nominating campaign. The Center for Media and Public Affairs found that television news stories covered the horse race six times as often as they reported on candidates' positions on issues.[7] However, horse-race journalism became less of a factor during the general election than it had been in the primary campaign. A much smaller percentage of stories featured the horse race in 2012 (38 percent) compared to 2008 (53 percent). Still the majority of stories in the period surrounding the presidential debates focused on the candidates' position in the polls.[8]

The tone of press coverage of the presidential campaign overall was more negative than positive. Reports about the Obama candidacy were generally more favorable than coverage of Romney. Over the course of the general election, 30 percent of stories about Obama were negative and 19 percent were positive. Thirty-eight percent of stories about Romney were negative while 15 percent were favorable. However, Obama's coverage in 2012 was notably less sympathetic than in 2008, when he received more than twice as much positive press. Democratic vice presidential candidate Joe Biden received more favorable press coverage than his opponent, Republican Paul Ryan. Biden's coverage was 16 percent negative compared to 28 percent negative for Ryan.[9]

The tenor of media coverage shifted markedly throughout the campaign in response to events. Romney was slammed by the media in mid-September after the left-leaning magazine *Mother Jones* released a video of him stating that 47 percent of Americans are dependent on government and feel they are victims entitled to assistance. The video had been surreptitiously recorded in May at a private Romney fund-raiser in tony Boca Raton, Florida. The story went viral, and generated bad publicity that Romney failed to neutralize when he stood behind the substance of his remarks. The incident played directly into the narrative of Romney as a candidate who favored the interests of the wealthy that was prominent during the campaign, and appeared to erode Romney's support in the polls.[10] Romney got better press following his performance in the first presidential debate where it was widely perceived that he had outperformed Obama. This debate sparked a media-assisted resurgence for the stagnant Romney campaign. The tide shifted once again during the last week of the campaign, when Obama experienced a positive boost in the tone of his coverage that was prompted largely by poll results indicating that he was the likely winner. The horse race managed to trump Obama's handling of Hurricane Sandy, which was praised by staunch Republicans like New Jersey governor Chris Christie, as the factor most responsible for the uptick in positive coverage.[11]

Journalists managed to turn reporting on issues into game frame coverage through the excessive fact-checking of campaign messages. Since the advent of the new media era in the 1980s, traditional notions of journalistic fact-checking and sourcing where reporters carefully verify information before publishing have been relaxed.[12] Fact-checking has been revitalized as a contemporary form of news where the statements of candidates, political organizations, and government leaders are subject to intense scrutiny by academics (FactCheck.org), news media personnel (PolitiFact.com), and the public (Snopes.com). In 2012, armchair journalists engaged in nonstop fact-checking of candidates' every claim in speeches, debates, position papers, and tweets. This new notion of fact-checking has become a major part of the media's game coverage of campaigns. Fact-check coverage comes complete with candidate scorecards and eye-catching graphics.

During the presidential debates, the major cable stations and other media organizations promoted fact-checking as a public enterprise. *Mashable*, a prominent blog covering developments in social media, encouraged citizens to use fact-checking websites and Twitter to validate the candidate's comments:

> Tonight marks the first of three presidential debates between President Barack Obama and GOP candidate Mitt Romney. It's the first time the two men will confront each other head-on about the rumors, issues and platforms from the campaign trail. But both men don't just have each other to fear—they have the entire Twitterverse to answer to. Social media has added a whole new, mammoth-sized layer to the way in which Obama and Romney field questions. Years ago, the candidates could fend off comments, re-interpret questions and captivate audiences until the newspapers hit the stands the next day, bringing to light the

errors and oversights. With Twitter and the real-time web, it takes only seconds for each candidate's words to be poked, prodded and scrutinized. If you're planning to keep the candidates honest as you watch the debates live, keep these websites and tools handy.[13]

Fact-checking as practiced by reputable organizations, such as the Annenberg Public Policy Center's FactCheck.org, offers citizens responsible, well-researched information that explains complex issues. However, some fact-checkers, including campaign operatives and political journalists, may have political agendas of their own. The quality of third-party sources used to verify facts varies greatly, and opinion is sometimes conflated with facts.[14] Competing data can be used to justify different interpretations of the facts.

Fact-checking in the 2012 campaign emerged as a form of gotcha journalism that put candidates on the defensive. Material that is subject to media fact-checking often consists of a brief summary statement or sound bite that encapsulates a complex issue position, and which has been taken out of context. Candidates and their representatives are rarely given the opportunity to clarify or expand upon their points before the fact-check goes public.

Fact-checking can result in a politician being labeled a "liar," even when there is no consensus. As Paul Ryan was giving his vice presidential speech at the Republican National Convention, journalists were engaging in real time fact-checking via Twitter. Ryan was accused by the Associated Press of taking "factual shortcuts" with issues including Medicare, the economy, and the closing of a GM plant in Janesville, Wisconsin. The speech was described as "the most dishonest convention speech ever" by the liberal media, prompting a backlash and counter-fact-check by conservatives.[15]

## ADVERTISING

Advertising in the 2012 presidential contest reached epic proportions. Records were set for the amount of money spent as well as the volume of ads produced and aired. Voters could access ads on television, on websites, through email messages, and on social media. The ad war was especially nasty, as the vast majority of ads were negative.

Over $1 billion was spent on advertising in the presidential election. Obama's campaign organization spent $333 million on ads, 82 percent of which were negative. Romney's campaign ad expenditures were $147 million, and 91 percent of his ads were negative.[16] In the final ten days of the campaign, the Romney and Obama campaigns spent over $40 million on ads in battleground states trying to win over the few remaining undecided voters.

Outside organizations spent an unprecedented amount of money on presidential campaign advertising. The Supreme Court decision in *Citizens United v. The Federal Election Commission* in 2010 prohibited restrictions on independent expenditures by corporations and unions. This opened the door for independent groups to run ads for and against candidates as long as they do not coordinate with candidate campaign organizations—a fuzzy standard that can be difficult to enforce. Super PACs, groups whose sole purpose is making independent expenditures in campaigns, and tax exempt advocacy organizations which engage in voter mobilization and issue awareness activities spent over $522 million on ads in the election, much of this during the nominating phase.[17] Outside groups greatly outspent the Democratic and Republican parties on ads.[18]

According to the Wesleyan Media Project, more than one million television presidential campaign ads were aired by the candidates, political parties, and interest groups between June 1 and Election Day, which was 39 percent more than in 2008 and 41 percent more than in 2004. Both the Romney and Obama campaigns produced over one hundred individual television spots during the 2012 campaign, compared to the fewer than thirty spots that the Reagan campaign made in 1984.[19] During the general election, the Obama campaign aired 503,255 ads, far outpacing Romney's organization, which aired 190,784 ads. However, Romney benefited from over 270,000 ads aired by Super PACs, like Restore Our Future, and supportive outside groups, such as American Crossroads, Crossroads GPS, and Americans for Prosperity.[20] Voters' exposure to television advertising differed radically by location. Ads were heavily concentrated in a handful of battleground states—Florida, Virginia, Ohio, Colorado, Nevada, New Hampshire, Iowa, and Wisconsin—while voters in other states received far less advertising attention.[21]

While television remains the gold standard for political advertising, newer technologies have made possible a plethora of digital advertising options that are less expensive, easier to produce, and more flexible. The Romney and Obama campaigns invested heavily in targeted online ads and videos that are created quickly and released at a rapid rate. These ads are targeted based on research on voters' political orientations and consumer behavior gleaned from social media, like Facebook and Google, and other sources. Some ads will pop up online when a term is typed into a search engine or particular content is accessed. Both campaigns made use of real time ad buys for display and video ads that appear on websites. Campaigns addressed salient issues and exploited the opponents' mistakes immediately by posting ads directed at specific audiences in target markets. For example, the Obama campaigns ran ads targeting women in swing states after the second debate when Mitt Romney used the unfortunate phrase, "binders full of women."[22]

Ten percent of the presidential campaign ad budgets were earmarked for online ads, up from 3 percent in 2008. The Obama campaign delivered over 800 million paid display ads per month beginning in January 2012, and earned more than 100 million additional impressions through viral distribution by his 27 million Facebook fans. In June alone, Obama ran over 1.2 billion display ads. There were ten times as many Obama display ads as Romney ads.[23]

Given the glut of ads, some campaigns and independent organizations ran controversial or bizarre ads to gain attention. This tactic was especially useful for driving traffic to online ads. During the primary campaign, a series of unusual ads in support of Republican candidate Herman Cain made headlines. In one, Cain's campaign manager, Mark Block, talks about Cain's qualifications for president, and concludes by taking a drag off of a cigarette. In another, a young girl talks about how the tax code is killing small businesses as her pet bunny is launched in the air and shot.[24] The Obama campaign sought to connect with young people in late October with a controversial ad featuring Lena Dunham, the star of HBO's edgy comedy *Girls*, riffing about her first time voting. "Your first time shouldn't be with just anybody. You want to do it with a great guy."[25]

Despite their abundance, it is unclear how much meaningful information voters gained from ads in the 2012 campaign. Research on election advertising comes to conflicting conclusions about the benefits and drawbacks of campaign advertising. Some studies indicate that ads provide useful information, and allow voters to contrast candidates' positions on issues and their public image. Negative ads, which were so prevalent in this campaign, allow the candidates to draw stark distinctions between themselves and their opponents. Ads also have the potential to reach disinterested voters, especially now that they are available on so many platforms.[26] On the other hand, ads are criticized for manipulating the electorate, trivializing campaigns, and promoting image-based, as opposed to issue-based, politics. Some studies argue that especially nasty advertising campaigns depress turnout as voters are turned off.[27] While ads may not have kept people from the polls in 2012, voters in battleground states grew tired of the advertising blitz. Ads also are derided for driving up the costs of elections, which was certainly the case in this past campaign.

## SOCIAL MEDIA

Social media, the signature new media contribution in the 2008 campaign, was a standard component of candidate strategy, media coverage, and voter media use in 2012. Social media offers voters novel ways to become involved in the presidential campaign through networking, collaboration, community building, and active engagement. In 2008, citizens, especially young people, innovated with social media outside of the purview of campaign committees, parties, and political organizations. They pioneered social media applications in elections, such as establishing peer-to-peer networks for electoral outreach using Facebook and Twitter. They created and distributed original content on YouTube and Hulu that gave candidates the equivalent of millions of dollars worth of free publicity. They organized online organizations around group identities and issues that performed functions similar to parties, including setting the media agenda, recruiting volunteers, and getting voters to the polls. The Obama campaign embraced the fact that voters were using social media independently to actively participate. The campaign encouraged supporters to use social media on behalf of the candidate without entirely co-opting their efforts.[28]

The social media campaign four years ago was remarkable for the degree to which it was sparked by citizens. In 2012, however, this populist social media imperative was replaced by higher levels of control by political and media organizations. Candidates' use of social media was aimed less at encouraging active voter engagement and more at pushing out information and fund-raising aggressively. The campaigns have adopted a strategy of jumping on the latest social media bandwagons, such as Tumblr, Pinterest, Instagram, and Reddit, without giving much thought to how voters will benefit. They posted hundreds of videos and ads to the candidates' YouTube channels and other video hosting sites. The candidates' organizations adapted content supplied by supporters to suit their objectives and distributed it through the campaigns' social media networks. A pithy caption might be added to a photo provided by a supporter and then circulated by the campaign. Both the Obama and Romney organizations implemented email outreach strategies that bordered on overkill, as voters on their lists received multiple messages per day from the candidates and their surrogates asking for money.

The Romney and Obama campaigns devoted significant resources to social media. They assembled social media staffs that coordinated their efforts across a range of platforms. The Obama campaign had an advantage as it was able to build upon its well-established social media infrastructure, while Romney's organization played catch-up. Adam Fetcher, Obama's deputy press secretary, emphasized the centrality of social media to the campaign: "Social media is a natural extension of our massive grass-roots organization."[29] Both campaigns used social media to humanize the candidates, and to share pseudo-personal information with voters, such as their music playlists and favorite foods. The campaigns' digital messaging reflected the image of the candidates that they sought to portray. Obama's social media attempted to be hip and free-wheeling with frequent references to popular culture and humorous parodies. Romney's digital postings were more buttoned-down and subdued, and often took the form of photos of his family or posters with slogans, like "No, we can't." However, neither candidate did much to converse personally with voters through social media other than the occasional tweet or rare Google hangout.[30]

With all of the attention to social media by candidates and journalists, the number of voters who use social media in presidential elections remains relatively small. According to the Pew Research Center, 12 percent of voters used Facebook for campaign purposes in 2012, 4 percent used Twitter, and 3 percent used YouTube. These figures have not increased much over the last presidential contest. The use of Twitter is up slightly from 2008, when it was used by less than 1 percent of the electorate.

## THE ELECTION NEWS AUDIENCE

Traditional mass media remain important to voters, even as many people go online for election information. Television news, especially cable, is still by far the most popular source of information for voters. Internet media have attracted a growing number of users since the 2000 election, and have begun to cut into the audiences for television and print newspapers. However, television experienced somewhat of a resurgence in popularity during the 2012 election. As table 6.1 indicates, television was the main source for 74 percent of the electorate compared to 68 percent in 2008. Television use was slightly higher at 76 percent in 2004.

A number of factors may explain the popularity of television presidential elections. Television is more effective at bringing the campaign to life than following Facebook posts or Twitter feeds. Watching the campaign unfold on television requires less work from voters than reading about it in a newspaper or following it online. Television news programs have become media hybrids as social media is incorporated into their election coverage. Voters can keep current on social media trends without having to negotiate

**Table 6.1.   Main Source of Election News in Presidential Elections**

|      | Television | Newspaper | Radio | Magazine | Internet |
|------|-----------|-----------|-------|----------|----------|
| 1992 | 82%       | 57%       | 12%   | 9%       | —        |
| 1996 | 72%       | 60%       | 19%   | 11%      | 3%       |
| 2000 | 70%       | 39%       | 15%   | 4%       | 11%      |
| 2004 | 76%       | 46%       | 22%   | 1%       | 21%      |
| 2008 | 68%       | 33%       | 16%   | 3%       | 36%      |
| 2012 | 74%       | 23%       | 17%   | 3%       | 36%      |

*Source*: Pew Research Center, Political Communication and Methods Study, January 2012; October 2012.
*Note*: Survey respondents could choose more than one main source.

the platforms themselves. Finally, television viewing options have become more convenient, as people can watch TV on their oversized flat screens at home or on their portable digital devices.

The print newspaper audience has been declining since the 2000 presidential contest. It reached an all-time low of 23 percent in 2012, down from 33 percent in 2008. A very small percentage of the population—3 percent in the last two presidential election cycles—considers print magazines to be their primary news source. The radio audience has increased in the new media era as talk radio has established a dedicated audience. Seventeen percent of voters relied on radio as a main election news source in 2012, which is consistent with its popularity in 2008. The percentage of people who rely primarily on the Internet for campaign news has increased steadily since 1996. However, the percentage of voters relying on Internet news remained stable at 36 percent over the past two elections.

## CONCLUSION

The fact that voters were awash in media during the 2012 election did not necessarily translate into a better informed or more satisfied electorate. Campaign communication was as noisy, nasty, and manic as in any election in recent memory. The incivility that permeates much political news was amplified through ads and social media. Voters were faced with the challenge of sorting through an enormous blur of information, most of it negative, much of it irrelevant, and some it false.

After pioneering mechanisms for active engagement through social media in 2008, citizens were viewed more as spectators in 2012. Campaign committees, media organizations, and independent political groups became more adept at targeting messages at voters, and asserted greater control over social media channels. Voters seemed to lack the motivation to push back.

In the end, voters were highly dissatisfied with election media. According to the Pew Research Center, 68 percent of voters in the 2012 campaign felt that there was more negative campaigning and mudslinging than usual, up from 54 percent in 2004. Voters gave low marks to the candidates, the press, pollsters, and campaign consultants for their performance in the campaign.[31] Many experienced election media fatigue and tuned out the campaign.

## NOTES

1. Jonathan Salant, "Obama Has Edge in Record Presidential Campaign Ads," *Bloomberg Business Week*, October 24, 2012, accessed October 26, 2012, www .businessweek.com/news/2012-10-24/obama-has-edge-in-record-presidential -campaign-ads.

2. Erving Goffman, *Frame Analysis* (Boston: Northeastern University Press, 1974); Joseph N. Cappella and Kathleen Hall Jamieson, "News Frames, Political Cynicism, and Media Cynicism," *Annals of the American Academy of Political and Social Science* 546 (1996): 71–84; Dietram A. Scheufele, "Framing as a Theory of Media Effects," *Journal of Communication*, Winter 1999, 103–22.

3. Stephen J. Farnsworth and S. Robert Lichter, *The Nightly News Nightmare* (Lanham, MD: Rowman and Littlefield, 2003).

4. Larry Sabato, *Feeding Frenzy* (New York: Free Press, 1991).

5. Thomas E. Patterson, *Out of Order* (New York: Knopf, 1993).

6. Rachel Weiner, "How Hurricane Sandy Could Affect the Election," *Washington Post*, October 26, 2012, accessed November 20, 2012, www .washingtonpost.com/blogs/post-politics/wp/2012/10/26/how-hurricane-sandy -could-affect-the-election/.

7. Center for Media and Public Affairs, "Study: TV News Bashes Romney, Boosts Horse Race," George Mason University, January 18, 2012.

8. Pew Center's Project for Excellence in Journalism, "Frame: Which Aspects of the Race Got Attention, and Which Ones Didn't?," *Winning the Media Campaign 2012*, November 2, 2012, www.journalism.org/analysis_report/ frame_which_aspects_race_got_attention_and_which_ones_didnt.

9. Pew Center, "Frame: Which Aspects."

10. Nate Silver, "September 27: The Impact of the '47 Percent'," *Five Thirty Eight* (blog), *New York Times*, September 28, 2012, accessed November 20, 2012, http://fivethirtyeight.blogs.nytimes.com/2012/09/28/sept-27-the-impact-of-the -47-percent/.

11. Pew Center, "Frame: Which Aspects."

12. Richard Davis and Diana Owen, *New Media and American Politics* (New York: Oxford University Press, 1999).

13. Neha Prakash, "5 Online Resources for Fact Checking the Presidential Debates," *Mashable*, October 3, 2012, accessed November 21, 2012, http://mashable .com/2012/10/03/debates-online-fact-check/.

14. L. Gordon Crovitz, "Double-Checking the Journalist 'Fact Checkers,'" *Wall Street Journal*, September 9, 2012, accessed November 20, 2012, http://online.wsj .com/article/SB10000872396390443686004577639743922340620.html.

15. Michael Calderone, "Paul Ryan's Convention Speech Ignites Media War over Facts," *Huffington Post*, August 30, 2012, accessed November 20, 2012, www .huffingtonpost.com/2012/08/30/paul-ryan-fact-checking-media_n_1844085 .html.

16. "Campaign 2012: Mad Money: TV Ads in the 2012 Presidential Campaign," *Washington Post*, accessed November 12, 2012, www.washingtonpost.com/wp-srv/ special/politics/track-presidential-campaign-ads-2012/whos-buying-ads/.

17. "Election 2012: Independent Spending, Week by Week," *New York Times*, November 4, 2012, accessed November 12, 2012, http://elections.nytimes .com/2012/campaign-finance/independent-expenditures/week/2012-10-29.

18. Center for Responsive Politics, "Outside Spending," OpenSecrets.org, accessed November 12, 2012, www.opensecrets.org/outsidespending/.

19. John G. Geer, "Were the Romney and Obama TV Ads a Total Waste?," *Daily Beast*, November 9, 2012, accessed November 22, 2012, www.thedailybeast .com/articles/2012/11/09/were-the-romney-and-obama-tv-ads-a-total-waste .html.

20. Laura Baum, "Presidential Ad War Tops 1M Airings," *Wesleyan Media Project: Political Advertising Analysis* (Middletown, CT: Wesleyan University, 2012).

21. Laura Baum, "2012 Shatters 2004 and 2008 Records for Total Ads Aired," *Wesleyan Media Project: Political Advertising Analysis* (Middletown, CT: Wesleyan University, 2012).

22. Brett Wilson, "US Presidential Election 2012: Targeted Online Video Ads Redefine Tactics," *Guardian*, November 1, 2012.

23. Zach Rodgers, "Obama Buys More Display Ads Than Romney, and in More Places," Ad Exchanger, November 5, 2012, accessed November 12, 2012, www.adexchanger.com/online-advertising/obama-team-buys-more-display-ads -than-romneys-and-in-more-places/.

24. Brian Naylor, "Herman Cain's Ads Unconventional if Not Effective," NPR, October 28, 2011, accessed November 12, 2012, www.npr .org/2011/10/28/141777382/herman-cains-ads-unconventional-if-not-effective.

25. Linda Feldman, "Lena Dunham's Sexy Obama Ad: Youthfully Alluring or Bad Taste?," *Christian Science Monitor*, October 26, 2012, accessed November 12, 2012, www.csmonitor.com/USA/Politics/The-Vote/2012/1026/ Lena-Dunham-s-sexy-Obama-ad-Youthfully-alluring-or-bad-taste.

26. John G. Geer, *In Defense of Negativity* (Chicago: University of Chicago Press, 2006).

27. Ted Brader, *Campaigning for Hearts and Minds* (Chicago: University of Chicago Press, 2006); Travis N. Ridout and Michael Franz, *The Persuasive Power of Campaign Advertising* (Philadelphia: Temple University Press, 2011).

28. Diana Owen, "New Media and Political Campaigns," in *The Oxford Handbook of Political Communication Theories*, ed. Kate Kenski and Kathleen Hall Jamieson (New York: Oxford University Press, 2012), chap. 53.

29. Jenna Wortham, "Campaigns Use Social Media to Lure Younger Voters," *New York Times*, October 7, 2012, accessed November 24, 2012, www.nytimes.com/2012/10/08/technology/campaigns-use-social-media-to-lure-younger-voters.html?_r=0.

30. "How the Presidential Candidates Use the Web and Social Media," Project for Excellence in Journalism, August 15, 2012, accessed November 20, 2012, www.journalism.org/analysis_report/how_presidential_candidates_use_web_and_social_media.

31. "Low Marks for the 2012 Election," Pew Research Center for the People & the Press, November 15, 2012, accessed November 24, 2012, www.people-press.org/2012/11/15/low-marks-for-the-2012-election/.

# 7

# AMERICA'S EVOLVING ELECTORATE

## Nate Cohn

When George W. Bush's brand of compassionate conservatism expelled Democrats from their traditional strongholds in the populist, upland South, the remaining elements of Bill Clinton's coalition—minorities, postgraduates, college-educated women, and less-religious voters—were insufficient to secure a majority in two straight presidential elections. But over the intervening eight years, demographic changes have shifted the playing field in the direction of Democrats, allowing President Obama to win with a majority of the popular vote with the rump Democratic coalition produced by the Bush elections.

Rather than broaden the Democratic coalition, a new generation of young and diverse voters has simply increased the weight of core Democratic constituencies. The nonwhite share of the electorate increased from 23 percent in 2004 to 28 percent in 2012, and President Obama carried 80 percent of nonwhite voters for the second consecutive election. The president's support among nonwhite voters was broad, with Obama exceeding historic Democratic benchmarks among African American, Hispanic, and Asian voters. While Republicans made further inroads in traditionally Democratic areas of the inland South, these gains were neither large enough to outweigh national demographic changes or well enough positioned to sway a truly competitive state. At the same time, Democrats held onto many of their gains among white voters outside of the south, especially in well-educated suburbs and among young white voters. These changes are not ephemeral or anomalous, but instead reflect underlying demographics shifts that will continue to advantage Democrats so long as elections are fought along the lines of the last two decades.

Although John Kerry won nonwhite voters by a 72–27 margin, Bush's 27 percent share of the minority vote represented an improvement over prior GOP efforts that augured well for the Republican Party's competitiveness as the electorate grew more diverse. But Obama made substantial improvements over Kerry's performance with nonwhite voters. According to exit polls, African Americans turned out at historic levels and offered 93 percent of their support to the president, up from Kerry's 89 percent in 2004. Obama also exceeded historic Democratic benchmarks with Asian and Latino voters. According to the exit polls, Obama won 71 percent of Hispanics—even more than the 67 percent that supported him during more politically favorable conditions four years earlier, let alone the 60 percent that supported Kerry in 2004. The initial exit polls also show that Hispanics represented 10 percent of the electorate, up from 8 percent in 2004 and 2008. Similarly, the exit polls suggest that 73 percent of Asian voters selected Obama, a striking increase from 62 percent in 2008 and 56 percent for Kerry in 2004. It should be emphasized that the exit polls are subject to a margin of error like any survey, especially in small samples like the Asian vote, but the exact figures are less important than the broader trend.

Higher minority turnout and support for Democratic candidates has reconfigured the electoral map, leaving Republicans imperiled in traditionally competitive states with large minority populations. Perhaps no state has undergone a more rapid transformation than Nevada, which tilted Republican with respect to the country in every election between 1964 and 2004. Nevada's Hispanic population increased by 82 percent over the last decade in America's fastest growing state, compared to just a 12 percent increase among whites over the same time period. As a result, the nonwhite share of the electorate surged from 23 percent of voters in 2004 to 36 percent in 2012—more than any battleground state. At the same time, Obama improved upon Kerry's performance, winning Latinos by forty-seven points, up from Kerry's twenty-one-point victory in 2004. Elsewhere in the southwest, Democrats reaped similar gains. New Mexico's Latino population reached 37 percent of the electorate, up from 32 percent in 2004. Obama won New Mexico's Latinos by a thirty-six-point margin, up from thirteen points in 2004. Even though Obama performed about as well among white voters as Kerry, these two Bush 2004 states voted for Obama by seven and ten points, respectively.

Increased Hispanic support for Democrats also allowed Obama to carry Florida, a must-win state for Republicans where Hispanics actually voted for Bush by a twelve-point margin in 2004. According to the initial exit polls, Obama won Florida Latinos by a twenty-one-point margin, a thirty-three-point shift over the last eight years. Many Democratic gains came from the Orlando-Kissimmee region, once heralded as the key swing city at the center of the country's key swing region, the I-4 corridor. But over the last decade, an influx of Democratic-leaning Puerto Rican voters has transformed the political character of the Orlando-Kissimmee metropolitan area, sending old bellwether counties into the Democratic column: Orlando's Orange County and Kissimmee's Osceola County voted for Obama by 18 and 25 points, up from Kerry's 0.2 and Bush's 5-point wins, respectively. A growing Mexican American and Venezuelan American population in the Tampa Bay–St. Petersburg metropolitan area gave the president victories in the largest counties outside of South Florida, and Obama's gains among third generation Cubans helped yield a decisive twenty-four-point victory in Miami-Dade County, up from Kerry's six-point win in 2004.

Obama benefited from strong black turnout and support in nearly every battleground state. According to the exit polls, African Americans represented 13 percent of the electorate for the second consecutive election, up from 11 percent in 2004. High black turnout was decisive in Ohio and Florida, where Romney would have prevailed if black turnout and support for the Democratic candidate declined to 2004 levels. Nationally, between 3 and 4 million new black voters joined the electorate over the last two cycles, and whether those voters stay home or turn out could easily decide future presidential elections, especially in states like Ohio, Virginia, Pennsylvania, North Carolina, and Florida.

To compensate for growing nonwhite support and turnout for President Obama, Romney needed to win white voters by twenty-four points to win the national popular vote, a feat no Republican presidential candidate has accomplished since Reagan in 1984. Remarkably, Mitt Romney managed to win white voters by twenty points—the best Republican performance since 1988. But while Republicans might initially take solace in Romney's strong national performance among white voters, Romney did not improve over Bush's performance in most battleground states. Instead, Romney's gains were almost exclusively driven by historic support from southern and Appalachian white voters. In many culturally southern counties with a history of offering even limited support to Democratic candidates, Obama's performance was the worst by any Democrat since McGovern or, in some places, ever.

Obama even lost more than fifty points compared to Kerry's performance in several "coal country" counties in southern West Virginia and eastern Kentucky, where cultural issues and the "war on coal" have combined to devastate Democratic fortunes in historically Democratic regions. While some have attributed Obama's struggles in "coal country" to race, Democratic Senate candidates like Tim Kaine in Virginia also performed well beneath historic Democratic lows. Romney's improvements over Bush's performance in Appalachia and the white South were more than enough to move "lean Republican" states like West Virginia and Arkansas to "solid Republican," but there weren't enough of these voters in sparsely populated but politically and culturally similar regions of southeastern Ohio, western Pennsylvania, and southwestern Virginia to sway the outcome of any competitive state.

If Romney preserved Bush's strong performance among non-southern whites, a few additional gains in the peripheries of eastern battleground states might have combined to leave the GOP relatively well positioned among white voters. But outside of Appalachia, Romney tended to run behind Bush's performance among white voters in the northern half of the country and especially in well-educated metropolitan areas.

Obama outperformed Kerry across the farmland of the rural Midwest from central and northwestern Ohio, across Indiana and Iowa, to the Red River Valley. These gains allowed Obama to comfortably carry white states like New Hampshire, Wisconsin, and Iowa by comfortable margins, even though they were among the closest states during the two Bush elections.

Obama also preserved many of his gains in well-educated and affluent northern suburbs, where many believed that Romney could perform relatively well. According to the exit polls, Obama lost voters making more than $200,000 per year by ten points, but that performance was far better than

**Table 7.1.   Democratic Share of White Voters**

|     | *2012* | *2004* | *Change* |
| --- | --- | --- | --- |
| VA | 38 | 32 | D+6 |
| NC | 31 | 27 | D+4 |
| IA | 51 | 49 | D+2 |
| CO | 44 | 42 | D+2 |
| NH | 51 | 50 | D+1 |
| MI | 44 | 44 | 0 |
| WI | 47 | 47 | 0 |
| **USA** | **39** | **41** | **R+2** |
| NV | 41 | 43 | R+2 |
| OH | 41 | 44 | R+3 |
| PA | 42 | 45 | R+3 |
| FL | 37 | 42 | R+5 |

Kerry's twenty-eight-point defeat in 2004. Similarly, voters with a postgraduate degree preferred Obama by sixteen points, up from Kerry's eleven-point victory in 2004. As a result, Obama maintained his hold on well-educated but traditionally Republican counties where Democratic presidential candidates lost every presidential election from 1968 through 2004, like Jefferson, Colorado; Loudoun, Virginia; Wake, North Carolina; and Somerset, New Jersey. Obama also performed near 2008 levels in moderate Democratic-leaning counties like Fairfax, Virginia; Polk, Iowa; Franklin, Ohio; Hennepin, Minnesota; and Oakland, Michigan. The president ran far ahead of Kerry and approached or exceeded his 2008 performance in highly educated, affluent, diverse, and socially progressive tech corridors, like Seattle's eastside, Silicon Valley, and Raleigh–Durham–Chapel Hill. It's also notable that many of these areas are home to a large Asian American population, which exit polls showed moving even further toward Democrats.

Obama's strength among affluent, well-educated, and diverse voters allowed the president to maintain most of his support in the critical suburbs and exurbs of northern Virginia: the country's best-educated region with the highest median income, where whites represent just 56 percent of the population. Obama won Fairfax, Loudon, and Prince William counties, as well as the independent cities within them, by 21 points, down only slightly from 22.6 points in 2008. An analysis by the *Washington Post* found that Obama won 52.5 percent of the vote in Washington-area precincts with a median income exceeding $180,000 per year, down just slightly from 55 percent in 2008.[1] Virginia was one of only a few states where Obama performed better among white voters than Kerry, and if Democrats continue to excel in northern Virginia, Republicans will have an extremely difficult time winning the Commonwealth's thirteen electoral votes in future elections. Although North Carolina rests on the GOP side of the ledger, Republicans face similar challenges in Raleigh–Durham–Chapel Hill, Greensboro, Winston-Salem, and Charlotte that might keep the Tar Heel State more competitive than Republicans hope.

But perhaps no state more completely captures the challenges facing Republicans better than Colorado, where the changes in the composition of the electorate and the two-party coalitions over the last decade have almost exclusively worked to the advantage of Democrats, who reap the benefits of a growing Hispanic population and gains among well-educated, socially moderate suburbanites without suffering the losses among white southern and Appalachian voters that cut against their gains in Florida, Ohio, Virginia, and Pennsylvania. Like Virginia, Obama's gains among affluent and college-educated voters meant that Obama performed better among white voters than Kerry, but the Latino share of the Colorado electorate nearly doubled from eight percent in 2004 to 13 percent in 2012. As a result, Colorado voted slightly more for the president over the last two elections than the nation as a whole, even though the state leaned Republican in all but one presidential election since 1948.

It is impossible to say whether Democrats can preserve their gains among nonwhite, well-educated, and affluent voters or whether the Democrats have hit their floor in the historically Democratic areas of the inland South and Appalachia. But the changes in the composition of the electorate over the last eight years represent a durable and lasting shift. With the important exception of African Americans, the growth of the nonwhite share of the electorate was due to demographic changes, not unusually high minority turnout rates. In 2012, whites represented 71 percent of the voting eligible population, down from 73 percent in 2008 and 76 percent in 2004. Unsurprisingly, the exit polls show that the white share of the electorate declined at a similar pace, from 77 percent in 2004, to 74 percent in 2008 and 72 percent in 2012. Indeed, if nonwhite minority turnout rates had fallen to 2004 levels, the 2012 electorate still would have become incrementally more diverse than it was in 2008. In the short term, one critical exception may be black voters, who truly did turn out at historic rates on behalf of the president. But even if black turnout rates return to 2004 levels, the growing nonwhite share of the voting eligible population will allow the total nonwhite share of the electorate to continue to increase in 2016.

The increasing nonwhite share of the voting eligible population manifests with the ascent of a diverse generation of young Americans. Just 60 percent of eighteen- to thirty-five-year-olds are non-Hispanic whites, and their younger brothers and sisters are even more diverse. As more young and diverse voters become old enough eligible to participate in elections, the nonwhite share of the voting eligible population drops further, especially as they replace overwhelmingly white seniors departing the electorate. In 2012, just 56 percent of eighteen-year-olds were white, and that figure will steadily decline through at least 2030, when 2012's infants—the first year of minority-majority births—become eligible to vote.

The mark of generational change is obvious in the exit polls. In 1988, George H. W. Bush defeated Michael Dukakis by 8 points, 53–45. Twenty-four years later, voters old enough to participate in the 1988 presidential election selected Mitt Romney by a similar 52–46 margin. The 2000 presidential election was one of the closest in history, and voters older than age twenty-nine—who were eligible to vote in 2001 or earlier—selected Romney by a

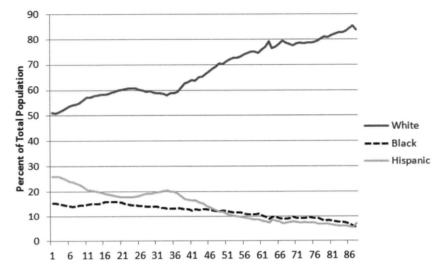

**Figure 7.1.   Race by Age**

1.9-point margin in 2012. Voters too young to participate in the 1988 election—aged forty-two years or younger—selected the president by a 57–41 margin, and eighteen- to twenty-nine-year-olds voted for the president by 24 points, 60–36. In both examples, the similarity of the 2012 exit poll figures with the results of the prior election obscures underlying changes, like the collapse of Democratic strength in the upland South. But both examples illustrate that Obama's margin of victory came from the ascent of a new and diverse generation of voters, with little help from older Americans.

These demographic changes will eventually produce more diverse electorates in midterm elections. Because minority turnout rates are lower in off-year elections, the white share of the electorate remains far higher during midterms than general elections. Just 31 percent of eligible Hispanic and Asian adults participated in the 2010 midterms, down from 50 percent and 48 percent in the 2008 presidential election. African American turnout also declined from 60 percent in the 2004 presidential election and 65 percent in the 2008 presidential election to just 44 percent. That 38 percent decline in Hispanic and Asian turnout and 32 percent decline in black turnout was far greater than the 20 percent decline in white turnout, resulting in a far less diverse midterm electorate; just 23 percent of voters were white in 2010, compared to 26 percent in the 2008 presidential election and 28 percent in 2012.

It is hard to say if or when minorities might begin to participate in midterm elections at higher rates. Even so, demographic changes are already diminishing the white share of the midterm electorate, which declined from 81 percent in 2002, to 79 percent in 2006 and 77 percent in 2010. At that pace, the GOP will face a midterm electorate reminiscent of 2008 in 2014 and more like 2012 by 2018. Of course, geography and redistricting combine to ensure that even a 2008-esque electorate and result might still maintain the GOP's House majority. In fact, Romney carried a majority of House districts despite losing the national popular vote by more than three points. Nonetheless, the decisive demographic advantage held by Republicans in midterm elections will fade to simply a relative advantage by the end of this decade.

The breadth of the GOP's demographic challenge requires equally broad gains across multiple demographic groups. While the GOP's struggles with Hispanics received considerable attention in the immediate aftermath of the election, it is important to recall that the GOP also fell short of their benchmarks with rural midwesterners, voters in well-educated and affluent suburbs, Asians, and African Americans. Hispanics only represent 10 percent of the electorate and they are distributed unevenly across the electoral map, including large populations in noncompetitive states like Texas, California, New York, and Illinois. Even if Hispanics swung 20 points in the GOP's direction in every battleground state, Obama still would have won the Electoral College by a 303–235 margin. While losses among Hispanics would cost Obama his narrow win in Florida, even a net twenty-point GOP gain wouldn't swing Colorado or Nevada. Even if it did, Obama would have still won through either Virginia or Ohio.

For Republicans to overcome demographic changes, the GOP's broad gains will need to be especially pronounced among young voters. Not only does the so-called millennial generation drive the growing nonwhite share of the electorate, but the youngest voters also tend to vote more for Democratic candidates after controlling for demographics. This is especially true for young white voters. Although eighteen- to twenty-nine-year-old white voters did not vote for the president, Romney only won by a modest 51–44 margin, far less than Romney's 61-38 lead among whites older than age thirty. If the GOP does not make inroads among millennial white voters, they will slowly reduce the GOP's share of white voters as they replace older and more conservative white voters departing the electorate. The GOP should not discount Democratic strength among young whites a fleeting product of college flirtations with liberal professors, or whatever the GOP's preferred interpretation of the countercultural forces that briefly overcame young voters in the late sixties and early seventies. The culture wars of the last few decades have divided white voters along religious lines, but young voters are less religious than their elders—ensuring a tough time for the GOP so long as the electorate re-litigates the religiously charged controversies of recent years.

The Republican formula for carrying white voters has been straightforward: decisively win white evangelicals, which make up about 33 percent of white voters; in exchange, lose non-Christian whites, who represent a far smaller 20 percent of white voters; and then fight for white non-evangelical Protestants and Catholics. Although Republicans tend to carry non-evangelical Christians, the principal source of the GOP's lead among white voters is their alliance with the largest group of white culture warriors. But a recent Pew Forum on Religion & Public Life study finds that only 22 percent of eighteen- to twenty-nine-year-olds consider themselves evangelical Christians, compared to 31 percent who are non-Christian. It should be noted that these figures are for all young voters, and minorities—disproportionately represented among young voters—are both less likely to identify as evangelical Christians or unaffiliated, so a larger share of young white voters are likely unaffiliated or evangelical than suggested by the numbers for all eighteen- to twenty-nine-year-olds.

The voting preferences of younger voters in controversial ballot initiatives on social issues demonstrate that young voters differ considerably from their elders on the cultural questions that have divided the two parties for two decades. Young voters supported gay marriage by decisive margins in Maine, Minnesota, Washington, and Maryland, with support for gay marriage even outpacing support for the president among eighteen- to twenty-nine-year-old voters in Minnesota. Young Coloradans also offered less support to the president than marijuana legalization, which earned the support of more than 70 percent of eighteen- to twenty-nine-year-olds.

Other demographic forces undermine the GOP's ability to make additional gains among white voters, including increased educational attainment and declining marriage rates. Republicans perform better among whites without a college education, but the white non-college share of the electorate is declining at a faster pace than the white share of the electorate, with the white non-college vote dropping from 65 percent of the electorate in 1980 to 39 percent in 2008. Democrats have also excelled among unmarried women, who also represent a growing share of eligible voters and the actual electorate. Educational attainment and marital rates are probably correlates of factors that contribute to Democratic success more than a cause, but it probably signals a white population likely to grow increasingly, if incrementally, more receptive to the current suite of Democratic messages. These forces do not prevent GOP gains among white voters—after all, Romney overcame all of these trends to do better than any Republican candidate in twenty-four years—but they cut against the possibility that Republicans could make big enough gains with white voters to singlehandedly outpace the growth of the nonwhite share of the voting eligible population.

The growing nonwhite share of the electorate has placed the GOP in an unenviable position. To compensate, Republicans will either need to markedly improve their performance among nonwhite voters or make additional gains among whites. There is certainly room for the GOP to improve among nonwhite voters; as recently as eight years ago, George W. Bush lost nonwhite voters by just forty-five points, compared to Romney's sixty-two-point defeat in 2012. There is even room for Republicans to improve among white voters, because Romney did not fare as well as President Bush among white voters outside of the South and Appalachia.

But demographics will make the math even more challenging for Republicans. If the nonwhite share of the electorate grows by another two percentage points over the next four years and the next Republican candidate repeats Romney's twenty-point win among white voters, then a Democratic candidate could prevail by winning minority voters by just forty-seven points, roughly equivalent to Kerry's victory and down considerably from Obama's sixty-two-point win. If Democrats approach 80 percent of the nonwhite vote, Republicans might need to win white voters by more than twenty-six points. Indeed, the GOP could match its best performances among white and nonwhite voters from the last seven presidential elections and only fight to a draw.

If re-litigating the issues of the last two decades seems to yield a Democratic advantage in a neutral political and economic climate, then the GOP may well need new issues and events to refigure the electorate along more favorable lines. Historically, elections following two terms of same-party control have resulted in the most significant shifts in the composition of the two party coalitions, making the 2016 presidential a critical opportunity for Republicans to redraw the battle lines of American politics on more favorable terms, much as Bill Clinton did in 1992.

## NOTE

1. Laris Karklis, Todd Lindeman, and Ted Mellnik, "How the Region Voted," *Washington Post*, November 10, 2012, accessed November 11, 2012, www.washingtonpost.com/local/how-the-region-voted/2012/11/10/1e66f3f0 -2b96-11e2-96b6-8e6a7524553f_graphic.html.

## 8

# CANDIDATES MATTER

## 2012's Senate and Gubernatorial Contests

*Geoffrey Skelley*

A year out from the 2012 election, most political analysts would have scoffed at the notion that Democrats would manage to pick up seats in the November contests. Faced with numerous seats to defend, unfavorable geography, and retirements, the Democrats' 53–47 edge in the Senate (including independent senators Bernie Sanders of Vermont and Joe Lieberman of Connecticut who caucused with the Democrats) appeared tenuous.

Of the thirty-three seats up for election in 2012, Democrats held twenty-three of them. Of those twenty-three, five were in states that John McCain had won in 2008: Missouri, Montana, Nebraska, North Dakota, and West Virginia. Knowing that the 2012 presidential election was unlikely to be as favorable a contest for Democrats as the 2008 edition, Democrats also feared losing contests in key swing states such as Florida, Ohio, and Virginia. Making their task even more difficult were the retirements of Democratic incumbents in Nebraska, North Dakota, and Wisconsin; many wrote off Democrats holding onto the former two from the start given their strong Republican lean in presidential elections. Needing only four seats to regain a majority, Republicans had more than enough targets to choose from in their search for a majority. Moreover, of the ten seats the GOP had to defend, only Massachusetts seemed especially endangered; most of the other seats were in ruby red states such as Texas and Wyoming.

But appearances can be deceiving. Despite unfavorable circumstances, Democrats managed to achieve a net gain of two seats in 2012 (counting independent Angus King, who announced after his victory in Maine that he would caucus with the Democrats), expanding their edge in the Senate

129

to 55–45. They accomplished this through a combination of superior candidates, luck, and presidential coattails. An unexpected retirement in Maine and self-inflicted wounds in races in places like Indiana and Missouri helped cost the GOP any chance of closing the margins in the Senate. Table 8.1 below summarizes the results of the 2012 senatorial elections.

Unlike the House, which saw a number of pickups on each side in the aftermath of decennial redistricting, few seats changed hands in the Senate. Of the four seats to switch parties, Republicans picked up only Nebraska while Democrats gained Indiana, Maine, and Massachusetts. All sixteen Democratic incumbents who opted to run for reelection won while Senators Scott Brown (R-MA) and Richard Lugar (R-IN) failed to garner another term (Lugar didn't make it to November, losing Indiana's Republican primary to Richard Mourdock). Thus, twenty-one of the twenty-three incumbents who sought reelection to the Senate this cycle won. Interestingly, the twenty-three incumbents seeking reelection were the lowest total since 2000 while the 91 percent incumbent reelection success rate was the highest since 2004 (96 percent).[1]

A key part of Democratic success was winning Senate elections in states where Republican presidential candidate Mitt Romney won at the top of the ticket. Despite Romney winning by at least nine percentage points in Indiana, Missouri, Montana, North Dakota, and West Virginia, Democratic candidates in all five states fought off Republican coattails to win. On the flip side, only Senator Dean Heller (R-NV) won despite Barack Obama carrying his state. In most of these six cases, the quality of the candidates played a decisive role in the outcome. The 2012 election proved once again that candidates do matter.

**Table 8.1.  Summary of the 2012 Senate Elections**

|  | *Democrats* | *Republicans* |
|---|---|---|
| Seats not up | 30 | 37 |
| Incumbents reelected | 16 (100%) | 5 (71%)[a] |
| Challenger victories | 1 (MA) | 0 |
| Open seats successfully defended | 6 (of 7) | 2 (of 4) |
| Open seats captured from opposition | 2 (IN, ME) | 1 (NE) |
| Total seats | **55**[b] | **45** |
| Net gain/loss | +2 | -2 |

[a] This percentage includes Indiana, where Senator Richard Lugar lost in his state's GOP primary to Richard Mourdock. Although he did not compete in November, Lugar sought reelection and is therefore counted.
[b] This includes Senators Bernie Sanders (I-VT) and Angus King (I-ME), who caucus with the Democrats.

Together, the races in Indiana and Missouri summed up Republican troubles in 2012. Conventional wisdom said that both should have ended up in the GOP column on Election Day: Senator Claire McCaskill (D–MO) was seen as perhaps the Senate's most vulnerable incumbent and Senator Richard Lugar (R–IN) seemed a sure bet for reelection. But as British prime minister Harold Macmillan is reputed to have once said, "Events, dear boy, events." First, Tea Party–backed Hoosier state treasurer Richard Mourdock (R) up-ended Lugar in the state's GOP primary. Then socially conservative Representative Todd Akin won the Show Me State's GOP nomination, with help from McCaskill, who ran an ad attacking Akin as a "true conservative" in a not-so-subtle effort to make him more attractive to Republican voters.[2] Less than two weeks later, Akin would speak the two most decisive words of his political career, answering a question in a debate that in instances of "legitimate rape," a woman's body can stop a pregnancy.[3] These comments turned the race upside down as national Republicans tried to get Akin to voluntarily drop out of the race; when Akin refused, he ended up losing much outside help in his race—pro-McCaskill groups spent two-and-a-half times as much as pro-Akin groups during the general election campaign.[4] Then at a late October debate, Mourdock was asked about abortion rights. His emotional answer defending his pro-life views included a belief that pregnancies resulting from rape were "something that God intended to happen."[5] The resulting firestorm probably doomed Mourdock's campaign. In Missouri, McCaskill went on to win by over 15 percent of the vote while Representative Joe Donnelly (D) claimed the Indiana seat by nearly six points, giving Democrats an unexpected hold and an nearly more unexpected pickup.

The closest race in the country this cycle occurred in North Dakota, where former state attorney general Heidi Heitkamp (D) edged Representative Rick Berg (R) by a little less than 3,000 votes. After Senator Kent Conrad (D) announced that he would not seek reelection in early 2011, Berg quickly threw his hat into the ring. Because he had only won election to the House in 2010, Democrats immediately attacked him for seeking higher office so soon after ascending to the House.[6] Democratic hopes fell to Heitkamp, a well-regarded former state officer who lost her 2000 bid for the Peace Garden State's governorship. In the campaign, Heitkamp overcame the state's presidential GOP tilt and attempts by Berg to tie her to Obama by stressing her political independence, criticizing the president's energy policy and emphasizing her support for gun rights.[7]

To the west in Montana, Senator Jon Tester (D) overcame a serious challenge from Representative Denny Rehberg (R) with a similar strategy to Heitkamp's. Despite having voted for the Affordable Care Act and

Dodd-Frank financial sector reform law, Tester crafted a centrist image built on his life as a farmer and support for the Keystone Pipeline, distancing himself from the president. Rehberg, like many other Republican candidates, attempted to hammer home a connection between Obama and Tester in voters' minds, while a conservative outside group targeted Tester as one of many "ObamaClones" in the Senate.[8] Providing assistance to Tester was the Libertarian candidacy of Dan Cox, who garnered over 6 percent of the vote. Tester's allies actually played a role in Cox's success, running ads (similar to McCaskill in Missouri) promoting Cox as a "true conservative" in an attempt to shift some GOP-leaning voters from Rehberg to the third-party candidate.[9]

Further west, Senate Republicans achieved their most precarious hold in Nevada, where Senator Dean Heller (R) narrowly won his first full term after being appointed to replace former senator John Ensign (R). Winning only about 46 percent of the vote, Heller overcame Obama's coattails in the Silver State to defeat Representative Shelley Berkley (D) by a little more than one percentage point. Unlike the races in Indiana, Missouri, Montana, and North Dakota, here the stronger candidate was the Republican. Berkley was plagued by ethics questions over whether she utilized her congressional post to assist her husband's medical practice.[10] The nature of this contest can perhaps be summed up by the fact that the Libertarian candidate and the "None of these candidates" ballot option combined to win nearly 10 percent of the vote. Despite Obama's coattails and being outspent by Berkley and her allies by over $3 million,[11] Heller survived.

Throughout the cycle, the Massachusetts showdown earned top billing on every "races to watch" list. Having won "Ted Kennedy's seat" in the heavily Democratic Bay State in a 2010 special election, Scott Brown (R-MA) was the number one Democratic target from the get-go. But Brown would be no pushover. While cultivating an image of pragmatism and moderation to appeal to working-class voters in the state, the incumbent also showed himself to be a prolific fund-raiser, warding off many possible challengers with his significant war chest. Possibly helping Brown was the fact that his opponent, consumer advocate and Harvard professor Elizabeth Warren, was anything but flawless as a candidate. This fact was most apparent when controversy arose over her claim to have Native American heritage, and disputes about whether or not she used that supposed ancestry to give herself a professional edge.[12] Nonetheless, Warren, a major figure in the progressive movement, remarkably turned out to be an even better fund-raiser than Brown, out-raising him by about $14 million.[13] Despite Brown's efforts, Warren's monetary advantage (a third-party spending truce limited outside spending in the race) and the deep blue hue of Massachusetts in a presidential year doomed the incumbent to an eight-point loss on Election Day in the most expensive Senate race in the country, with over $81 million in candidate spending.[14]

Next door, Representative Chris Murphy (D-CT) triumphed over businesswoman Linda McMahon (R-CT) and her gigantic war chest to succeed retiring senator Joe Lieberman (I-CT). McMahon sought a Senate seat in the Nutmeg State for the second straight election, having lost to now senator Richard Blumenthal in 2012. Much like Brown, McMahon lost not because she was a notably bad candidate but because firmly Democratic Connecticut lacked enough ticket-splitters to elect her—on Election Day, Murphy underperformed Obama by three percentage points. For a time, it looked as if McMahon might have a chance. A Quinnipiac poll in late August found her narrowly ahead of Murphy, 46–43.[15] Complicating matters, Murphy had a number of problems early on in his campaign, particularly personal finance issues regarding his mortgage and a foreclosure. But he rallied behind solid debate performances and aid from the Democratic Senatorial Campaign Committee. All in all, in her two bids in 2010 and 2012, McMahon spent almost $100 million of her own money in failed efforts, losing by about twelve points both times.[16]

Two states in the Midwest offered possible pickup opportunities for Republicans heading into 2012. In Wisconsin, Senator Herb Kohl (D) decided to retire, creating another open seat for Democrats to defend. At the same time, embattled populist senator Sherrod Brown (D) looked vulnerable to a challenge in Ohio. But Democrats managed to retain both seats. Brown's opponent, youthful Ohio state treasurer Josh Mandel, never led a single poll released between March 2011 and Election Day,[17] signaling how his candidacy never truly took off. Brown fought off attacks on his record to win by six percentage points on Election Day, running evenly with Obama. In the Badger State, an ugly four-way GOP primary battle resulted in a win for moderate former governor Tommy Thompson (R-WI). But during the primary, Thompson was forced to move to the right to win the nomination and had to expend precious resources to earn his hard-fought victory. His general election opponent, Representative Tammy Baldwin (D-WI), had no challenger in her primary, allowing her to save up for the main event. In the campaign, Baldwin hammered Thompson for his years in Washington as a lobbyist, an approach that helped her overcome the former governor's attacks on her liberal House record. For Baldwin, Obama's win in Wisconsin also aided her victory—the two won similar percentages on Election Day.

Baldwin made history, becoming the first openly gay member of the U.S. Senate.[18]

In the South, two other seemingly winnable campaigns for Republicans failed to materialize in Florida and Virginia. A Quinnipiac poll in January showed incumbent Senator Bill Nelson (D–FL) in a near dead heat with eventual challenger Representative Connie Mack IV (R–FL) in the Sunshine State.[19] But Mack was troubled by attacks on his character, particularly for a number of bar brawls and road rage incidents when he was younger.[20] The baseball scion lost momentum throughout the summer and never really recovered, losing by thirteen points to Nelson. The contest in the Old Dominion proved to be far closer than the one in Florida. With the impending retirement of Senator Jim Webb (D), Tim Kaine (D) and George Allen (R) faced off in a battle that many thought might decide control of the Senate. Both candidates tried to cast the other as fiscally reckless. Allen, who was seeking to regain the seat he lost to Webb in 2006, tried to link the former DNC chairman to Obama's stimulus and health care laws. But Kaine campaigned as a moderate, highlighting his success at controlling the size of the state budget as governor while attacking Allen for supporting President George W. Bush's tax cuts during his previous term in the Senate.[21] Kaine carried the day, outperforming Obama's Virginia percentage by nearly two points.

There were other races around the country that held the potential to be competitive, filling watch lists and garnering oodles of dollars from the national committees and outside groups. In the southwest, former surgeon general Richard Carmona (D) gave Democrats hopes of capturing the open seat in reddish Arizona. A month out, polls had Carmona neck-and-neck with libertarian-minded Representative Jeff Flake (R).[22] But the political reality in the Grand Canyon State kept the seat in the Republican column on Election Day. New Mexico, next door, proved to be more or less the opposite of Arizona. In an open-seat battle, ex-representative Heather Wilson (R) looked to be the strongest Republican candidate available but the increasingly Democratic Land of Enchantment handed the seat to Representative Martin Heinrich (D). To the east, the race in Pennsylvania seemed to be tightening close to Election Day, but Senator Bob Casey (D) held off a challenge from businessman Tom Smith (R).

None of the other races were particularly competitive. Democratic holds in California (Dianne Feinstein), Delaware (Tom Carper), Maryland (Ben Cardin), Michigan (Debbie Stabenow), Minnesota (Amy Klobuchar), New Jersey (Bob Menendez), New York (Kirsten Gillibrand), Rhode

Island (Sheldon Whitehouse), Washington (Maria Cantwell), and West Virginia (Joe Manchin) were always in the cards, as was the reelection of Senator Bernie Sanders (I-VT). On the Republican side, results in Mississippi (Roger Wicker), Tennessee (Bob Corker), Utah (Orrin Hatch), and Wyoming (John Barrasso) never lacked certainty. Open seat wins for Republicans in GOP-strongholds Nebraska and Texas by Deb Fischer and Ted Cruz, respectively, also surprised few, though Democrats had hoped that former senator Bob Kerrey (D-NE) would be able to keep the Cornhusker State blue despite the retirement of incumbent Senator Ben Nelson (D). An unexpected and unfortunate development for Republicans was the retirement of Senator Olympia Snow (R-ME), a moderate who would have easily won reelection. Her decision to exit politics opened up the Maine seat for independent former governor Angus King to comfortably win the seat. Leading Democrats got out of the way, anticipating that King would caucus with the Democrats. They were prescient: King did as they expected just a few days after winning on Election Day.

Similar to the presidential contest, it was a banner year for political money in Senate races: All forms of spending this cycle totaled nearly $1 billion. Outside groups, including party committees, expended around $350 million, while candidates spent more than $625 million. There will be a lot of debate about the impact of spending on the presidential race but the importance of spending in down-ticket races was generally reconfirmed. Just examining candidate spending, in twenty-four of thirty-three races, the candidate who spent more won. But the election results also indicated that candidates and fundamentals can still matter more than money. In Nevada, Heller won reelection despite being outspent; in North Dakota, Berg's monetary advantage did not help him carry the day; and in Connecticut, despite being outspent nearly five-to-one by McMahon, Murphy won because the Nutmeg State is still very Democratic.[23]

Overall, whether it was luck (e.g., Snowe's retirement), mediocre-to-poor Republican candidates (e.g., Akin, Mack, Mourdock), strong Democratic standard-bearers (e.g., Heitkamp, Tester), or help from the top of the ticket (e.g., Connecticut, Massachusetts), Democrats overcame significant geographic and numerical obstacles to actually net two seats in 2012. Looking forward to 2014, the unexpected Democratic gains in 2012 have left a thornier path to a Senate majority for Republicans, although Republicans do again start with an advantage: Democrats must defend twenty of the thirty-three seats up in 2014, while Republicans only have to defend thirteen.

## 2012 GUBERNATORIAL AND
## STATEHOUSE CONTESTS

Gubernatorial races during presidential elections are typically footnotes—nearly three-fourths of those tilts are held during midterm cycles—but the outcomes of those elections, as well as those in state legislatures, greatly impact public policy decisions across the country. There were eleven gubernatorial elections in 2012, five of which were open seat contests. Republicans achieved a net gain of one seat by winning North Carolina, the only seat to change party hands in what proved to be a relatively uneventful gubernatorial cycle. With the win in the Tar Heel State, the GOP now controls thirty governorships nationally, marking its highest total since 2000.[24]

As table 8.2 below shows, in the six contests featuring incumbents, all six won fairly handily; only Governor Earl Ray Tomblin (D) in West Virginia failed to win by double digits, winning by just shy of five points. Only Governor Jay Nixon (D-MO) won reelection despite winning a smaller percentage of the vote in 2012 than in 2008. As for Governor Jack Dalrymple (R-ND), he won his first full term after becoming governor when then-governor John Hoeven (R-ND) won a Senate seat in 2010.

Most of the action in the gubernatorial contests occurred in the open seat races. As Election Day neared, question marks only really surrounded

**Table 8.2.    Incumbent Performance in 2012 Gubernatorial Races**

| State | Incumbent | Vote % | Challenger | Vote % | Margin | Incumbent Change from Last Election |
|-------|-----------|--------|------------|--------|--------|--------------------------------------|
| DE | Jack Markell (D) | 69.3 | Jeff Cragg (R) | 28.6 | 40.7 | +1.8[a] |
| MO | Jay Nixon (D) | 54.8 | Dave Spence (R) | 42.5 | 12.3 | -3.6[a] |
| ND | Jack Dalrymple (R) | 63.1 | Ryan Taylor (D) | 34.3 | 28.8 | NA[b] |
| UT | Gary Herbert (R) | 68.4 | Peter Cooke (D) | 27.6 | 40.8 | +4.3[c] |
| VT | Peter Shumlin (D) | 57.8 | Randy Brock (R) | 37.6 | 20.2 | +8.3[d] |
| WV | Earl Ray Tomblin (D) | 50.5 | Bill Maloney (R) | 45.6 | 4.9 | +0.9[e] |

*Sources*: Electoral data as of Dec. 19, 2012, via Dave Leip's Atlas of U.S. Presidential Elections (http://uselectionatlas.org/RESULTS/) and "Statewide Results Special Gubernatorial General Election—October 4, 2011," West Virginia Secretary of State (http://apps.sos.wv.gov/elections/results/results.aspx?ye ar=2011&eid=10&county=Statewide).

[a] First elected in 2008.
[b] Originally appointed to office, won first election in 2012.
[c] Originally appointed to office, won first election in 2010.
[d] First elected in 2010.
[e] First elected in 2011 special election.

the outcomes in Montana, New Hampshire, and Washington. In Big Sky Country, polling showed a very tight race, with the final two polls in the week leading up to the election showing either a tie or former representative Rick Hill (R) holding a slight lead.[25] But on Election Day, state attorney general Steve Bullock (D) triumphed by a percentage point. In what wound up being the closest gubernatorial race in 2012, Bullock likely triumphed for a couple reasons. First, Bullock had stronger approval ratings among likely voters than Hill.[26] Just as important, having served as a governing partner with outgoing governor Brian Schweitzer (D) as attorney general, Bullock likely benefited from Schweitzer's popularity, appearing to enough voters to be the appropriate successor.

In Washington, fundamentals claimed another victim, this time state attorney general Rob McKenna (R). While McKenna ran well ahead of Mitt Romney on Election Day, the strong Democratic tilt of the Evergreen State again proved too much for GOP hopefuls: It has now been thirty-two years since a Republican won a gubernatorial contest in Washington. The benefactor of this streak, former representative Jay Inslee (D), will be the fifth consecutive Democratic governor, following the retiring governor Christine Gregoire (D). Early on, it appeared that McKenna might have a shot at breaking the longest gubernatorial dry spell in the nation for Republicans, as he led most polling into mid-July. But once Inslee's campaign kicked into high gear, following his resignation from the House of Representatives in March to fully focus on the campaign, he pulled ahead of McKenna in the polls.[27] The Democratic campaign sought to make McKenna appear too conservative for the left-leaning Washington electorate, particularly emphasizing the fact that McKenna had joined other Republican attorneys general in challenging Obama's health care law. Though he was criticized for an insufficiently specific economic plan and lost the endorsement of most major state newspapers, Inslee eked out a victory.[28]

The other race considered fairly competitive occurred in New Hampshire, where four-term governor John Lynch (D) decided to retire after eight years in Concord. Conservative Ovide Lamontagne (R) made another attempt at winning the governorship in New Hampshire, having lost to now senator Jeanne Shaheen (D) in the state's 1996 gubernatorial race. Opposing Lamontagne was former state senator Maggie Hassan (D), who argued that the Tea Party–backed Republican was too extreme for the swingy Granite State. Lamontagne embraced his conservative image, promising to cut taxes and arguing that Hassan would attempt to propose an income tax or sales tax, an issue of great importance in New Hampshire (it has neither).[29] Polling in the race initially went back and forth, but by late

October, Hassan held a small but steady lead in most surveys. On Election Day, Hassan outperformed Obama by around 2.5 points, winning nearly 55 percent of the vote and by a much larger margin, around 12 points, than polling indicated.[30]

North Carolina's seat switched hands as former Charlotte mayor Pat McCrory (R) easily dismissed Lieutenant Governor Walter Dalton (D). While McCrory had previously lost to incumbent Governor Bev Perdue (D) in 2008 by a narrow margin, Perdue's unpopularity in the Tar Heel State and ethics questions led her to not seek reelection, thereby avoiding a rematch with McCrory.[31] In nearby West Virginia, Governor Earl Ray Tomblin (D) had to endure his second election in as many years after winning a special election in October 2011 to replace now senator Joe Manchin. Seeking a full term this time, Tomblin faced off against his previous opponent, businessman Bill Maloney (R). Despite the red hue of the Mountaineer State at the presidential level, Tomblin managed to increase his share of the vote by about one point, winning a full four-year term in Charleston. West Virginia wasn't the only place to split tickets: Along with Tomblin, Bullock in Montana and Governor Jay Nixon (D-MO) also won despite Mitt Romney easily carrying their states at the presidential level. Much like in the Senate, Democrats managed to win a number of seats in states that were no-goes for Barack Obama at the top of the ticket.

In the remaining gubernatorial contests, Democrats held onto seats in Delaware (Jack Markell) and Vermont (Peter Shumlin) while Republicans kept their hands on Indiana (Mike Pence), North Dakota (Jack Dalrymple), and Utah (Gary Herbert). Interestingly, few outside observers ever expected the Hoosier State contest to be very close, but it narrowed in the end, with Representative Mike Pence (R) only edging former Indiana House Speaker John Gregg (D) by less than three percentage points.

As for the state legislative contests, Republicans entered the 2012 cycle holding both chambers in twenty-six of forty-nine states (Nebraska has a nonpartisan unicameral legislature) while Democrats controlled fifteen and eight were split.[32] But the 2012 result was slightly favorable to Democrats: they retook control of seven chambers, including the Houses in Colorado, Oregon, and New Hampshire; and both chambers in Maine and Minnesota. It appeared that Democrats had also taken control of the New York State Senate for only the second time since 1966, but a group of independent Democrats instead chose to caucus with the GOP to form a controlling coalition. Similarly, on the other side of the country, two maverick Democrats joined with Republicans to form a one-seat majority in the Washington Senate, one of the five chambers Republicans took control of in 2012. The GOP won a historic victory in Arkansas, earning Republican majorities in both houses of the state's general assembly for the first time since Reconstruction. Remarkably, the GOP now controls every single legislative chamber in the formerly Democratic Solid South. Along with Arkansas, the GOP also took control of the Alaska Senate and regained a majority in the Wisconsin Senate. Divided legislatures are nearly no more: Only in Iowa, Kentucky, New Hampshire, New York, and Washington does one party not assert control over both chambers of their state houses (Virginia's Senate is split 20-20 but Republicans control the tie-breaking lieutenant governor vote, allowing them to organize it). The final state legislature tally: Republicans now control both chambers in twenty-seven states, Democrats in seventeen, with five others split.[33]

While Democrats are thrilled with their presidential result as well as their success in the Senate, an additional Republican governorship and continued full control by the GOP of the majority of state legislatures indicates that the United States truly remains a purple nation.

## NOTES

1. "Table 1-18 House and Senate Incumbents Retired, Defeated, or Reelected, 1946–2010," *Vital Statistics on American Politics 201–2012* (Thousand Oaks, CA: CQ Press, 2011), 43–44.

2. Dave Catanese and Alex Isenstadt, "Missouri GOP Senate Primary: McCaskill Gets Her Opponent, Akin Wins," *Politico*, August 8, 2012, accessed November 28, 2012, www.politico.com/news/stories/0812/79467.html.

3. John Eligon and Michael Schwartz, "Senate Candidate Provokes Ire with 'Legitimate Rape' Comment," *New York Times*, August 19, 2012, accessed November 28, 2012, www.nytimes.com/2012/08/20/us/politics/todd-akin-provokes-ire-with-legitimate-rape-comment.html.

4. Amanda Terkel, "John Cornyn: Todd Akin Unlikely to Get Any Help from NRSC," *Huffington Post*, September 28, 2012, accessed Nov. 28, 2012, www.huffingtonpost.com/2012/09/28/john-cornyn-todd-akin-nrsc_n_1922756.html; "2012 Outside Spending, by Races," OpenSecrets.org, accessed December 19, 2012, http://opensecrets.org/outsidespending/summ.php?cycle=2012&disp=R&pty=A&type=G.

5. Lucy Madison, "Richard Mourdock: Even Pregnancy from Rape Something 'God Intended,'" CBS News, October 23, 2012, accessed November 28, 2012, www.cbsnews.com/8301-250_162-57538757/richard-mourdock-even-pregnancy-from-rape-something-god-intended/.

6. Shira Toeplitz, "House Freshman Berg Will Run for Senate in North Dakota," *Roll Call*, May 16, 2011, accessed November 29, 2012, www.rollcall.com/news/house_freshman_berg_will_run_for_senate_in_north_dakota-205672-1.html.

7. Dale Wetzel and Dave Kolpack, "Democrat Heidi Heitkamp Wins Senate Race in North Dakota," *Washington Times* (AP), November 7, 2012, accessed November 29, 2012, www.washingtontimes.com/news/2012/nov/7/berg-concedes -us-senate-race-heitkamp-north-dakota/.

8. Mark Barabak, "Winning the West, Montana Style," *Los Angeles Times*, February 27, 2011, accessed November 29, 2012, http://articles.latimes.com/2011/feb/27/nation/la-na-campaign-2012-west-20110227; Patrick Svitek, "Jon Tester Touts Taking on Obama in New Ad," *Huffington Post*, August 7, 2012, accessed November 29, 2012, www.huffingtonpost.com/2012/08/07/jon-tester -obama_n_1751524.html.

9. Mike Dennison, "Group Sympathetic to Tester Drops $500K on TV Ad—for Libertarian," *Billings Gazette*, October 26, 2012, accessed November 29, 2012, http://billingsgazette.com/news/state-and-regional/montana/group-sympathetic-to-tester -drops-k-on-tv-ad-for/article_44197da9-b6d2-5e8a-ae05-7442aef0a45d.html.

10. John Bresnahan, "Shelley Berkley Ethics Case Shakes Up Nevada Race," *Politico*, July 9, 2012, accessed November 29, 2012, www.politico.com/news/stories/0712/78308.html.

11. Based on OpenSecrets.org data, Berkley and her allies spent about $25 million, Heller and his allies about $21.9 million. "Total Raised and Spent 2012 Race: Nevada Senate," OpenSecrets.org, accessed December 19, 2012, www .opensecrets.org/races/summary.php?id=NVS1&cycle=2012; "2012 Race: Nevada Senate Outside Spending," OpenSecrets.org, accessed December 19, 2012, www.opensecrets.org/races/indexp.php?cycle=2012&id=NVS1.

12. Josh Hicks, "Everything You Need to Know about Elizabeth Warren's Claim of Native American Heritage," *Washington Post*, September 28, 2012, accessed November 29, 2012, www.washingtonpost.com/blogs/fact-checker/post/everything-you-need-to-know-about-the-controversy-over-elizabeth-warrens -claimed-native-american-heritage/2012/09/27/d0b7f568-08a5-11e2-a10c -fa5a255a9258_blog.html.

13. "Total Raised and Spent 2012 Race: Massachusetts Senate," OpenSecrets .org, accessed December 13, 2012, www.opensecrets.org/races/summary.php ?id=MAS1&cycle=2012.

14. "Most Expensive Races," OpenSecrets.org, accessed November 29, 2012, www.opensecrets.org/overview/topraces.php.

15. John Brandt, "McMahon Leads Dem Rival in Connecticut Senate Race Poll," Fox News, August 28, 2012, accessed November 29, 2012, http://politics.blogs .foxnews.com/2012/08/28/mcmahon-leads-dem-rival-connecticut-senate-race-poll.

16. Kate Nocera, "Chris Murphy Tops Linda McMahon in Conn. Senate Race," *Politico*, November 6, 2012, accessed November 29, 2012, www.politico .com/news/stories/1112/83434.html; McMahon's two-cycle spending based on

data from "Total Raised and Spent 2012 Race: Connecticut Senate," OpenSecrets .org, accessed December 19, 2012, www.opensecrets.org/races/summary .php?id=CTS1&cycle=2012, and "Total Raised and Spent 2010 Race: Connecticut Senate," OpenSecrets.org, accessed December 19, 2012, www.opensecrets .org/races/summary.php?cycle=2010&id=CTS2.

17. "Ohio Senate—Mandel vs. Brown," RealClearPolitics, accessed November 29, 2012, www.realclearpolitics.com/epolls/2012/senate/oh/ohio_senate _mandel_vs_brown-2100.html#polls.

18. Kate Nocera, "Tammy Baldwin Tops Tommy Thompson in Wisconsin," *Politico*, November 7, 2012, accessed November 29, 2012, www.politico.com/ news/stories/1112/83453.html.

19. "January 11, 2012—Obama Ties Romney, Santorum in Florida, Quinnipiac University Poll Finds; Nelson, Mack Senate Race Too Close to Call," Quinnipiac University, January 11, 2012, accessed November 29, 2012, www.quinnipiac.edu/ institutes-centers/polling-institute/florida/release-detail?ReleaseID=1689.

20. "Connie Mack's Past Altercations Again a Campaign Issue," *Tampa Bay Times* (AP), March 12, 2012, accessed November 29, 2012, www.tampabay .com/news/politics/elections/connie-macks-past-altercations-again-a-campaign -issue/1219639.

21. Bill Sizemore and Julian Walker, "Results: Kaine Beats Allen for U.S. Senate Seat," *Virginian-Pilot*, November 7, 2012, accessed November 29, 2012, http:// hamptonroads.com/2012/11/results-kaine-beats-allen-us-senate-seat.

22. "Arizona Senate—Flake vs. Carmona," RealClearPolitics, accessed November 30, 2012, www.realclearpolitics.com/epolls/2012/senate/az/arizona_ senate_flake_vs_carmona-3005.html#polls.

23. Based on OpenSecrets.org data, compiled from "Congressional Races," OpenSecrets.org, accessed December 19, 2012, www.opensecrets.org/races/ index.php, and "2012 Outside Spending, by Super PACs," OpenSecrets.org, accessed December 19, 2012, www.opensecrets.org/outsidespending/summ.php? cycle=2012&disp=R&pty=A&type=S.

24. Brian Chappatta, "Republicans to Hold Most Governor Offices Since 2000," *Bloomberg*, accessed November 30, 2012, www.bloomberg.com/news/2012-11-07/ republicans-to-hold-most-governor-offices-since-2000.html.

25. "Montana Governor—Hill vs. Bullock," RealClearPolitics, accessed November 30, 2012, www.realclearpolitics.com/epolls/2012/governor/mt/montana_ governor_hill_vs_bullock-1839.html.

26. Polling results from Public Policy Polling, "Tester Leads MT Senate Race, Flake Up in AZ, Romney by 7," November 4, 2012, accessed November 30, 2012, www.publicpolicypolling.com/main/2012/11/tester-leads-mt-senate-race -flake-up-in-az-romney-by-7.html#more.

27. "Washington Governor—McKenna vs. Inslee," RealClearPolitics, accessed November 30, 2012, www.realclearpolitics.com/epolls/2012/governor/wa/ washington_governor_mckenna_vs_inslee-2202.html.

28. "Inslee Secures Victory in Wash. Governor's Race," *USA Today* (AP), November 10, 2012, accessed November 30, 2012, www.usatoday.com/story/news/politics/2012/11/10/inslee-washington-politics-mckenna/1696263/.

29. Norma Love and Holly Ramer, "Breaking News: Democrat Maggie Hassan Wins N.H. Governor's Race over Ovide Lamontagne," *Concord Monitor* (AP), November 6, 2012, accessed November 30, 2012, www.concordmonitor.com/home/2679302-95/hassan-state-lamontagne-hampshire.

30. "New Hampshire Governor—Lamontagne vs. Hassan," RealClearPolitics, accessed November 30, 2012, www.realclearpolitics.com/epolls/2012/governor/nh/new_hampshire_governor_lamontagne_vs_hassan-2804.html#polls.

31. Gary Robertson, "Bev Perdue Retiring: North Carolina Governor Reportedly Won't Seek Reelection," *Huffington Post*, January 28, 2012, accessed November 30, 2012, www.huffingtonpost.com/2012/01/26/bev-perdue-retiring-north-carolina-governor_n_1233586.html.

32. Tim Storey, "Expect Turnout—but Not a Wave—in State Legislative Races," Sabato's Crystal Ball, October 11, 2012, accessed November 30, 2012, www.centerforpolitics.org/crystalball/articles/expect-turnover-but-not-a-wave-in-state-legislative-races/.

33. "Democrats Make Substantial Gains, But GOP Holds onto 2010 Victories and Adds Four Chambers," National Conference of State Legislatures, November 7, 2012, accessed November 30, 2012, www.ncsl.org/press-room/history-holds-true-in-2012-legislative-races.aspx; Thomas Kaplan and Danny Hakim, "Coalition Is to Control State Senate as Dissident Democrats Join with Republicans," *New York Times*, December 4, 2012, accessed December 5, 2012, www.nytimes.com/2012/12/05/nyregion/malcolm-smith-defects-joining-dissenting-democrats.html; Brad Shannon, "UPDATE—Republican-Led Coalition Takes Control of State Senate," *Olympian*, December 10, 2012, accessed December 19, 2012, www.theolympian.com/2012/12/10/2348825/republican-led-coalition-takes.html.

*9*

# REPUBLICANS HOLD THE LINE

## 2012's National House Contest

### *Kyle Kondik*

As the dust settled from 2012's battle for the United States House of Representatives, operatives at both the Democratic Congressional Campaign Committee and the National Republican Congressional Committee had reasons for optimism.

Democrats had outperformed most pre-election projections by netting a gain of eight seats, putting them over the two hundred mark in the House (Republicans won 234 seats to the Democrats' 201). They also knocked off sixteen Republican incumbents and won the popular vote for the House nationally.

Republicans, meanwhile, had won the most important prize—obviously, retaining the House—and, despite their losses, maintained a majority that not only was bigger than any of the House Republican caucuses during the party's 1995–2007 period of control, but was also the third-largest Republican caucus in the post–Great Depression era (the GOP only had bigger caucuses after the 1946 and 2010 elections).

All in all, a net change of only eight seats represents a fairly high level of stability; in the seventeen postwar presidential elections (including this one), there was an average of about a seventeen-seat net change in seats, which is more than double the net level of change in this election.[1]

That stability came in spite of an unpopular Congress. In September 2012, the Gallup polling organization reported that congressional approval was the lowest it had ever measured in an election year, going back to 1974: Only 13 percent of Americans approved of the job Congress was doing.[2]

But it's important to remember that Congress is usually unpopular, though perhaps not this unpopular—of the nineteen elections where Gallup measured congressional popularity going back to 1974 (there was no poll in 1984), only twice (in 1998 and 2002) was congressional approval over 50 percent. While Americans generally express disdain for Congress, they typically send their own representative back to Congress—in the post–World War II era, about 92 percent of House members who sought reelection did in fact return to the House.[3]

That figure was slightly lower this time—about 90 percent of House incumbents who sought reelection were reelected—but many incumbents faced extenuating circumstances. Of 390 House members who sought another term in the House—that is, those who did not retire or otherwise leave the House—40 lost. But eight lost to other members in member versus member primary contests (brought about by redistricting), and another three lost to fellow members in member versus member general election contests. In non-redistricting years, there aren't member versus member races. Hence, the incumbent reelection rate this year is at least slightly artificially low because of the special circumstances of redistricting and reapportionment.

That incumbency reelection advantage is of course helpful for the incumbent party, particularly when that party already holds a forty-nine-seat advantage (as Republicans did heading into the 2012 election). Incumbency, combined with a lack of a national wave and control of redistricting in some key states, allowed Republicans to again win the House despite the reelection of a Democratic president and Democratic gains in the U.S. Senate.

## DEMOCRATS WIN POPULAR VOTE, BUT NOT BY ENOUGH

It is something of a historical fluke that Democratic House candidates actually won more total votes—about a million more—than Republican House candidates in 2012 but failed to win the House; Democrats won the House while losing the national House vote in 1914 and 1942, while Republicans pulled off the feat in 1952, 1996, and in 2012.[4] Obviously, the percentage of total House votes won does not perfectly translate to the number of seats each party wins, to the disappointment (this time) of Democrats.

One possible factor in that discrepancy is that Democrats, partially because of redistricting but also partly because of lifestyle choice, appear to be clustered closer together than Republicans, which helps dilute their House performance. Political scientists Jowei Chen of the University of Michigan and Jonathan Rodden of Stanford University have argued that this clustering puts Democrats in a structural disadvantage in House races: "In many states, Democrats are inefficiently concentrated in large cities and smaller industrial agglomerations such that they can expect to win fewer than 50 percent of the seats when they win 50 percent of the votes," they write.[5]

That might help explain why Democrats in 2012 won a significantly greater number of seats in blowouts—defined here as a winner getting 70 percent of the vote or more (or being unopposed) in a House race—than Republicans. In 2012, Democratic candidates either won 70 percent or more of the vote or were unopposed in eighty-two House races, while Republicans won 70 percent or more of the vote or were unopposed in just forty-six House races. Those wasted votes in blowout races make winning a House majority more difficult for Democrats.

## REDISTRICTING: SETTING THE STAGE FOR STABILITY

The seeds of the Republicans' 2012 House victory were sown in 2010, when the Republicans picked up a remarkable sixty-three net seats and also their biggest share of state legislative seats since 1928.

If there's ever a year to have a big state and federal legislative election victory, it's in the first year of a decade. That's because the new census is released the following year, which prompts changes to the nation's apportionment of U.S. House seats and spurs states to redraw their districts to reflect population change.

The 2010 census provided more evidence of the nation's shifting population. Frost Belt states New York and Ohio both lost two congressional seats apiece because of stagnant population growth, while fast-growing Florida gained two seats and megastate Texas added four. All in all, as figure 9.1 shows, the South and West gained seats at the expense of the North and Midwest.

Ultimately, the shifting seats resulted in no partisan change. By the University of Virginia Center for Politics' calculations, of the twelve seats eliminated, Democrats lost eight and Republicans lost four (that includes

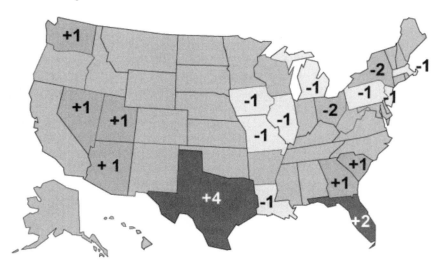

**Figure 9.1.   Congressional Reapportionment after the 2010 Census**
*Source*: University of Virginia Center for Politics.

Republican general election victories in two member-versus-member contests: one in Ohio and one in Iowa). Of the twelve seats added in other
parts of the country, Democrats effectively won eight and Republicans
won four.

Congressional redistricting did, however, set the stage for big swings
in individual states. Republicans picked a good time, the 2010 elections,
to win unified control of the state legislature in North Carolina for the
first time since Reconstruction. That allowed them to dramatically redraw
the state's congressional map (returning the favor to Democrats, who gerrymandered the map after the 2000 census). Democrats had a 7–6 majority
in the Tar Heel State's House delegation going into the 2012 elections, but
Republicans picked up three seats and almost won another—Democratic
representative Mike McIntyre barely hung on against a stiff Republican
challenge. Meanwhile, Democrats in Illinois blew up the Land of Lincoln's
congressional map, eliminating one Republican seat to comply with the
census (Representative Adam Kinzinger defeated Representative Don
Manzullo in a member-versus-member primary race) and altering several
other districts to make them more favorable to Democratic candidates. On
Election Day, Democrats defeated four Republican incumbents, thanks in
no small part to the redraw. A new way of drawing House seats in California also helped Democrats make gains there (the California story is explored
in further depth below).

## A MIDWEST CASE STUDY

But in most places, the Republicans' state legislative advantage was brought to bear, and they used that dominance not necessarily to target congressional Democrats, but rather to solidify Republicans, many of whom were freshmen elected in the 2010 wave.

Republicans controlled redistricting in several key midwestern states after 2010 that voted for Barack Obama in 2008 and would later support the president again in the 2012 election: these included Michigan, Ohio, Pennsylvania, and Wisconsin. Republicans netted fourteen seats out of these four states in 2010—or nearly a quarter of their total midterm gain. The GOP went to work to solidify these gains through redistricting, redrawing the congressional maps to add at least slightly more Republican votes to the potentially swingy districts of freshmen such as Representative Sean Duffy in Wisconsin and a handful of newly elected representatives in Ohio and Pennsylvania. The remap helps explain why Democrats didn't defeat a single Republican incumbent in any of these states in 2012; so too, however, does the simple fact that President Obama did worse in all of these states than he did in 2008. For example, Obama won six of Wisconsin's eight congressional districts in 2008; this time, Obama won only three (despite comfortably carrying the state).[6] Those three districts that flipped from Obama to Romney between 2008 and 2012 were the ones held by Republican representatives Paul Ryan (Romney's running mate and a veteran House member) and Duffy and Reid Ribble, two 2010 freshmen winners. An Obama-style 2008 wave might have allowed Democrats to win back these seats, but in this case—and in the other states—the Republican maps held up quite well.

All told, in 2008, Obama won 55 percent of the vote in these four states, and Democrats captured thirty-five of the sixty House seats in those states (58 percent). In 2012, Obama won 52 percent of the vote in these states, but Democrats won only 30 percent of the House seats (seventeen of fifty-six; Ohio lost two seats after the census and Michigan and Pennsylvania each lost one apiece). Winning a future Democratic House majority will presumably require the party to unlock at least some of these seats in states that were friendly to Obama in his two presidential victories.

## CALIFORNIA'S BRAVE NEW WORLD

Congressional redistricting is not controlled by state legislators in all states. In 2010, California voters dramatically altered not only how the Golden

State drew its congressional districts, but also how voters select general election candidates. Those decisions made formerly sleepy California into a major congressional battleground, with results that were largely—but not uniformly—positive for Democrats in this deep blue state.

From 2002 to 2010, there were 265 individual U.S. House general elections in California (53 seats contested over 5 elections). In that time period, only once did one seat change hands from one party to the other—in 2006, Democrat Jerry McNerney unseated Representative Richard Pombo (R) in a Northern California district. That means in all other 264 elections, the incumbent party that controlled the seat going into the election controlled it afterward.

But after a nonpartisan commission—as opposed to the incumbent-protecting state legislature—redrew the state's districts thanks to the 2010 voter-initiated reforms, both parties recognized that there were new opportunities to alter the nation's largest U.S. House delegation.

A few incumbents found themselves forced to run against each other, such as Democratic representatives Howard Berman and Brad Sherman in a Los Angeles-area district. Other representatives did not have much of a chance to win in the new districts, such as powerful Republican representative David Dreier, who elected to retire. Beyond that, several districts were redrawn, with the effect of increasing competition; about a quarter of the seats featured at least some level of credible real two-party competition throughout 2012 (as measured by the University of Virginia Center for Politics' House ratings).

Beyond the creation of the redistricting commission, California voters also elected to adopt a system where all candidates run in a single "jungle" primary, with the top two finishers advancing to the general election (Washington state has a similar system). This led to several districts where two Democrats—like Berman and Sherman—or two Republicans advanced to the general election. All in all, eight of the fifty-three races featured general election opponents from the same party.

That included one race where Democrats kicked away a golden opportunity to pick up a Republican seat, illustrating the challenges posed by the new system. After redistricting, Representative Gary Miller (R) elected to run in the new, Democratic-leaning Thirty-First District, which he did not live in or represent under the old map. Redlands mayor Pete Aguilar was the Democratic challenger, but he ended up finishing third in the primary, behind Miller and state senator Bob Dutton (R). Miller prevailed in the general election, and district voters—57 percent of whom voted for President Obama—probably wondered where the Democrat was on their

House ballot. Unsurprisingly, Democrats have named this district as one of their top pickup opportunities for 2014.[7]

Going into the election, Democrats held thirty-four of the state's fifty-three seats, and after knocking off several Republican incumbents—Representatives Brian Bilbray (CA-52), Dan Lungren (CA-7), and Mary Bono Mack (CA-36)—Democrats ultimately netted four seats out of California, for a lopsided 38–15 advantage in the delegation. Republicans might be able to chip away at that advantage, as there are several Democratic seats in the state's Central Valley (stretching from Sacramento to Bakersfield) that could be competitive in future cycles, in addition to the seats that changed hands in this past election. After a remarkably stable last decade, it's likely that we'll see more competition in the Golden State going forward.

By comparison, note that the United States' other megastate, Texas, will have twenty-four Republicans and twelve Democrats in its congressional delegation (partially balancing out California for Republicans), and that only two of the state's thirty-six races produced victors who won with less than 55 percent of the vote. The Lone Star State's Republican-controlled House remap produced a flurry of court challenges—which ended up pushing back the 2012 primary several months—and it's possible that the map will be redrawn later in the decade.

## THE HEART OF THE TWO HOUSE CAUCUSES

Despite hearty challenges from Republicans Richard Tisei in Massachusetts' Sixth District (against Democratic representative John Tierney) and Andrew Roraback in Connecticut's open Fifth District (against Democrat Elizabeth Esty), the GOP was unable to win any New England seats outside of New Hampshire for the third straight cycle. Meanwhile, in the Granite State—the region's most Republican-friendly state—Democrats retook both House seats. The Republicans are again shut out of New England; Democrats now control all twenty-one of the region's House seats. Add that New England bloc to the Democrats' House advantages from the West Coast (48 of 67 seats in California, Oregon, and Washington state) and New York (21 of 27 seats), and one can account for 45 percent of the Democrats' 201 House seats.

Meanwhile, Republicans now hold 98 of 138 House seats (71 percent) in the 11 states of the old Confederacy; those 98 members from the South represent 42 percent of the 234-member Republican House caucus.

While Republicans probably will have some chances in New Hampshire and California going forward, and Democrats should be more competitive in states like Florida and Virginia (where Obama won twice) and North Carolina (where Obama won once), the bedrock of both parties' House delegations pretty clearly comes from the West Coast and Northeast (for the Democrats) and from the South (the Republicans), which perhaps not coincidentally also represent their Electoral College bases.

## CONCLUSION

For Democrats and Republicans, their most obvious targets in the 2014 election are the incumbents that they failed to defeat in 2012. Republican challengers, despite having the aid of Mitt Romney at the top of the ticket, were unable to dislodge a handful of Democratic incumbents that occupy conservative districts, including Representatives John Barrow (D-GA), Jim Matheson (D-UT), and Mike McIntyre (D-NC). Expect all three to remain targets. Republicans will also surely make a run at winning back the two lost seats in New Hampshire—the Granite State is notably frenetic in its politics and would surprise no one by swinging back to Republicans in 2014—and will also have to consider whether they want to spend the resources in California and Illinois to try to win back the many seats they lost in those states to Democrats in 2012. While both those states are Democratic, midterm electorates are typically older, whiter, and—hence—more Republican than presidential electorates.

Democrats, meanwhile, will continue to try to squeeze more seats out of California and New York, where they left opportunities on the board in 2012. The gerrymanders of midwestern states such as Michigan, Ohio, Pennsylvania, and Wisconsin might take those states largely out of play for both sides, but there will be potential opportunities in certain places across the Midwest; Democrats will certainly take another run at Representative Dan Benishek (R-MI) and newly elected representative Rodney Davis (R-IL), both of whom they nearly defeated in 2012. One test as to whether Democrats can compete in territory hostile to President Obama will be in West Virginia's open Second District, where Representative Shelley Moore Capito (R) is attempting to move up to the Senate. The Mountain State, once reliably Democratic in presidential contests (and still fairly Democratic on the state level), is now heavily Republican in presidential contests. Winning back the House will require Democrats to compete in places where President Obama did poorly.

As Sean Trende of RealClearPolitics points out elsewhere in this book, the immediate prospects for Democrats to net the seventeen seats they need to retake the House are grim, at least in 2014: Since the Civil War, no president has seen his party gain more than ten seats in a midterm election. And two-term presidents frequently see their party perform poorly in midterm elections. Presidents Dwight Eisenhower (1958), Ronald Reagan (1986), and George W. Bush (2006) all suffered significant congressional losses in their "sixth-year itch" midterm elections. So did Presidents Harry Truman (1950) and Lyndon Johnson (1966), who were only elected once but were serving their party's fifth and second consecutive term, respectively, in the White House; President Gerald Ford (1974) also presided over big losses for his party in what would have Richard Nixon's final midterm. Bill Clinton, thanks to a booming economy and Republican overreach on impeachment, actually saw his party make small gains in the House in 1998 and play to a draw in the Senate.

Democrats made some strides in 2012, but if they are to retake the House, they are going to have to overcome not only history, but also the Republicans' dual advantages of redistricting and incumbency.

## NOTES

1. "Table 1.1—Gain or Loss for President's Party: Presidential Election Years," *Pendulum Swing* (New York: Pearson Education, 2011), 9.

2. Jeffrey M. Jones, "Congress' Approval Poised to Be Lowest in an Election Year," Gallup, September 14, 2012, accessed December 3, 2012, www.gallup .com/poll/157475/congress-approval-poised-lowest-election-year.aspx.

3. "Table 1-18: House and Senate Incumbents Retired, Defeated or Reelected, 1946–2010," *Vital Statistics on American Politics 2011–2012* (Thousand Oaks, CA: CQ Press, 2011), 43–44.

4. Hendrik Hertzberg, "Mandate with Destiny," *New Yorker*, accessed December 21, 2012, www.newyorker.com/talk/comment/2012/12/03/121203taco_talk _hertzberg.

5. Jowei Chen and Jonathan Rodden, "Unintentional Gerrymandering: Political Geography and Electoral Bias in Legislatures," *Quarterly Journal of Political Science* (forthcoming), accessed December 3, 2012, www-personal.umich.edu/~jowei/florida.pdf.

6. David Nir, "Daily Kos Elections' Presidential Results by Congressional District for the 2012 and 2008 Elections," *Daily Kos Elections*, accessed December 3, 2012, www.dailykos.com/story/2012/11/19/1163009/-Daily -Kos-Elections-presidential-results-by-congressional-district-for-the-2012-2008 -elections?detail=hide.

7. Alex Isenstadt, "House Dems Waste No Time Plotting for 2014," *Politico*, accessed December 5, 2012, www.politico.com/news/stories/1112/84360 .html?hp=l2.

# 10

# FORWARD: THE FUTURE OF THE DEMOCRATIC PARTY

*Jamelle Bouie*

Every so often, political parties score decisive wins in presidential elections, and like clockwork, this leads observers and commenters to speculate about a coming "realignment" in American politics. In 2004, commentators wondered if George W. Bush and Karl Rove had ushered in a period of conservative ascendancy. Rove told reporters that his goal was to make the Republican Party "the dominant party for whatever time history gives it the chance to be."

Likewise, in 2008, pundits declared that Barack Obama had assembled a coalition that would mark the beginning of a new liberal age in American life. "A Democratic majority is emerging," wrote James Carville in his book *40 More Years: How the Democrats Will Rule the Next Generation*, "This majority will guarantee that the Democrats remain in power for the next forty years." And this year, following President Obama's successful bid for reelection, any number of pundits have wondered if the GOP was running up against its demographic doom. "The Republicans' Southern strategy, of appealing mostly to white voters, appears to have run into a demographic wall," wrote the *New York Times* in its analysis of the 2012 election.

What these declarations always miss, however, is the fact that no victory is permanent, and each win contains the seeds of its eventual defeat. The Affordable Care Act was a tremendous achievement for President Obama and the Democratic Party—the culmination of a decades-long effort to extend health care coverage to all Americans—but the cost of passing that bill was a conservative backlash, and a Republican House majority larger than the one Newt Gingrich led after the Republican Revolution sixteen years earlier.

During the 112th Congress, Republicans managed to block Obama from pursuing major objectives, and forced him to either play "small ball," or negotiate on their turf—hence the fight over the debt ceiling. But the cost of this was to destroy Congress' approval rating, bringing it to an all-time low, and give Obama the space to run a campaign against GOP obstruction.

The 2012 elections were a big victory for Obama and the Democratic Party. With his 51 percent margin in the popular vote, Barack Obama became one of four presidents in the last century to win reelection *and* break 50 percent in both elections. Far from a movement for change, his reelection campaign was a defensive action—a slow-moving, tenacious attempt to defend his accomplishments, and move the political winds in his direction.

And despite the similarities of the combatants—Harvard-educated lawyers with technocratic streaks—it was also an ideological battle of the kind not usually seen in American politics. As Obama put it throughout the campaign, both he and former Massachusetts governor Mitt Romney held "fundamentally different" views of where the country should go. For Romney, America's future looked much like its past—a smaller government with fewer obligations would allow business to flourish and succeed. Traditional social values—around marriage and abortion—would encourage stable families and prosperous communities.

Obama didn't offer a break from the past so much as a promise to protect government's "commitments" and "investments"—to social insurance, to programs for poor and middle-class families, to a broader federal role in the economy. But this status quo orientation shouldn't obscure the extent to which Obama was also promising to implement a far reaching agenda that would transform our health care system (the Affordable Care Act), financial system (Dodd-Frank), and the way we produce energy (the stimulus).

This "fundamental" divide extended itself to the coalitions of both candidates. If Mitt Romney's campaign sought to mobilize the mass of white America—he won 59 percent of the white vote overall—Barack Obama's was an attempt to shift the composition of the electorate to something a little browner, and a little less traditional. He was successful.

African Americans were 13 percent of the electorate (he won 93 percent of them), Asian Americans were 3 percent of the electorate (he won them, 73 percent to 26 percent), women were 53 percent of the electorate (he won them, 55 percent to 44 percent), and Latinos—long considered the "sleeping giant" of American politics—were 10 percent of the electorate. They went for Obama, 71 percent to 27 percent.

None of this is to say that there's *actually* been a realignment, or to say that Obama has shifted the dynamics of American politics. He hasn't—the pendulum will swing again, it's simply a question of "when." In the meantime, we have entered an unfamiliar world, where Democrats seem to have the upper hand, or at least, are riding a whole host of trends, policies, and ideas that put them in a strong position for the near term.

Or, to put this in another form, now that Obama has won the election and—temporarily, at least—the fight over the role and direction of government, what comes next for his administration, and what comes next for the Democratic Party that will carry his legacy forward in four years?

## WHAT DOES THE FUTURE LOOK LIKE?
## A NEW (OLD) COALITION

We can't talk about the future of the Democratic Party without first looking at the particulars of the electoral coalition that will—in all likelihood—sustain it for the next twenty years. Ten years ago, in their book *The Emerging Democratic Majority*, demographers John Judis and Ruy Teixeira described it as such: A "strengthening alliance between minorities, working and single women, the college educated, and skilled professionals." This coalition has existed in some form since the 1972 election, but—until recently—has not been large enough to sustain the Democratic Party without considerable support from working and middle-class whites—the party's traditional base.

In 2004, one could see the outlines of a majority coalition—John Kerry outperformed the fundamentals of that election year, and came close to unseating George W. Bush, but fell short. It wasn't until 2008 that the emerging majority came into its own, elevating Barack Obama to the Democratic nomination for president, and giving him a landslide victory over John McCain.

Of course, those were unusual times. Bush's long, controversial presidency was coming to a close, and Democrats were eager to have their shot at governing the country. A last-minute financial collapse—and a blundered response by McCain—nearly ensured that Obama would cruise to victory. Unlike 2008, 2012 was a more normal election year, and a test of whether this "new coalition" could stand in the face of economic headwinds and an energized opposition.

And it did.

Obama's margin among blacks is the reason he scored consecutive victories in Virginia and Ohio—the former a once-traditionally Republican state and the latter one that has long had a slight GOP lean. His margin among women moved Iowa and New Hampshire from toss-ups to solid wins. And his margin among Latinos pushed Colorado, Florida, and Nevada out of the reach of former Massachusetts governor Mitt Romney.

This coalition will only continue to gain strength as the economy recovers and current population trends continue. Latino immigrants are flocking to states like Georgia, Florida, and North Carolina, college-educated workers are either moving to or staying in Virginia, North Carolina, and Colorado, and two generations after the Great Migration brought millions of African Americans to the nation's industrial centers, their descendants are moving back to the South in search of education, housing, and history.

The Census Bureau projects a swelling of the nation's nonwhite population over the next twenty years. By 2025, more than 66 million Americans—or nearly a fifth of the population—will be of Hispanic descent—a quarter increase from 2010. The black community will grow just enough so that African Americans will come in at 12 percent of the population—which is where they stand now—and the Asian American community will grow to more than 21 million people, or 7 percent of the population.

Unless something dramatic happens—like these people moving inwards to Wyoming and Missouri—odds are good that the bulk of this population growth will happen where we expect: the Southeast and the Southwest (the Sun Belt), otherwise known as the states where Democrats have made their greatest inroads.

If you project the current electoral map forward, it looks great for Democrats: Virginia and North Carolina, for instance, become reliable blue states. Already, they fall into the "purple" column, with Virginia leaning slightly to Democrats and North Carolina leaning slightly to Republicans. Obama won the former by a modest margin in 2008 and 2012, while he lost ground in the latter, moving from a slight win to a small loss. But if the nonwhite share of the population continues to grow in both states, it's a sure bet that—eventually—both will become states that lean reliably Democratic.

The same is true in Georgia. Right now, the state is solidly Republican and its share of the Electoral College vote has steadily grown, making it the Republican equivalent of Michigan—a must-have state. But like its neighbors in the upper South, demographic change has improved Democratic chances in the state, and brought them closer and closer to striking distance. John Kerry's paltry 41.3 percent of the vote in 2004 became Barack Obama's 46.9 percent in 2008 and 45.5 percent in 2012. And neither Mitt Romney nor John McCain was able to replicate George W.

Bush's 57 percent share in 2004, or 54 percent share in 2000. It's not at all hard to see Georgia become a state where Democrats can compete, and possibly win.

You can also add Texas and Arizona to the list. Texas has always had a large Latino population, but it's only in recent years that the state has become majority-minority. This hasn't stopped Republicans from making earnest attempts gain Latino votes. GOP groups like Hispanic Republicans of Texas—led by George P. Bush, son of former Florida governor Jeb Bush—have successfully elected Latino Republicans to Congress, the Texas Supreme Court, and the state's House of Representatives. Nevertheless, Latinos in the state have only grown more Democratic as time has gone on. In 2004, George W. Bush won nearly half of Texas Latinos, 49 percent to 50 percent. Just four years later, Obama would win 63 percent.

And in Arizona, the Latino population is large, Democratic, and growing. For each statewide election, including the most recent Senate race, Democrats get closer and closer to winning. And some election analysts believe that—if native son John McCain weren't on the ticket—Obama would have won the state in 2008.

There are a few important caveats to all of this.

First, it presumes that Republicans won't have been able to forge a majority coalition of their own, or make gains in states that are traditionally Democratic. Remember, for at least the next thirty years, the American electorate will remain majority white. And in mostly white, working-class states like Wisconsin, Michigan, Pennsylvania, and Ohio, Republicans have made steady gains. It's possible that Republicans will begin to win those states at the same time that Democrats make traditionally GOP states more competitive, thus resulting in something that looks like a stalemate, where Democrats stand on slightly higher ground.

Second, every action is met with a reaction. When one considers that political parties, above all, want to win, odds are good that Republicans will learn how to tailor their message and ideas to the concerns of their base—middle-class whites—and the voters they'll need to convince—nonwhites and immigrants. Indeed, integration and assimilation among immigrants will eventually create a group of voters who identify with the white mainstream, and are more amenable to conservative ideas on the size and scope of government.

And finally, it doesn't account for possible fissures and fractions in the Democratic coalition itself. It goes without saying that different groups want different action out of the government, and while President Obama has been able to reconcile some of these competing pressures, they will arise in future presidential contests. These fissures have real electoral implications; if progressive Democrats feel that their best path toward influence is to stand against more centrist Democrats—à la the Tea Party in 2010—then it could jeopardize the party's standing in legislative races around the country. Which is to say that if the future of the Democratic Party contains a strong and competitive majority, then it also includes growing fights over the direction of the party, and its priorities.

## FRACTURES IN PARADISE: WHAT MIGHT THOSE FISSURES LOOK LIKE?

It's worth going back to the aftermath of the 2004 election, when Democrats—much like Republicans today—were trying to chart a path forward for their party. The "netroots"—a growing group of online-based activists, galvanized by the Iraq War, and represented in the Democratic primary by former Vermont governor Howard Dean—urged a strategy of base building, rooted in progressive policy. The idea was straightforward: Democrats were losing because they refused to distinguish themselves from the other party, or in the words of Barry Goldwater, voters didn't want an echo, they wanted a choice.

The 2012 outcome offered a vindication, of sorts, for this view. Beginning with his speech in Osawatomie, Kansas in January, and continuing throughout the year, Barack Obama ran a surprisingly populist campaign for president, defending the traditional investments of the federal government in education, research, economic development, and the social safety net, while pushing for higher taxes on the rich—a formerly taboo subject for Democrats (see "tax and spend liberal" as an insult), which became the most popular of Obama's pitch to voters.

Given what we know about the fundamentals of this election—political scientists predicted a slight Obama win as early as February—it's hard to draw a causal relationship between the president's rhetoric and his reelection victory. But in terms of the election narrative, it was understood—by all sides—that Obama had a mandate of sorts for raising taxes on the highest earning Americans. Or, as he told reporters during a press conference following the election, "I didn't get reelected just to bask in reelection."

Again, this is something progressives count as a victory—lawmakers are arguing over which taxes to raise, and not which programs to cut.

But it wasn't just the presidential election that—according to liberals—has validated their approach to politics. In the Ohio Senate race, progressive stalwart Sherrod Brown won reelection—against a torrent of outside money—on an unabashed message of economic aid for working class Ohioans, and higher taxes on the rich. In Massachusetts, liberal icon Elizabeth Warren won a tough race against the popular Scott Brown, a moderate Republican who won election in 2010 as part of the backlash against health care reform. In Montana, incumbent Democrat Jon Tester prevailed over challenger Denny Rehberg with a promise to raise taxes on the rich and protect entitlements for "ordinary Americans," and in Wisconsin, a left-wing House member—Tammy Baldwin—prevailed over former governor Tommy Thompson to become the first openly gay member of the Senate.

What unites each race is the explicit commitment to progressive rhetoric—an approach that would have been unusual in years past. As Adam Green, head of the Progressive Change Campaign Committee, said in an interview with *The Atlantic*, "When Democrats stand up boldly on economic issues, even conservative voters will vote for them."

The more centrist wing of the Democratic Party, on the other hand, has seen its numbers dwindle since 2008. The "Blue Dog" caucus in the House, for example, had fifty-four members in the 111th Congress. When the new Congress meets in January, it will have fourteen. Bill Clinton played a prominent role in the presidential campaign, but he merely offered a version of Obama's message—a centrist veneer, of sorts. And the policies favored by centrist Democrats—deficit reduction, tax reform, and charter-school based education reform—have little traction with progressives. Indeed, if Obama accepts benefit cuts to Social Security, Medicare, or Medicaid as part of a "grand bargain" on debt reduction—a bargain favored by moderate Democrats—he'll almost certainly face a revolt from left.

If Obama had lost reelection, then the centrists would have cause to argue that the progressive message is an electoral loser. For now, they'll have to wait until 2016, when the party begins to search for Obama's successor. Then, it's almost certain that the tensions between both sides will flare into an outright battle. Even a candidate like Hillary Clinton—widely seen as the "next in line"—could prove divisive; her 2008 candidacy aroused liberal discontent, and played a large part in Obama's rise. The same goes for politicians like New York governor Andrew Cuomo, whose liberal-friendly credentials on social issues—he pushed same-sex marriage through the state's legislature—are balanced against his tight connection to Wall Street and his actions in office, including moves against public employee unions.

These battles will play out across a range of issues. On climate change, ambitious liberals are pitted against more conservative Democrats from coal-producing areas of the country, which—in the case of Ohio and Pennsylvania—are also areas key to success in presidential elections.

On immigration, there's a split between activists—who seek a less punitive enforcement regime, and a path to citizenship for undocumented immigrants—and the politicians who represent low-wage workers and others who feel threatened by mass immigration.

On health care, liberals want to expand the government's role beyond the Affordable Care Act, with a public option and experiments in single-payer on the state level, while moderates and centrists seek to preserve more elements of the status quo, and trim benefits in Medicare and its assorted programs. And on education, liberals who seek to strengthen traditional public education—and preserve a place for teachers' unions—are pitted against centrists who want to bring market mechanisms to bear on education, with charter schools, weaker unions, and programs like "Race to the Top."

These differences extend beyond bread and butter issues. Over the last two years, there's been growing progressive discontent with Obama's foreign policy, its continuation of the war in Afghanistan, its use of continuous drone strikes in Pakistan, its whistleblower prosecutions, its embrace of targeted assassinations, and its continued support for high defense spending. Much in the same way that Barack Obama ran for president in 2008 as a defender of civil liberties—and someone who could reverse the legacy of George W. Bush—there will be room for a Democratic presidential candidate to run *against* Obama's continuation of Bush-era national security policy.

On top of all of this, there are the issues that have yet to enter the national consciousness, but are bubbling beneath the surface. In 2012, Internet activists rallied against the Stop Online Piracy Act (SOPA), which would attempt to combat online copyright infringement by allowing people and companies to sue websites that distributed such content, or directed users to potential distributors. Activists on the left and right attacked it—and a similar bill, the Protect IP Act—as an intolerable infringement on Internet freedom, and while the Obama administration promised to veto either bill, it remains true that the chief backers of both measures—the movie and music industries—are major donors to the Democratic Party. Four or eight years from now, this could be the basis for another split between liberals and centrists.

## CONCLUSION

It should be said that any number of things could happen over the next decade that would shift the position of either party and dramatically change the electoral landscape. Still, there are a *few things* we can predict about the next few years of American politics.

First, with the promise of economic fairness for its more vulnerable members—and social equality for the more materially secure—the Democratic Party mixed a potent electoral cocktail that will help it win for the foreseeable future. Like the Reagan coalition of evangelicals, working-class whites, and upper-income voters, this nationally competitive coalition of minorities, young people, women, and professionals is ascendant. The immediate effect of this ascendancy is to shake up the electoral map. States like Virginia, North Carolina, Georgia, Arizona—and possibly Texas—will become more Democratic and more competitive, thus depriving the GOP of a key path toward national victory. At the same time, Republicans are likely to expand their gains in the Midwest, thus compensating for their diminished position in the Southwest and parts of the Southeast.

Second, this coalition—while stable—isn't unified, and there are real tensions within it. With Obama's reelection, liberals see themselves as having vindicated an approach to politics that emphasizes progressive policy and a less cooperative message. They remain opposed to the goals of Democratic centrists—namely entitlement cuts and deficit reduction—and are ready to fight against President Obama should he go down that path. Indeed, a much larger battle over the goals of the Democratic Party, between liberals and centrists, will almost certainly occur during 2016, as Democrats look forward to find a successor to President Obama.

And finally, there are a whole host of issues where the Democratic Party lacks a consensus, and in the next decade, different factions will hash out their differences and establish new battle lines.

In the end, predicting the future, even for the short term, is difficult. In 1956, no one could predict that in seven years the president of the United States would be killed by an assassin's bullet. In 1968, few people imagined that Richard Nixon would end his political career under a cloud of scandal and abuse. And in 1996, no one thought that the United States would—just seven years later—find itself embroiled in two wars, and fighting a "global war on terror."

Which is to say that for as much as we can know about the present, or the even the overall short term, the longer term is incredibly difficult to anticipate. Where the Democratic Party goes, and what it becomes is—for anything but the near future—an open question.

# 11

# A TIME FOR CHOOSING

## The Future of the Republican Party

### Robert Costa

For much of the year, Mitt Romney and his advisers spoke about the presidential campaign as a referendum on President Barack Obama's economic record. "Our view is that this is a very simple election," a senior Romney strategist told *U.S. News & World Report* in June. "It's a referendum on Obama's handling of the economy."[1] As a Harvard Business School graduate and a former private-equity executive at Bain Capital, Romney was comfortable making a numbers-driven case against the president. Initially, he wasn't looking to lead a movement; he aspired to be an even-tempered alternative to a likable Democratic incumbent. "Don't forget, [Obama] has been president for three and a half years, and talk is cheap," Romney told a Cincinnati crowd in the early summer, at the peak of his push to frame the race as a clinical review. "If you want to see the results of his economic policy, look around Ohio, look around the country."[2]

"The conventional wisdom about this presidential election . . . is that it represented a competition between two competing paradigms," says Nate Silver, the *New York Times* election analyst. "Mitt Romney, this theory held, would seek to make the election a referendum on President Obama's performance—hoping that voters' dissatisfaction with the direction of the country in general, and the economy in particular, would lead them to vote him out of office, almost regardless of what the alternative was."[3] Romney's approach was partly a product of his experience in the Republican presidential primaries, where he outpaced conservative crusaders such as former Speaker Newt Gingrich, former Pennsylvania senator Rick Santorum, and

Tea Party star Representative Michele Bachmann of Minnesota. During those contests, his reputation as a competent manager was critical, and his aides predicted that he could sweep into office with a similar general election campaign.

That strategy changed in August when Romney tapped Representative Paul Ryan of Wisconsin, the House Budget Committee chairman, to be the Republican Party's vice presidential nominee. Quite suddenly, the Romney campaign's message shifted from a near-constant focus on economic matters to a broader and fiercer debate about a choice between "two futures," as Ryan often described it in his speeches. "The election is now a choice, not a referendum; a contest between two clearly and sharply different policy visions and views on the role of government," wrote Ben Smith, the editor of BuzzFeed, soon after the Ryan pick.[4] David Frum, a former speechwriter for President George W. Bush, agreed, noting that with one decision, Romney put conservatism on the ballot.[5] No longer was the election about the politics of economic data; it was about the size and scope of government.

Many conservative leaders publicly applauded the selection, because Ryan is a rising star. "It was foremost a shrewd acknowledgment on Mr. Romney's part that his path to the White House is going to take more than pointing out the obvious," wrote Kim Strassel in the *Wall Street Journal*.[6] But privately, the reaction was far more mixed. Romney had abruptly injected a full dose of conservative ideology into a campaign that had been studiously avoiding ideology. In the political press, there were whispers about whether Romney could pull it off. "American politics is littered with bold and improbable decisions that don't work out very well," wrote Peter Beinart in the *Daily Beast*. "With this one, the chances of failure look pretty good. Mitt Romney has now tied his presidential fortunes to Paul Ryan's budget plan. He may say he doesn't endorse all the plan's specifics, but as a matter of political reality, he already has."[7] Soon after, the questions began to mount: With Ryan at his side, would Romney be able to both excite the base and woo the suburban moderates? Would he be able to balance his appeal as a northeastern businessman with Ryan's fiscal bravado? At first blush, the juxtaposition of an experienced former governor with a young and dynamic legislator made for compelling political theater, but its political viability was a variable that weighed upon Romney's advisers.

Months later, it's evident that Romney struggled to make the Ryan pick an election-defining moment. Romney and Ryan enjoyed a personal rapport, but they rarely managed to present a coherent message about what they represented. At times, both candidates were quite vocal about being a "choice" ticket, but in other instances, they ducked ideology and reverted back to Romney's earlier, simpler theme about an economic "referendum." Less than three weeks after the Ryan selection, Romney barely touched upon conservative ideology in his acceptance speech at the Republican convention. In short, the campaign never found its political footing. On the stump, Romney and Ryan largely avoided making major blunders, but they had difficulties communicating a vision. Whereas Obama ran a full-throated and consistent campaign for expanding the federal government, Romney unsuccessfully strove to be simultaneously an ideological conservative to his base and a centrist to undecided voters.

Ryan's selection and its influence on the campaign remains a prism for interpreting Romney's defeat and thinking about the GOP's future. At the time of the pick, it was an understandable maneuver to balance the ticket, but later, it became indicative of an uneasy strategy. The pair hoped to build a coalition among the GOP's various wings, but, ultimately, they failed to weave a thread through those groups. The challenge for the Republican Party in the second Obama term is figuring out how to succeed where Romney and Ryan could not. How does the party increase its ranks and raise its poll numbers while sustaining its core principles? In making its case to the country, does it need to focus more on the Obama record and less on ideology? Or does it need to explain, more coherently and in greater detail, the ideological "choice," the core difference between present-day Democrats and Republicans? Can the party eventually find the equilibrium that Romney and Ryan sought?

As Republicans grapple with these questions and plot a renewal, they will have to make decisions in three distinct areas: policy, demographics, and leadership. When Romney picked Ryan, he looked out at the field of veep contenders and tried to pick the person who could attract the most support. According to Romney's advisers, those three areas were also top considerations. Indeed, Romney's vice presidential calculus, calibrating and strategizing about how best to move forward, is akin to what the Republican Party will be doing in the two years before the 2014 midterms.

It is again, as Ronald Reagan said in 1964, a time for choosing for the party and the conservative movement. The coming debates within the party about its platform, its constituencies, and its leading figures, both in Washington and in the states, will say much about its potential success. The debates will sometimes be heated, but they are critical, since the takeaway from the Romney-Ryan experience is that the party is in flux. It wants to blend its Tea Party vigor (represented by the Ryan pick) with more traditional values (represented by the Romney nomination), but it is unsure of how to do this.


## THE POLICY WARS

Throughout the 2012 general election campaign, Ryan frequently spoke about the looming fiscal crisis. He proclaimed the values of the budget he had authored in the lower chamber as evidence of Republican seriousness about the larger spending issues of our time. Even in the swing state of Florida, which is home to millions of retirees, Ryan campaigned hard on the theme of reforming Medicaid and Medicare through policies, including what he calls "premium support," that would encourage more individual control of health-care spending. Part of the larger Romney-Ryan ambition was to lead a legislative charge to overhaul these federal programs, and Romney told his advisers that he admired Ryan's ability to boldly take on the biggest and often most politically complicated problems. But although conservative intellectuals celebrated the tenaciousness of Romney and Ryan on entitlement reform, many retirees were less appreciative. When Ryan spoke to the AARP in late September, he was booed when he talked about tackling the entitlement issue. On Election Day, Romney and Ryan lost Florida after months of leading the president in Florida polls.

The Romney-Ryan entitlement endeavor was a key part of the campaign's policy strategy, which looked to the intellectual and legislative leadership of Ryan and his allies in the House as inspiration for the party at large. On other issues, such as foreign policy and taxes, Romney and Ryan held traditional Republican positions (a strong, well-funded military; lowering tax rates), but the campaign's platform generally mirrored the move by House Republicans in 2011–2012 to shift the party to the right. Now, as Ryan returns to the chairmanship of the Budget Committee, he will be in a position to continue the House-driven molding of national Republican policy, but the stakes and the composition of the debate have changed. The coming policy wars are likely to be less about how Ryan is positioning the party to take on entitlements and more about whether the party even wants to lead its policy agenda with the issue, and whether on other issues, such as taxes and foreign policy, we will begin to see a drift back toward the center.

"The test will be whether Mr. Ryan . . . can make the transition from House budget philosopher to governing heavyweight who can help negotiate a bipartisan deal and sell it to his colleagues," wrote Jennifer Steinhauer, a *New York Times* reporter, in late November.[8] But Ryan will not be the only force in the debate about the direction of policy. As an influential congressman fresh off the GOP ticket, he'll be a player, but the party is no longer subject to the leadership of the presidential candidate. For instance, House Speaker John Boehner, who has led the Republican conference since 2007, said in a speech after the election that he is willing to make concessions on tax revenue. This is evidence of an almost immediate change in the policy talks within the party. Romney and Ryan were wary of ever discussing a Republican agreement about revenue increases, but Boehner interpreted the election as a clue to the future. "That is the will of the people, and we answer to them," Boehner said at a Capitol news conference. "For purposes of forging a bipartisan agreement that begins to solve the problem, we're willing to accept new revenue, under the right conditions."[9]

"Not since the 1970s have Republicans been so weak on the tax issue," says David Weigel, a *Slate* writer. "Like Romney said, in his way, they're victims of their own success. They've lowered rates to the extent that voters don't fret about them. So they're no longer talking about the Dec. 31 deadline for the tax rates as a Masada, a full-bore defense of the old rates. They're talking about what they can get if they accede to the Democrats."[10] The famous tax "pledge" many Republican lawmakers have made, working with anti-tax activist Grover Norquist, now seems to be less of an issue. Before the election, breaking the Norquist pledge could be a perilous political move. Now, in the post-Romney era, many Republicans see moving toward more revenue options as living within the new political reality. They are quickly realizing, as Lloyd Grove wrote in the *Daily Beast*, that the "grubby business of entitlement reform,"[11] which they had hoped would be the central project of 2013, would have to be temporarily shelved as they look to protect the tax rates established a decade ago.

Beyond the initial policy battles over tax rates and revenue, Republicans will also have to face daunting questions on a variety of other fronts. Social conservatism remains an important part of the national Republican platform, but some leading conservatives are asking whether the GOP approach to gay marriage, abortion, and drugs fits the times. "The speed with which civil unions and same-sex marriage have become debatable topics and even mainstream policies is astonishing," wrote George F. Will in the *Washington Post* after the Romney defeat. "As is conservatives' failure to recognize this: They need not endorse such policies, but neither need they despise those, such as young people, who favor them."[12] The GOP Senate candidacies of Todd Akin in Missouri and Richard Mourdock in Indiana, which were both seriously hurt by the candidates' comments about rape, did not help the Romney-Ryan cause, and they damaged the Republican objective of using social issues, especially family values and life issues, to win over select groups of undecided voters. Look for the debate about social conservatism in the coming months and years to be just as volatile and unpredictable as the debate over tax revenues. Republicans are not likely to abandon their conservative positions on the key social issues, just as they won't abandon their wish for lower tax rates, but there will be ample debate in the halls of Congress and in statehouses about how best to hold onto Republican principles while appealing to the Obama generation.

Immigration, too, will find itself back in the center of the Republican debates. "For the party in general, however, the problem is hardly structural. It requires but a single policy change: border fence plus amnesty," argues Charles Krauthammer in the *Washington Post*. "Yes, amnesty. Use the word. Shock and awe—full legal normalization (just short of citizenship) in return for full border enforcement."[13] The position on the opposite side of the argument, against amnesty, is just as robust as Krauthammer's. "Having suffered not one but several humiliating defeats on Tuesday, Republicans are in danger of embracing 'comprehensive' immigration reform—which is to say, amnesty—out of panic," wrote the editors of *National Review*, a few days after Krauthammer's column was published. "The GOP does need to do better among Hispanics and other voters, but this is not the way to achieve that—and, more important, it is bad policy."[14]

On foreign policy, the path ahead is murkier, especially because Romney's defeat is not blamed on his positions, but rather on his critique of the Obama administration's handling of foreign crises, especially the attack on American diplomatic officials in Libya. There is discussion among pundits about whether Republicans need to move closer to Ron Paul, the libertarian Texas congressman and presidential candidate. Speaking on Fox News after the election, Bill Kristol, the *Weekly Standard* editor and a supporter of President George W. Bush's foreign policy, predicted that future Republican leaders would pay greater attention to the Ron Paul wing of the party. "I'm not a fan of Ron Paul," Kristol said. "But I do think, analytically, that Rand Paul [Republican senator from Kentucky and Ron Paul's son] could be a formidable presence in the Republican Party over the next three or four years."[15]

But it will be domestic policy where the party will see the greatest tension. Overall, there will undoubtedly be tensions. While the Ron Paul faction is ascending on foreign policy, the GOP establishment in Congress and in the party ranks remains mostly committed to the Reagan approach of fostering American strength in the world and a strong military. To at least some extent, this will be challenged. And on social issues, the party doesn't seem ready, for the moment, to jettison its traditional positions on marriage and abortion. But these positions will also be questioned. As conservative intellectual Reihan Salam said in a speech at the American Enterprise Institute in mid-November, the party desperately wants to re-formulate its methods. "[That] doesn't entail jettisoning social conservatism and cultural populism, but rather reframing them in the interests of mak-ing them relevant to the lived experience of middle America," he said.[16] Ramesh Ponnuru, a *National Review* editor, concurs. "The Iraq War, the financial crisis, and other issues specific to the late Bush years obviously did play a huge role" in the Republican defeats in 2006 and 2008, he writes. "But it's also true that Republicans weren't even arguing that they had a domestic agenda that would yield any direct benefits for most voters, and that has to have hurt them."[17] The same was true in 2012.

## THE DEMOGRAPHIC DEBACLE

The Republicans' demographic problem, exposed by the 2012 exit polls, is hardly a surprise to party grandees. "The numbers tell a clear story; the demographics of America are changing in a way that is deadly for the Re-publican Party as it exists today. A GOP ice age is on the way," wrote Mike Murphy, a longtime Republican consultant, in 2009.[18] Though policy de-bates will form the center of the Republican transition from the Romney campaign to the future, finding a way to reconcile the party's policies with the country's changing demographics will be another challenge. There is a growing concern within the party that the older white voters who helped elect Reagan, George H. W. Bush, and George W. Bush to the White House over the past three decades can no longer form an electoral majority, so the party must find a way to reach out to minority voters, young voters, and other Americans who have not traditionally identified themselves as conservatives or Republicans.

According to NBC News, party leaders are citing demographics as the reason for Romney's defeat in behind-the-scenes conversations with donors and strategists. "This RNC report of exit-poll data, which NBC News has obtained and which RNC Chair Reince Priebus presented to GOP senators on Wednesday, states that 'demographic change' in the United States 'is real,'" reported NBC's Mark Murray. "It notes that the white share of the electorate has declined from 81 percent in 2000 to 72 percent in 2008. And it points out that '3 in 10 voters will be minorities in 2016.'"[19] But most politicos do not think this challenge is insurmountable. "While demographic and population trends are clearly working against Republicans—Texas as a swing state in 2020, anyone?—the party is not that far, electorally speaking, from creating a credible path back to 270 electoral votes," says the *Washington Post*'s Chris Cillizza. "Find a way to make the industrial Midwest—Ohio, Iowa, Wisconsin and even Pennsylvania—competitive again and the map suddenly doesn't look so bad for the GOP."[20]

That said, Hispanics are going to see a great deal of outreach from Republicans in the next year, and the immigration-policy debate will be part of that effort. Republicans are very worried that states such as Florida and Texas, which have large blocs of Hispanic voters, may be lost to the party permanently unless a fresh message can be offered. Still, "outreach is not done in a single awkward lunge," says Michael Gerson, a former Bush speechwriter. "It will involve more than endorsing comprehensive immigration legislation, though that is necessary. Hispanic voters have a series of concerns typical of a poorer but economically mobile community: working schools, college access, health care, a working safety net."[21] The same strategy is also likely to apply to Roman Catholic voters. This group, like Hispanics, gave the president strong support, and Republicans are eager to bring them back into the GOP fold. Catholics represent "more than a quarter of the electorate," according to CNN, and have backed Obama for two straight cycles.[22]

But while Republican leaders feel the demographic problem keenly, they also understand that demographics alone can't take all the blame for Romney's loss. The shift away from the GOP among certain groups is seen as a symptom of the larger policy and leadership problems in the party. "It's clear that with our losses in the presidential race and a number of key Senate races, we have a period of reflection and recalibration ahead for the Republican Party," said Senator John Cornyn of Texas, the outgoing chairman of the National Republican Senatorial Committee, in a post-election statement. "While some will want to blame one wing of the party over the other, the reality is candidates from all corners of our GOP lost. Clearly we have work to do in the weeks and months ahead."[23] Putting a Hispanic or another minority politician on the ticket next time, adds Ross Douthat of the *New York Times*, won't solve anything unless Republicans understand the political and economic reasons for the Romney defeat. "Both shifts, demographic and economic, must be addressed if Republicans are to find a way back to the majority," he says. "But the temptation for the party's elites will be to fasten on the demographic explanation, because playing identity politics seems far less painful than overhauling the Republican economic message."[24]

Nonetheless, something must be done to address the Republicans' demographic debacle. Romney won white evangelical voters in strong numbers, and he won churchgoing Catholics easily, too. But growing numbers of secular, younger, and minority voters are staying away from the GOP. "A version of his coalition in Virginia—a combination of minorities, women and younger adults—also helped Mr. Obama win Colorado, Nevada [and] Florida," reports Michael Shear of the *New York Times*.[25] Addressing demographics will be partly a matter of policy, partly a matter of politics. Republicans were out-campaigned by the Obama team when it came to organizing among African Americans, Hispanics, and Asian Americans. Finding a way to win over these voters will take time, but it will almost certainly be a major part of the Republican rehabilitation between now and the next presidential campaign. The party sees that Romney's model was not sufficient this time, and will be even less so four years from now.

## THE LEADERSHIP VACUUM

Yet before the horse race for the 2016 Republican presidential nomination begins in earnest around late 2014, the party will have to fill the leadership vacuum left by the Romney defeat. Who will step up and become a new national leader for a party in the wilderness? That is a critical question as the party moves forward. The early favorites for the 2016 GOP nomination, such as Florida senator Marco Rubio and New Jersey governor Chris Christie, will continue to be described as leading figures. Rubio is considered to be a potential point person on immigration reform, and many Republicans admire Christie as a moderate and a tough executive. But beyond the pull of certain personalities, the real leadership debate will be between the Tea Party wing of the party and the more centrist leadership on Capitol Hill. On policy and on demographics, as previously discussed, Republicans are adjusting to the election by changing their tone and approach. The same can be said for how Republicans on Capitol Hill are adjusting in terms of leadership. Though the top tier of Republican House and Senate leaders remains unchanged, there are signs that the party is having internal debates about the tone and style of its leadership.

Speaker Boehner, House Majority Leader Eric Cantor, and House Whip Kevin McCarthy all kept their spots on the Republican leadership team following the election, but the House GOP's fourth leadership spot—conference chairman—saw a fight for the party's future. Representative Cathy McMorris Rodgers of Washington and Representative Tom Price of Georgia ran against each other for the position and, although the vote tally has not been made public, McMorris Rodgers won. Price, a former chairman of the conservative Republican Study Committee, had the support of Ryan and other Tea Party Republicans but was unable to beat McMorris Rodgers, a Boehner ally and one of the House GOP's leading women. "Price, for instance, tied for most conservative House member . . . while McMorris Rodgers ranked 117," according to *National Journal*'s 2011 ratings.[26] The early message was that House Republicans did not want to present an all-male leadership team to the country mere days after losing among women. It was also a sign that though Ryan and his conservative allies remain the driving force on public policy, they don't hold total control.

On the other side of the Capitol, Senator-Elect Ted Cruz of Texas, a Hispanic Republican and Tea Party favorite, was named vice chairman of the National Republican Senatorial Committee, and Senator Rob Portman of Ohio, an even-tempered Republican who is popular with policy wonks and donors, was also named vice chairman. Senator Jerry Moran of Kansas, a low-key midwesterner, was elected NRSC chairman. Senator Mitch McConnell of Kentucky, a soft-spoken conservative, kept his position as minority leader, even though Republicans had a net loss of two Senate seats in 2012. Moran, Cruz, and Portman will be major players in the coming year as the GOP tries to win back seats in the 2014 cycle and build toward a potential majority. Several Democratic senators will be up for reelection in 2014, and Republicans are already strategizing about how to win back the upper chamber. These three new members of the Senate leadership will be parts of the puzzle, but look for Ryan, Rubio, and other legislators who are not part of the official leadership structure to continue to influence the party's direction from various media and other platforms.

For the moment, there is no obvious party leader, either in the presidential discussion or inside the Beltway. "The party finds itself in the unenviable position of having to reinvent itself—something most top GOP strategists and lawmakers agree needs to be done—without an obvious standard-bearer to carry that message on a daily basis," says Aaron Blake in the *Washington Post*. "That could be less than ideal for a party in need of cohesion, leadership and a steady hand."[27] At a GOP post-election gubernatorial retreat in Las Vegas, former Republican National Committee chairman Haley Barbour said that the party should take its time in settling on a new spokesman post-Romney. He said there are too many potential stars to rush to judgment about the future of the party. "We've got to give our political organization a very serious proctology exam," Barbour said. "We need to look everywhere."[28]


## CONCLUSION

When Mitt Romney won the nomination, he first tried to run his campaign as a referendum on Obama. Then, when he began to slide in the national polls, he decided to switch to what pundits described as a "choice" campaign, which put ideology and bold ideas on the ballot, and not just an argument about a sagging economy and failed steward-ship in the Oval Office. Paul Ryan, as the vice presidential pick, was the keystone to that strategy. In some ways, Romney did manage to elevate the discussion on entitlements, but he was not able to successfully build a national majority with his policies or his appeals to various demographic groups. In the wake of Romney's defeat, the party is beginning to review his decisions and outlook and to ask itself questions about where to go on those three issues—policy, demographics, and leadership. As the 2012 political season closes, the answers are unclear, but the debate has begun. Already there are brewing discussions in Congress and in the states about who should lead, what the party should run on, and how it will survive in a changing electoral landscape. These are serious questions, and the post-Romney period will be "a time for choosing" about how the party needs to evolve.

When Romney tapped Ryan, he had a certain rationale: He wanted to frame the election as an ideological choice. He knew he needed to be more than an alternative to a Democratic incumbent who wasn't shy about his desire to expand the federal government. Romney lost, but the Repub-lican Party will need to address considerations akin to the ones Romney faced in the course of his veep search. The party needs new faces and new ideas, but deciding which faces, and which ideas, will be complicated. As Obama is inaugurated and pushes his second-term agenda, Republicans will need to do more than elevate one politician or another into the void. Before they choose their next nominee, Republicans have to decide, once again, who they are.

# NOTES

1. Kenneth T. Walsh, "Team Romney: Election a Referendum on The Economy," *U.S. News & World Report*, accessed December 20, 2012, www.usnews.com/news/blogs/Ken-Walshs-Washington/2012/06/15/team-romney-election-a-referendum-on-the-economy.

2. Christina Bellatoni and Terence Burlij, "Romney Bus Tour Begins after Day of Economic Debate," PBS.org, June 15, 2012.

3. Nate Silver, "Referendum or Choice, Which Candidate Will Show Fighting Spirit?," *New York Times*, October 22, 2012.

4. Ben Smith, "Ryan Pick Means a New Campaign for Romney," BuzzFeed, August 10, 2012.

5. David Frum, "Why Ryan?," *Daily Beast*, August 11, 2012, www.thedailybeast.com/articles/2012/08/11/paul-ryan.html.

6. Kimberly A. Strassel, "Why Romney Chose Ryan," *Wall Street Journal*, August 14, 2012.

7. Peter Beinart, "Mitt Romney's Pick of Paul Ryan: Bold Doesn't Always Work," *Daily Beast*, August 13, 2012.

8. Jennifer Steinhauer, "Back on Hill, Ryan Remains a Fiscal Force," *New York Times*, November 18, 2012.

9. John A. Boehner, "Speaker Boehner Calls for Bipartisan Action to Avert the Fiscal Cliff," Office of the Speaker of the House of Representatives, November 7, 2012, accessed December 20, 2012, www.speaker.gov/speech/full-text-speaker-boehner-calls-bipartisan-action-avert-fiscal-cliff.

10. David Weigel, "Tax Hike Nation," *Slate*, November 16, 2012.

11. Lloyd Grove, "Grover Norquist Sees the Fiscal Cliff and Guns It," *Daily Beast*, November 16, 2012, www.thedailybeast.com/articles/2012/11/16/grover-norquist-sees-the-fiscal-cliff-and-guns-it.html.

12. George F. Will, "A Reformed Republican Party," *Washington Post*, November 16, 2012.

13. Charles Krauthammer, "The Way Forward," *Washington Post*, November 9, 2012.

14. "The Amnesty Delusion," *National Review*, November 12, 2012.

15. William Kristol, *Fox News Sunday* interview, Fox News, November 11, 2012.

16. Reihan Salam, remarks at the American Enterprise Institute, November 16, 2012.

17. Ramesh Ponnuru, "The Party's Problem," *National Review*, November 14, 2012.

18. Mike Murphy, "For Republicans, the Ice Age Cometh," *Time*, June 22, 2009.

19. Mark Murray, "RNC Report Suggest Other Reasons Why Romney Lost," NBC News, November 16, 2012.

20. Chris Cillizza, "Future for Republicans Is Not So Bad," *Washington Post*, November 18, 2012.

21. Michael Gerson, "Shifting Demographics Will Force GOP's Hand," *Washington Post*, November 18, 2012.

22. Dan Gilgoff, "6 Ways Religious Demographics Could Determine Tuesday's Winner," CNN.com, November 6, 2012.

23. Michael Cooper, "G.O.P. Factions Grapple over Meaning of Loss," *New York Times*, November 7, 2012, accessed December 20, 2012, www.nytimes.com/2012/11/08/us/politics/obama-victory-causes-republican-soul-searching.html.

24. Ross Douthat, "The Demographic Excuse," *New York Times*, November 10, 2012.

25. Michael Shear, "Demographic Shift Brings New Worry for Republicans," *New York Times*, November 7, 2012.

26. Michael Catalini, "McMorris Rodgers vs. Price: Leadership Race a Study in Contrasts," *National Journal*, November 12, 2012.

27. Aaron Blake, "The Republican Party's Leadership Vacuum," *Washington Post*, November 16, 2012.

28. Karen Tumulty and Dan Eggen, "GOP Governors Back Away from Romney's Remarks," *Washington Post*, November 15, 2012.

# 12

# ARE WE IN AN ELECTORAL REALIGNMENT?

## *Sean Trende*

In 1955, V. O. Key wrote a short article in *The Journal of Politics* entitled "A Theory of Critical Elections." Key examined the elections of 1896 and 1928 in New England, and concluded that there were certain elections that could be described as "critical" elections. These critical elections are marked by changes in the electorate that are, in Key's memorable phrase, "sharp and durable."[1]

This wasn't an entirely new idea. Journalists such as Samuel Lubell had described certain elections as "realigning" elections several years earlier.[2] But Key provided quantitative proof that suggested Lubell really was onto something.

Key's article spawned hundreds of others, as political scientists sought to identify what a realigning election looked like, categorize certain elections as realigning, and ascertain what drives these realigning elections. Opinion eventually more or less coalesced around the idea that a few important elections formed what we might call the "canonical" realignments: 1800, 1828, 1860, 1896, and 1932. Political scientists further speculated that there was a "periodicity" to realignments: They occurred roughly every thirty years or so.

The problem here should be immediately obvious: The list stops in 1932. There are no agreed-upon realignments after the 1932 election. Years like 1968, 1980, 1992, 1994, 1996, and the entire series from 2000 through 2010 have been proposed as potentially realigning elections. But none of these elections truly fits the definition of realignments set forth by political scientists.

So one possible answer to the question of whether 2012 is a realigning election is to critique the underlying question. Instead, perhaps the question should be "do realignments exist at all?" In 2004, Yale's David Mayhew wrote a blistering, controversial critique of realignment theory, *Electoral Realignments: A Critique of an American Genre*, which argues that American elections from 1828 through 1932 actually fit the realignment narrative much worse than realignment theorists allow.[3] In *The Lost Majority*, the author of this chapter sought to pick up where Mayhew's work left off, and to suggest that realignment theory fails to explain post-1932 elections well.[4]

Nothing has changed that would suggest realignment is anything less than a false concept that should be abandoned. Political coalitions are constantly in flux, and confining our expectations of major change to particular elections cramps our understanding of history, condescends to the American people, and even encourages bad policymaking. This chapter focuses on the five most common claims of realignment theory.

But, recognizing that this is a minority view, this chapter will largely devote itself to engaging realignment theory on its own terms. Even with this broad concession, 2012 is a poor fit for a realignment. Indeed, even if we reframe the idea of realignment to be a sort of slow-moving, "secular" realignment later posited by Key,[5] we would still struggle to explain the relevant time period in terms of realignment theory.

## EXAMINING THE 2012 ELECTION

We first must set some boundaries as to what constitutes a "realignment." Sloppy usage of the term is one of the main reasons that every election is seemingly followed by a claim of realignment. As John Sides has aptly observed, "The term 'realignment' gets thrown around casually, sometimes suggesting nothing more than 'something big is happening.' But the term has a more precise meaning—indeed, it must have a precise meaning in order for it to mean anything."[6]

Most accept the basic definition of a "critical," or realigning election as set forth by Key: that there be a "sharp and durable" change in the electorate. Beyond that, there is little agreement. For purposes of this chapter, we can turn to Mayhew's book, which helpfully collects fifteen broad claims made by various realignment theorists over the years. This chapter focuses on what we might consider the five "major" claims of realignment theory.

*A realignment gives rise to new dominant voter cleavage over interests, ideological tendencies, or issues.* For example, in 1828, we see the rise of the Second-Party System and the beginnings of the "Bank War." In 1860, the Third-Party System arrives, along with the Civil War. Then the 1896 election sees the end of the debate over the Civil War and the rise of the populist wing of the Democratic Party. Lastly, 1932 obviously brings about the New Deal and its eponymous coalition.

What new dominant voter interest, ideological tendency, or issue arose in the recent election? Perhaps we could say the Democrats' health care law. But this has been a goal of liberals for almost one hundred years, and has been a part of the Democratic Party platform for over sixty years. While it is an extremely important law, it isn't the type of fundamental re-definition of the relationship between the individual and the state that we find with, say, the New Deal or the onset of the Civil War.

Perhaps the fight over the Bush tax cuts for high earners? This is a variant of a fight we've been having since 1993, or even since 1980. If anything, the fact that both sides remain engaged in a death match over whether the top rate should be 39.6 percent or 35 percent illustrates just how little change we're really talking about. Perhaps we might find a fundamental issue-shift in Americans' increasing acceptance of marriage equality? This is certainly an important change in our county's attitude, but wasn't particularly a focal point of the campaign.

While we need to be careful not to diminish Obama's achievement in being reelected, it is also noteworthy that he will be the first president re-inaugurated with a lower share of the popular vote, smaller number of Electoral College votes, and lower number of total votes in our nation's history. The contrast with the other critical elections and their immediate successors is stark.

The polling also suggests that there has been very little change in Americans' attitude toward government. Gallup found that only 39 per-cent of Americans believed that Americans should do more to solve our country's problems.[7] This is consistent with the long-term trend in Gallup, which has found 50 percent support for a more active government only a handful of times since the early 1990s. Likewise, the Pew Center has asked various questions regarding people's attitudes toward business, government, and society, which exhibit little movement since the late 1980s (again, outside of a handful of social issues).[8] This doesn't mean that America is center-right or center-left or anything of that nature. It just suggests that its attitudes today aren't that different than they were even a few decades ago.

*A realignment is preceded by—or contemporaneous with—a good showing by a third party,* such as the rise of Free Soilers in the 1840s and 1850s, the People's Party in 1892, and the Progressive/Republican split of 1924. Of course, nothing of the sort has happened recently. The most recent third-party campaign to garner a significant share of the vote was Ross Perot's in the 1990s; his focus on the debt and deficit, his economic nationalism, and his strength among working-class whites make him an ill-suited candidate for a precursor to the Obama campaign.

*Turnout is up in a realigning election.* Because a realigning electorate shifts to address previously unmet needs, we see an increase in turnout. As of this writing, all the votes cast in 2012 have not year been counted, so it is difficult to know precisely what percent of the voting eligible population voted. Regardless, the following chart proceeds under the assumption that there will be 129 million votes counted when the final vote counts are certified.[9]

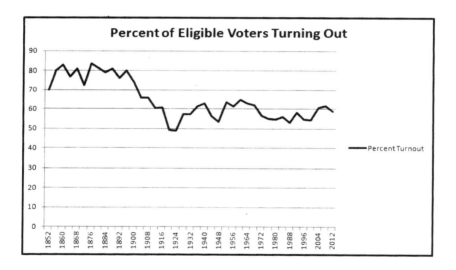

As you can see, turnout was actually down this election. Even 2008 shows a modest increase in turnout, at best. The big spike in turnout occurs in 2004, which would have actually suggested a realignment pointing toward Republicans.

*Electoral realignments bring about long spans of unified party control of the government.* The twelve years from 1828 through 1840 are the shortest period of unified control to follow a canonical realignment. This tendency makes any Democratic realignment in the past two decades problematic.

Republicans have controlled the House now for eight of the past ten Congresses. Included in this list are Republicans' second-biggest and third-biggest House wins since 1928, which they achieved in the 2010 and 2012 elections. Given that no president since the Civil War has seen his party gain more than ten House seats in a midterm election, it seems unlikely that this streak will be broken in the near future.

This is a major problem for proponents of the "Obama realignment" thesis. Years like 2010 simply don't occur in the early stages of a realignment. While we could arguably be arriving at a time where separate "presidential" and "midterm" electorates result in alternative good and bad years for each party, that does not help the realignment case. As Sides aptly observed, "a realignment doesn't take midterm elections off."

*A realignment brings about sharp and durable changes in the electorate.* This is really the central claim of realignment theory. The First-, Second-, and Third-Party Systems are the major outcomes of the 1800, 1828, and 1860 elections. The solidification of Republican strength in the Northeast is the aftermath of the 1896 election, which helped enable the party to win seven of the nine succeeding elections. The Democrats became a truly national party in 1932, in turn winning seven of the next nine elections.

This is also the claim that most proponents of the "Obama realignment" hypothesis are really making. Under this narrative, the superficial closeness of the 2012 election belies a changing electorate. Obama's co-alition of African American, Latino, liberal, and white suburban voters propelled him to victory, and will propel future Democratic candidates to victory in similar fashion.

It is possible. But from a realignment perspective, there are two problems. First, the recent changes in the electorate are not sharp. Second, it is far from certain that they will be durable.

To see what I mean by "sharp" changes in the electorate, consider the following map. It shows the change in the partisan "lean" of the various states from 1924 through 1932. By partisan lean, I mean how the state voted relative to the national average, similar to the Partisan Voting Index (PVI) designed by psephologist Charlie Cook. So if a Democratic candidate won a state with 53 percent of the vote, and won nationally with 51 percent of the vote, the state is assigned a two-point Democratic lean.

In the following three maps, states that swung at least five points toward the Democrats from 1924 to 1932 are assigned a charcoal color, while states that swung at least five points toward Republicans are assigned a light gray color:

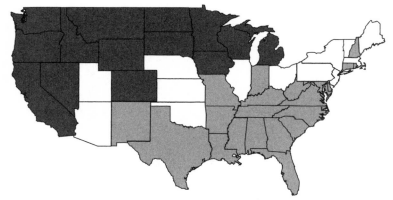

**States Where Partisan Lean Changed >5 points, 1924–1932**

All but thirteen states moved at least five points relative to the national average. Moreover, the movement has a sharp regional component. This is what the changes in the canonical realignments look like. The maps were obviously redrawn in 1800, 1828, and 1860, since entirely new political parties were rising to the forefront. Twenty-six of the forty states that had been in existence in the 1888 elections shifted at least five points toward one party or the other by 1896.

What about 2012? Examine the following map, which shows shifts from 2004 through 2012.

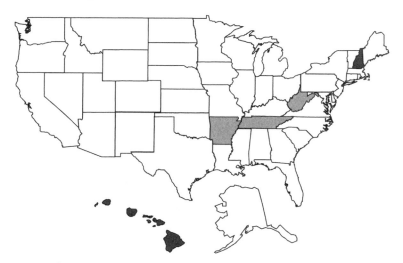

**States Where Partisan Lean Changed >5 points, 2004–2012**

The contrast with 1932 is sharp. We basically see the same map as we saw in 2004, relatively speaking. We can see this in even starker contrast if we narrow our field of consideration to states where the partisan lean changed more than two points from 2004 to 2012.

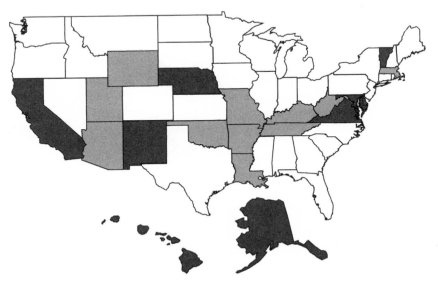

**States Where Partisan Lean Changed >2 points, 2004–2012**

Twenty states—less than half—have made these sometimes incremental moves toward one party or the other since 2004. By contrast, from 1924 to 1932, only eight states out of forty-eight failed to move by less than two points relative to the nation. From 1888 to 1896, all but eleven of the forty states that voted in 1888 moved by that much. Perhaps most importantly, the present moves have been largely concentrated in the very red or very blue states. Since 2004, Virginia became a purple state and New Mexico became relatively blue, while Missouri and West Virginia moved entirely out of the "competitive" category to become solidly red.

To really drive this point home, and to negate the possibility of a secular realignment, let's take things back to 1988. Here are the states where the partisan lean has moved by more than five points since that election:

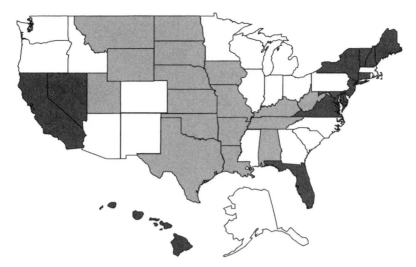

**States Where Partisan Lean Changed >5 points, 1988–2012**

Even here, only thirty-one of fifty states moved substantially toward Democrats or Republicans. A higher percentage of states shifted by a similar amount in the eight-year windows from 1888 to 1896 and from 1924 to 1936. Consider what a twenty-four-year period means too; we should be preparing for our second realignment using this temporal frame; but we can't clearly see a single one.

What's more, only a few states have dramatically changed their partisan orientation, even in the twenty-four-year time frame. Missouri, Montana, and South Dakota went from having marginal Democratic leans to having solid Republican leans according to the PVI. West Virginia was the biggest mover of all the states, going from a solidly Democratic lean to a solidly Republican lean. Delaware, Maine, and New Jersey went from having mildly Republican leans to having solid Democratic leans, while New Hampshire, Virginia, Florida, and Nevada transformed from solidly Republican states to swing states. Other than that, we've mostly seen red states become redder, and blue states become bluer.

If the changes marked by the past few elections were not sharp, then perhaps they are durable? Maybe Obama's reelection marks a new era where Democrats continue to win elections narrowly, akin to the 1876 to 1896 period for Republicans? Perhaps the influx of young voters, single women, and minorities into the electorate creates something of a "Big Blue Wall" that now extends to the "tipping point" state—that state which gives the winner electoral vote number 270—to Democrats?

This demographic argument is necessarily speculative. But it runs into three potential problems. The first is that what we're seeing might be Obama's coalition, rather than a Democratic coalition. While it is incorrect (and more than a little condescending) to suggest that that Obama's strong showing with blacks, Latinos, and other groups is due to his standing as the nation's first African American president, for African Americans to make up 13 percent of the electorate and to give 95 percent of their votes to a Democratic presidential candidate is an historical anomaly. The traditional numbers are more like 11 percent and 90 percent, respectively.

Could African American participation sink back to pre-2008 levels without Obama atop the ticket? It's by no means a given, but it is a possibility. Political scientist Matt Barreto notes that 79 percent of African Americans are "very enthusiastic" about the Democratic Party now, but only 47 percent say they will be after Obama's presidency ends.[10] Obviously a lot can change in four years. But the substantial drop-off in African American participation that occurred from 2009 through 2011 is at least a warning sign that this could happen.

What would this mean? It would have potentially crippling effects on the Democrats. Assume, for a moment, that with Obama off the top of the ticket, the African American vote returns to 2004 levels of turnout and support for Democrats. Even if everything else in the electorate stayed exactly the same as 2012, Florida and Ohio would flip to Republican support, and Pennsylvania would be less than a point away from giving the Republican candidate electoral vote number 270.

Second, the demographic hypothesis immediately runs into the reality of 2009 through 2011. During this time, the "coalition of the ascendant" simply failed to show up, even in many of the "red-to-blue" states. In 2009, Bob McDonnell won the Virginia governorship by the same margin that Republican George Allen had enjoyed twenty years earlier in a similar political environment. In 2011, Republicans won control of the Virginia State Senate under a map that had been gerrymandered by Democrats. In New Hampshire in 2010, Kelly Ayotte won a Senate race by twenty points. Richard Burr of North Carolina won by the largest margin of any North Carolina Senate candidate since 1974. Nevada and New Mexico both elected Latino Republican governors; Nevada did so by a healthy margin. Republicans swept most of the competitive races in the upper Midwest that year.

In the 2010 race for Congress there was a huge gender gap of twelve points. But Republicans actually carried women by two points, the first time that they had done so in House races on record. African Americans fell back to 10 percent of the electorate, and Republicans captured 9 percent of their vote. Republicans won college graduates by sixteen points, suburban-ites by twelve points, and Independents by eighteen points—all groups that are supposed to be a part of the emerging Democratic majority.

Put differently, 2008 and 2012 happened, but so did everything in between, and the idea that we have necessarily distinct midterm and presi-dential electorates now is only a theory that hasn't really been tested. Even after the intervening 2012 elections, Republicans find themselves with an unusually high number of House, Senate, gubernatorial, and statehouse seats to be at the beginning of a realignment; they are proving more durable than the Democratic gains from 2006 and 2008. Consider the following table, which shows the percentage of seats held by the "out-party" even four years after the critical elections of 1896 and 1932 (this excludes third parties):

**Table 12.1.   Share of Seats for "Out-Party," after 1900, 1936, and 2012 Elections**

|  | *1900*<br>*(Democrats)* | *1936*<br>*(Republicans)* | *2012*<br>*(Republicans)* |
|---|---|---|---|
| Senate | 36% | 19% | 45% |
| House | 42% | 24% | 54% |
| Gubernatorial | 40% | 17% | 60% |
| State House Seats | 46% | 30% | 53% |
| State Senate Seats | 46% | 34% | 54% |

Finally, this ignores other changes that are less salutary for Democrats in the electorate. In particular, here is the Democratic lean of whites com-pared to the country as a whole in presidential races.

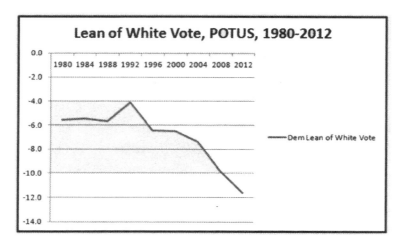

For Congress:

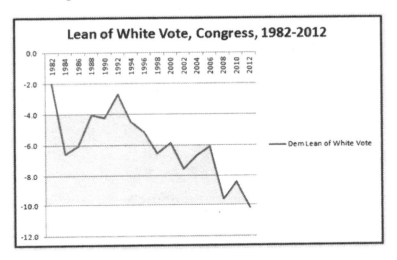

Now this trendline might continue, or it might stop. But it is the reason why the Republicans have remained competitive in presidential races, even as the white share of the vote has dropped significantly since 1992. If Republicans continue to win 60 percent of the white vote for Congress and the Presidency, they will continue to be competitive in presidential races for a very long time.

This is because the decline in the white share of the electorate has actually been rather slow. In recent years it has likely been accelerated by two factors. First, Obama obviously energized minority constituencies; as noted this may or may not outlast his presidency. Second, the number of white votes has been down significantly in recent years. Assuming that whites made up 72 percent of the electorate in 2012, and assuming that there 129 million votes end up being included in the final vote count, this would imply that 5.7 million fewer whites cast ballots in 2012 than in 2008.

This isn't due to increased death rates among whites. There are actually around 2.6 million more whites aged twenty and up than there were in 2008, which makes the drop-off all the more surprising.[11] In fact—and this is a critical fact that is frequently overlooked—the "bulge" in the white population is only now preparing to reach "peak" voting age. The following chart shows the distribution of the non-Hispanic white, black, and Hispanic populations by age in this country:

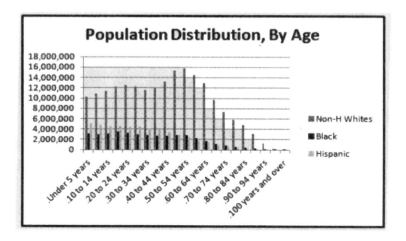

In ten to fifteen years, the Baby Boomers, just now hitting retirement age, will begin to die. At that point, the makeup of the electorate will likely change rapidly. But until then, we might actually see an increase in the white vote.

So it is far too early to declare that the Republican Party, at least as we know it, is about to become overwhelmed by a demographic tide that makes elections like 2012 the norm. At the very least, we need to wait until 2016 to find out (a) if minority participation continues at historically outsized rates with Obama off the ticket; (b) if whites' voting rate increases in 2016; and (c) if the anti-Democratic trend in white voting persists. All of these may well turn out in Democrats' favor. But we've already seen that simply changing (a) would have almost handed the election to Mitt Romney. If (b) and (c) change as well, a lot of these predictions of durability will look pretty weak.

## IS "REALIGNMENT" REALLY A USEFUL CONCEPT?

Up until now, we've engaged realignment on its own terms. But I think a lot of this discussion is beside the point. Even if Republicans win the presidency in 2016, it is still important that Obama won reelection by a nice margin in 2012, from both historical, policy and, not least of all, social perspectives.

More importantly, the historical record suggests that our ability to predict what elections will look like even two years in the future is weak at best. The 2004 and 2008 elections were both accompanied by a burst of triumphalist analysis proclaiming realignments that seemed to rule out the possibility that elections such as 2006 and 2010 were lurking around the corner.

A lot of these predictions came from partisans. But consider 1977, when political scientist Everett Carll Ladd, probably the most prominent election analyst of his day, had this to say about the 1976 elections:

> The Republican party cannot find, outside of the performance of its presidential nominee, a single encouraging indicator of a general sort from its 1976 electoral performance. . . . We have criticized the common tendency of political commentators to overreact to the last election, but . . . [t]he Democrats have emerged almost everywhere outside the presidential arena as the "everyone party."[12]

This assessment was not without support. Democrats had massive majorities in the House and Senate. Jimmy Carter had swept the South, suggesting that the Republicans' wins in the 1950s and early 1970s had more to do with Eisenhower's popularity and the fights over civil rights than actual Republican strength. Perhaps most ominously for the GOP, eighteen- to twenty-nine-year-olds—the most numerous demographic group in that election—had given Carter a 51 percent to 47 percent win. Ford's strongest group? Voters over sixty, who were half as numerous as the eighteen- to twenty-nine-year-olds.

Of course, 1976 reflected a low point for the GOP, and was actually followed by a steady progression of improving electoral fortunes. Because humans are very bad at predicting the short-term contingencies that truly drive elections a few months in advance, much less four years in advance, Ladd's projections fell apart. There was simply no way that he could see stagflation, the Iran hostage crisis, or killer bunnies. While an observer in 2004 might see the downturn in the Iraq war coming, the 2008 implosion of the economy, timed six weeks before the election, was outside the realm of foreseeability. An analyst in 2009 could be excused for missing the stagnant economy of 2010, the rise of the Tea Party, the unpopularity of the health care bill, or the Obama administration's inability to reenergize its base.

But this is just exactly the point. Realignment theory tells us that these sorts of things don't matter much, and that elections are more driven by demographics and the medium-term orientation of the parties. This doesn't square with the wild swings of the past few election cycles. For that matter, realignment theory doesn't even square up well with the parameters it has set for itself. When viewed across the broad expanse of American history, realignment theory becomes simultaneously overinclusive and underinclusive. That is to say, the canonical elections don't fit into the various realignment requirements that we sketched out particularly well. At the same time, other, noncanonical elections fit the requirements equally well, if not better.

We initially noted that realignments brought new issues to the forefront. But is that really more true, say, of 1860, than it is of 2012? Slavery had been rising as an issue since the "bank wars" concluded in the 1830s, and the Republican Party first performed well in House elections in 1854. What of 1896? Republicans and Democrats had been fighting about the coinage issue for decades, and agrarian third parties were nothing new. The New Deal was often explicitly grounded in Woodrow Wilson's "New Freedom."

At the same time, there are elections that bring up new, important issues, but that aren't included in the canon. In particular, as Mayhew notes, 1876 saw the end of Reconstruction and the beginnings of a major fight over the nation's political economy that stretches through today. The 1920 election saw a fight over the League of Nations and America's place in the world. In 1844, as well as 1900, debate raged over whether America should be an imperial power. The Korean conflict and trust dominated politics in 1952. The 1892 and 1964 elections were important inflection points regarding civil rights. It's not entirely clear why 1896 is more important to our nation's history than any of these years, other than that's what we've mostly been taught now for fifty years. The canonical realignments are a decent summary of important inflection points in our nation's fight over haves versus have-nots, which greatly interested the New Deal–era historians and political scientists who framed realignment theory. This is hardly the only important fight we've had in our nation's history though.

What of third parties? There were major third-party efforts in the 1848, 1880, 1912, 1948, 1968, and 1980 elections. Yet none of these elections are seen as preceding realigning elections. Turnout? Looking at the figure on page 166, one would struggle to identify 1932 or 1860 as particularly high turnout elections. Indeed, if one were trying to pick the realignments, the noncanonical years of 1876 and 1952, which saw huge turnout spikes, would be likely focal points.

Finally, the idea that there are long, durable times of single-party control, which are sharply denoted by realigning years, is belied by the history. In the 1860 to 1896 realignment, Republicans lost control of the House halfway through, and never really regained it. The continuity between the pre-1874 and post-1874 presidential elections is tenuous at best, with Republicans going from broad victories in between 1860 and 1872, to losing the popular vote in four of five elections from 1876 through 1892 (and winning the popular vote in 1880 by only a few thousand votes).

The 1896, 1900, and 1908 Republican wins might best be thought of as "anti-Bryan" coalitions; the maps in 1904 and those post-1908 look quite different. The 1920, 1924, and 1928 elections were all massive landslides, unlike the relatively close turn-of-the-century elections. Even within these three elections there are important differences in the party coalitions.

As for the New Deal coalition, we might ask whether it was really born in 1932. After all, the Northeast had swung Republican in 1928, and this is where Key initially identified the critical election as occurring. Moreover, how long did it really last? Democrats might have controlled Congress, at least nominally, after the 1938 elections. But New Dealers certainly did not; the "conservative coalition" of conservative southerners and Republicans determined which bills passed and which bills failed. Harry Truman's 1948 map actually looks more like Wilson's 1916 map than any of Roosevelt's. Johnson's 1964 win, with its solid showings in the Northeast and weak results in the South and West, is more of a precursor to the later Clinton/Obama maps than it is a successor to FDR's coalition. In between, we have to contend with Eisenhower's landslide wins in 1952 and 1956. Political scientists dismiss these wins as "deviating elections," but they were strongly similar, down to the county level, to the Nixon and Reagan maps that showed up several decades later.

Rather than looking for broad, lasting wins in a vain attempt to scry the future, perhaps we should content ourselves with the realization that elections are governed largely by short-term forces that are largely unpredictable. Yes, Republicans won seven of ten elections from 1952 through 1988, and now Democrats have won the popular vote in five of six. But which of those elections, really, were the victorious parties supposed to lose? Do we need a construct regarding lasting majorities to explain them adequately?

Indeed, most elections, including the last one, can be projected reasonably well given a few structural data points, such as economic growth and whether an incumbent is seeking reelection. But if realignment theory were true, our econometric models should cease functioning at some point. In present terms, that means that Republicans should start running substantially behind what the models project. Instead, Republicans ran ahead of the models in 2000 and 2002, slightly behind in 2004 and 2006, about even in 2008 and 2012, and well ahead in 2010.[13] We simply don't see any evidence that demographics or voter preferences are overriding short-term contingencies in the medium term, in a way that systematically harms either party.

None of this would matter if the concept of realignments didn't distort our understanding of elections. Realignment projects an apathetic electorate, one that comes alive only once every three decades to demand change. On the contrary, the record reflects an electorate that is active and constantly in flux, even if the shifts aren't always as dramatic as what we saw from 1924 through 1932.

Perhaps most perniciously, realignments can drive bad policy. Republicans famously sought a realignment in 2000 and 2004, and believed they had achieved it in the latter election. This encouraged a fair bit of hubris, which led to their pursuit of unpopular policies and arguably delayed the realization that something needed to change in the Iraq War. In 2008, Democrats were convinced that the Republicans were headed the way of the Whigs, and came across as absorbed with health care reform when most people were concerned with the economy. This has fed the overall impression that Washington is out of touch with the American people, and that our leaders are incapable of governing in a way that reflects the concerns of the American people.

In short, we should always be mindful of two things. First, as E. E. Schattschneider famously put it, "The people are a sovereign whose vocabulary is limited to two words, 'Yes' and 'No.' This sovereign, moreover, can speak only when spoken to."[14] Second, the Founders set our government up such that the people get to speak relatively frequently. In other words, it is often difficult to translate the verdict rendered by the people, and probably impossible to do so at a level that would allow us to determine a realignment is taking place. Perhaps more importantly, another election is always just twenty-two months away from the swearing in, so even if we could translate accurately what an election "means," the people can always decide they want something else in fairly short order. That they exercised that option so frequently between 2004 and 2012 should give pause to anyone seeking to give an upper hand to either party. That they have exercised it so frequently, so consistently, with such sensitivity to short-term forces across history probably means that we should not confine our caution to the present day.

# NOTES

1. V. O. Key Jr., "A Theory of Critical Elections," *The Journal of Politics* 1 (1955): 11; see also Walter Dean Burnham, *Critical Elections and the Mainsprings of American Politics* (New York: W. W. Norton, 1971), 4–5.

2. Samuel Lubell, *The Future of American Politics*, 2nd ed. (Garden City, NY: Doubleday Anchor Books, 1956).

3. David R. Mayhew, *Electoral Realignments: A Critique of an American Genre* (New Haven, CT: Yale University Press, 2002).

4. Sean Trende, *The Lost Majority: Why The Future of Government Is Up for Grabs—and Who Will Take It* (New York: Palgrave Macmillan, 2012).

5. V. O. Key Jr., "Secular Realignment and the Party System," *The Journal of Politics* 2 (1959): 198.

6. John Sides, "The Perils of Democrats' Euphoria, or Why the 2012 Election Is Not a Realignment," *The Monkey Cage* (blog), November 12, 2012, http:// themonkeycage.org/blog/2012/11/12/the-perils-of-democrats-euphoria-or-why -the-2012-election-is-not-a-realignment/.

7. Frank Newport, "Majority in U.S. Still Say Government Doing Too Much," Gallup, September 17, 2012, www.gallup.com/poll/157481/majority-say -government-doing.aspx.

8. Trende, *Lost Majority*, 108–9.

9. I use the following source to estimate the voting eligible populations for 2008 and 2012: http://elections.gmu.edu/Turnout_2008G.html and http://elections .gmu.edu/Turnout_2012G.html. All other data are from Walter Dean Burnham, *Voting in American Elections: The Shaping of the American Political Universe Since 1788* (Bethesda, MD, and Palo Alto, CA: Academia Press, LLC, 2010).

10. Ben Jealous, Silas Lee, and Matt A. Barreto, "NAACP Battleground Poll," November 8, 2012, www.slideshare.net/JamiahAdams/naacp-2012-battleground -poll-15102981, slide 18.

11. "National Intercensal Estimates (2000–2010)," U.S. Census Bureau, www .census.gov/popest/data/intercensal/national/nat2010.html.

12. Everett Carll Ladd Jr. with Charles D. Hadley, *Transformations of the American Party System: Political Coalitions from the New Deal to the 1970s*, 2nd ed. (New York: W. W. Norton, 1976), 293.

13. Jacob M. Montgomery, Florian M. Hollenbach, and Michael D. Ward, "Ensemble Predictions of the 2012 US Presidential Election," in "Symposium: Forecasting the 2012 American National Elections," *PS: Political Science and Politics* 45, no. 4 (October 2012): 651–54, http://mdwardlab.com/sites/default/files/ Symposium.pdf; Alfred G. Cuzán, "The 2006 House Elections: Forecasts and Results," www.apsanet.org/~lss/Newsletter/jan07/Cuzan.pdf.

14. Elmer Eric Schattschneider, *Party Government: American Government in Action*, 3rd ed. (New Brunswick, NJ: Transaction Publishers, 2004) 52.

# 13

## FROM 2012 TO 2016

### Concluding Thoughts on the Permanent Campaign

*Susan MacManus*

*With the assistance of David J. Bonanza and Ashleigh Powers*

[I]n an election season that brought the oft-repeated adage "it's the economy, stupid" to new levels, analysts had predicted the national unemployment . . . and slow recovery numbers would be Obama's Achilles' heel. Poll after poll had indicated a sour mood in America with majorities believing the country was on the "wrong track." But a combination of silver-lining economic statistics released [the Friday before the election], plus positive reporting about the federal government's response to Hurricane Sandy, a lauded "ground game" and an opponent [Romney] who was unable to capitalize on the uncertain fiscal landscape, combined to give the president [Obama] the boost he needed in the 11th hour.

—Kelley Beaucar Vlahos,
FoxNews.com, November 7, 2012[1]

[C]ommunities of color, young people and women are not merely interest groups, they're the "new normal" demographic of the American electorate.

—Janet Murguia, President of the
National Council of La Raza, November 7, 2012[2]

In the days following the closely contested 2012 presidential election, numerous analyses focused on what President Barack Obama's campaign did right and where Governor Mitt Romney's went wrong. Such postmortem debates occur after every election. As *Wall Street Journal* reporter Janet Hook noted: "Post-election second-guessing is as common as worms after a spring rain."[3]

Predictably, there was agreement by both sides on some aspects of the long, grueling campaign season (Democrats' superior organization and voter mobilization data base; Romney's superior first debate performance; the changing demographic face of Americans), but sharp disagreement on others (the candidates' relative campaign skills, fund-raising, ad placement, intra-party schisms, the "demise" of the Republican Party).

But perhaps more than in any presidential campaign in recent history, Election 2012 elicited major debates about how future campaigns should be run in an era of constantly changing technology affecting candidates' communication with voters and in a country experiencing major demographic shifts that are yielding a deepening generational political divide (young— Democratic; old—Republican). Post-election analyses of major events (the party nominating process, the national party conventions, the presidential and vice presidential debates) have raised some interesting questions about choices that must be made by candidates and parties in 2016. So, too, have analyses of the relative effectiveness of various voter mobilization efforts that occurred right up through Election Day, November 6, 2012 (the opening and location of campaign offices at the grassroots level, voter registration efforts, polling, message formation, ad content and placement, visits by candidates and their surrogates to key swing states and/or to big donor states, getting less-than-enthusiastic voters and late deciders to the polls, among others).

As the campaigns began winding down, the issues of election reform and privacy protection started to heat up. Problems with long lines, late vote counts, equipment failures, and claims of voter suppression and fraud across the states prompted President Obama to raise anew questions about the need for national-level election reform and a pledge to tackle the issue in his second term.[4]

The highly probative efforts the campaigns engaged in to generate micro-targeted ads and GOTV (get out the vote) efforts raised concerns among privacy advocates as discussions about whether and how to maintain these extremely valuable, highly invasive contact lists got underway. According to some critics, "a big problem with efforts to protect personal information . . . is that the politicians are not guarding the chicken coop.

They are the foxes. . . . It's not clear who is positioned to protect the rights of voters at a time when politicians from both parties increasingly build their campaigns on the insights that commercial data brokers provide."[5]

In this chapter, we look at some of the major events and voter mobilization activities of the 2012 election and briefly discuss the questions each generated about future presidential campaigns.

## MAJOR EVENTS: KEY QUESTIONS RAISED

### The GOP Party Primary

As the incumbent in the 2012 election, President Obama faced no serious challengers for his party's nomination. But on the other side of the aisle, Republicans knew, beginning with Senator John McCain's defeat in 2008, that the 2012 GOP nominating process would be a crowded affair. Changes in party rules governing the primary schedule and the method of awarding delegates led many to predict a long, drawn-out nominating process that might ultimately end in a brokered convention in Tampa for the first time since 1952:

> [T]he 2012 primary calendar is heavily back-loaded, with major states such as California and New York going much later in the process than in 2008 and far fewer delegates up for grabs through Super Tuesday. In fact, the altered calendar will create the most spread-out contest since the 1970s. And more states than in the past will award delegates based on each candidate's portion of the vote, rather than all of a state's delegates going to the winner of the popular vote. All together, it will be mathematically impossible for Romney—or anyone—to eliminate opponents early on. . . . There are approximately 2,427 delegates up for grabs in the 2012 Republican primary, but a number of states who broke Republican National Committee rules and moved their primaries forward will likely see their delegate totals halved. So the actual number of total delegates will probably be 2,284, meaning a candidate will have to win 1,143 to clinch the nomination.[6]

Neither the Republican National Committee's well-intentioned effort to reduce the number of states holding their presidential preference primaries early (front-loading) to better vet their ultimate nominee nor its decision to award delegates in states proportionally instead of by winner-take-all was effective.[7] The key swing state of Florida ignored the calendar rule and scheduled its primary for January 31 in spite of party rules calling for its delegation to the GOP convention to be cut in half (which it was).[8] And Governor Romney virtually sewed up the nomination by April 2012—rendering talk of a brokered convention moot. His closest competitor, Rick Santorum, withdrew on April 10—well in advance of the California and New York primaries.

What was perhaps the most unexpected dimension of the GOP primaries was the record number of high-profile TV debates featuring GOP candidates, the first of which occurred on May 5, 2011![9] (See figures 13.1 and 13.2.) By the time Mitt Romney had virtually secured the party nomination, he had participated in twenty televised debates!

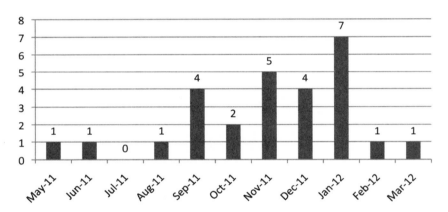

**Figure 13.1.   Twenty-Seven GOP Presidential Debates**

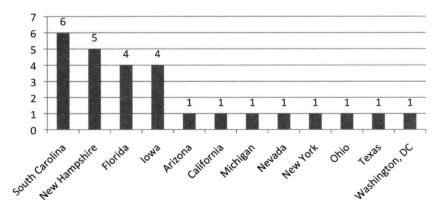

**Figure 13.2.   GOP Presidential Debates: 2011–2012**

As a result of the most grueling primary battles in modern history, the 2012 GOP nominating process raised several key questions:

*Can national political parties really control the timing of individual states' decisions to hold presidential primaries, caucuses, and state-level party conventions?* Two election cycles in a row have seen states ignore national party rules in spite of being punished. Will it happen again in 2016? As one analysis of Florida's maverick behavior has pointed out, "Florida Republicans largely got what they wanted, as their primaries in both years were fiercely contested, closely watched, and ultimately became pivotal victories for eventual nominees John McCain and Mitt Romney."[10]

*Is front-loading the primaries or stringing them out the better strategy? Winner-take-all or proportional delegate allocation rules?* Proponents of front-loading primaries and winner-take-all allocation rules argue that stringing them out costs too much, thereby putting unnecessary pressure on the eventual nominee to spend funds that could be better used in the general election phase. Opponents of front-loading and winner-take-all rules are convinced that each winnows down the field too quickly without vetting the candidates thoroughly enough.

*In an election that proved population composition (demographics) matters (see figure 13.3), is it wise for parties, especially Republicans, to stick to the tradition that puts Iowa and New Hampshire (predominantly white electorates) first in the nominating process?*

Historically, the rationale for these two states going first is their size; they are both small states that allow a look at how well a candidate can engage in retail politics—selling themselves via personal contact. That argument still has some validity in light of the fact that exit polls showed that

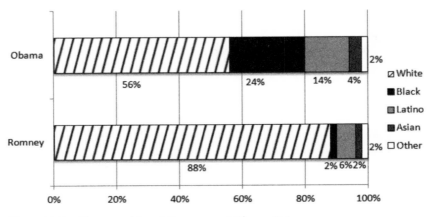

**Figure 13.3.   Demographics of Romney and Obama Voters**

the ability to connect with voters (creating the image that a candidate cares about people like you) was a key factor in reelecting President Obama.[11]

But winning primaries in diverse, often larger, critical swing states is critical to determining whether a nominee can successfully appeal to younger, more racially/ethnically and ideologically diverse electorates. In 2012, Romney fared poorly in those types of states because of having to move further right on *social* issues in the smaller, more rural, Anglo-dominated states.[12] In the words of one analyst: "Republican primaries have become Tea Party litmus tests, forcing candidates to audition for a lily-white, anti-urban base that feels like Archie Bunker and Ward Cleaver in an era of Modern Family and Dora the Explorer."[13]

Romney ended up losing the swing states of Florida, Virginia, Colorado, Nevada, and others. And just a few short weeks after Obama was reelected, the Republican governor of Iowa was proposing to eliminate the state's "quadrennial pre-caucus beauty contest known as the Ames Straw Poll" because of its poor record of predicting the party's eventual nominee.[14] (Michele Bachmann won the August 13, 2011, straw poll but came in last in the Iowa caucus in January 2012.)

*Is the net impact of an extensive series of televised primary-stage debates on a party's ultimate nominee more positive or negative? Will there be as many in 2016 when* **both** *parties may have competitive primaries because there will be no incumbent in the race?* Proponents of a lot of TV debates at the primary stage argue that it helps the eventual nominee to hone his or her debating skills and positions the candidate to be better prepared for the general election debates. As proof positive, they point to Romney's superior performance at the first debate against Obama, labeled a "game changer" by many analysts.[15]

Opponents of a seemingly endless number of intra-party debates strung out for months on end complain that they aid the opposition party's nominee by supplying that candidate with all the ammunition he or she needs to craft effective negative ads against the debate survivor. Certainly Obama was given general election ammunition to use against Romney by the governor's fellow Republicans on a wide range of issues, ranging from immigration, taxes, energy, and health care, to women's issues such as pay equity and reproductive rights.[16] On a number of these issues, Romney, more of a moderate, was forced to move right to prove himself a true conservative, opening himself up to attacks by the Obama camp for being a flip-flopper. Over time, these TV debates effectively "pinned [Romney] down at the 2-yard line on the conservative end of the field rather than positioning him between the 40-yard lines."[17]

*In a year when one party has a heavily contested and contentious primary and the other has no competitive primary (an incumbent president running for reelection), should the incumbent's campaign, party, or supportive PACs run negative TV ads **during the primary** designed to take out the strongest potential opponent?*

A trend observed in some competitive congressional primary races across the country is for a candidate to run negative ads against a potentially formidable opponent competing in the opposite party's primary, with the intent of keeping him or her from getting the nomination. A well-known example of the use of this tactic involved Democrat Alan Grayson, a flamboyant candidate for Florida's Ninth Congressional District seat. His campaign financed highly negative—and successful—mailers against a popular Puerto Rican candidate (state legislator John Quinones) running in the GOP primary.[18] The candidate who ultimately prevailed posed little threat to Grayson in the general election, thereby virtually assuring the former congressman of election. (He had lost his bid for reelection in 2010.) Some fear that this technique of candidate intervention in another party's primary may ultimately be used in presidential contests. As it was, the Obama campaign began developing messages to run in ads against Romney when it became clear he was the nominee (April), even before the last state had held its GOP primary or caucus (June 26, 2012).

### The Party Nominating Conventions

Republicans held their party convention in Tampa, Florida, in late August (27–30); Democrats followed a week later (September 4–6) with theirs in Charlotte, North Carolina. Both states had gone for Obama in 2008, although narrowly. Each state was considered a swing state in 2012. Both conventions cost millions, at the same time that networks were cutting back their primetime coverage, fears of violent protests were on the rise, and their late summer dates raised concerns about Mother Nature's intervention as well as questions related to delays in receiving federal funds needed for the general election campaign. (Candidates are not eligible to receive federal campaign funds until officially nominated by their party.)

While some cast conventions as no longer necessary or exciting, Molly Ball of *The Atlantic* disagrees:

> Sure, the conventions are a manufactured event, more infomercial than news, with nothing of consequence decided. But here's why you shouldn't be too cynical about them: **★They're for the delegates**. . . . Talking to delegates, from the 10-time veteran to the first-time participant, you

get a sense of the grassroots energy that powers American politics at the most basic level. ★**They're for the voters at home**: Tens of millions of viewers will tune in to see the primetime speeches. . . . It's a rare chance to see the candidates unfiltered, as they wish to be seen, and the way they present themselves sends an important, if one-sided, message. ★**They're for history**: Formalities like the party platform don't actually dictate what politicians on either side believe—Romney, for example, has said he disagrees with the GOP platform's no-exceptions opposition to abortion. But the platforms, along with the speeches, are significant in tracking the movement of the parties over time. This year, the Democratic platform will include a plank supporting gay marriage for the first time ever. ★**They launch stars**. . . . If history is any guide, by the time the confetti has fallen and the balloons have been dropped from the ceiling, there will be a new name on the lips of the political world.[19]

Significant differences of opinion about the timing, staging, and structure of the 2012 national party conventions have already raised questions about what will happen to them in 2016:

*Does the city or state selected really help a party win that state in the fall?* Republicans chose Tampa, located in the state's largest media market, and in Hillsborough County—historically, the state's best bellwether—anticipating that the convention could turn the area—and state—red again. Democrats chose Charlotte hoping to prove that the state's transition to a blue state in 2008 was complete and that the increasingly diverse South was becoming more Democratic-friendly territory. Neither state ended up voting as the convention-site selectors had projected.

*Should conventions be shortened considerably?* Florida Republicans' worse fears seemed likely to come true—an August hurricane headed toward the Tampa area. The storm never really hit the area, but rain and winds forced the party to cancel the first day of the convention, leaving the host city, the delegates, and hundreds of vendors holding their breath that the storm would veer away from the area by the next day. It did. But the cancellation of events and the successful readjustment of the schedule raised anew questions of whether four-day conventions are really necessary anymore or even desirable with networks offering fewer hours of prime time coverage. Many post-election analyses have predicted that party conventions in 2016 might be one-day events to save money . . . and minimize the number of hours a TV network must set aside for primetime convention coverage.[20]

*Are outdoor venues during summer months the best acceptance speech venues?* As it turned out, Mother Nature affected both party conventions. In Charlotte, President Obama's planned nomination acceptance speech had to be moved from the large outdoor Bank of America Stadium back to the Charlotte Convention Center due to potential rain, thunder, and lightning from the same storm system that canceled the first night of the GOP convention in Tampa. This late move cost millions of dollars, prompting questions about the pragmatism of holding these events in large outdoor stadiums during the summer. It is highly likely that the TV networks will lobby long and hard against such a proposed location in 2016.

*Is it better to schedule the conventions midsummer or late summer?* It is not just weather-related concerns that have some party officials rethinking late summer/early fall conventions. Under federal campaign finance rules, a candidate cannot receive federal funds to be used in the general election phase of a presidential campaign until he or she is officially nominated by the party. Romney really felt the pinch of the campaign finance rule holding back federal funds until official nomination because it deprived him of resources to counter the massive number of attack ads the Obama campaign launched against him in the summer before the GOP convention. In virtually every post-election analysis, the barrage of unanswered Obama ads against the governor was mentioned as a major factor contributing to the president's victory. Democratic operative Paul Begala acknowledged that the successful pro-Obama Super PAC (Priorities USA Action) took "Go Ugly Early" as its operative mantra. The founders, two former Obama White House aides, never wavered in their strategic vision. "They had one hill to take—Mount Bain—and they did it by taking Romney's greatest strength—his business record—and making it a weakness."[21] In 2016, it is likely that both parties will have contested primaries and will revisit their 2012 decisions to hold the conventions in late summer.

*How much security should there be in a post-9/11 era, and should certain locations be avoided due to greater security vulnerabilities?* Delegate security concerns in the post-9/11 era intensified in both cities in the face of widely publicized promises by anarchist groups to disrupt convention activities. Those concerns put both cities on edge and vastly ran up the costs of the conventions. As it turned out, most of the violent protests fizzled, leaving peaceful protesters to fully express their free speech rights—not a bad outcome from the perspective of either convention city. While some criticized the expenditures and the fortress-like appearance of the convention sites, public opinion polls showed the public more supportive of the security expenditures than critical. The old adage that it's better to be safe than sorry held true.

It is important to note that security concerns loomed larger in Tampa than in Charlotte for two reasons: (1) the Tampa area's greater vulnerability due to its access via multiple waterfronts and (2) the presence of MacDill

Air Force Base, home to CENTCOM—U.S. Central Command—with responsibilities for twenty countries in the Middle East. In the future, debates over where to hold the national party conventions will certainly include discussions about the relative security-related vulnerabilities and costs of proposed convention sites.

*Should there be a longer time between the two conventions? And what gives a party the bigger convention bounce: The party holding its convention last? Primetime speakers? Delegate diversity revealed in camera shots? Media bias? Or the candidates?* CNN reported that 2012 marked the fifth time that the two major party conventions were held on back-to-back weeks, most recently in 2008.[22] This also happened in 1912, 1916, and 1956. Since 1956, the incumbent's party has gone second. Going second has generally been seen as an advantage and as yielding a bigger post-convention bounce when time between the conventions is so short.

In 2012, Republicans pointed to their storm-shortened convention, cutbacks in primetime media coverage, and overly negative media coverage due to the storm and extensive visuals of security barricades, along with the short time between conventions as reasons why Romney got no convention bounce. Democrats countered that their primetime speakers, most notably former president Bill Clinton, were bigger draws than those who appeared at the Republican convention (including Marco Rubio), *and* that the camera shots panning over the Democratic delegates revealed a much more diverse America than similar shots of GOP convention delegates. The latter, in combination with the increases in the minority (especially Hispanic and Asian) and youth shares of the electorate, will undoubtedly raise debates among Republicans about how to recruit and select a more diverse-looking array of Republican convention delegates.

Party activists and strategists are more likely than others to see and defend conventions as consequential—as potential turning points in any election cycle. Republican Alex Castellanos remarked to Democrat Paul Begala that Clinton's speech to the delegates would probably be the moment that reelected Barack Obama: "Bill Clinton saved the Democratic Party once, it was going too far left, he came in, the New Democrats took it to the center. He did it again tonight." Begala described the Democrats' decision to let Clinton speak as "giving Elvis the microphone," a more effective strategy than the Republicans handing it to Clint Eastwood, along with an empty chair.[23] (Actually, the chair episode later produced a widely circulated *New Yorker* cartoon after the first presidential debate when Obama appeared to many as "absent" from the debate.)

*Do the costs of conventions outweigh the benefits?* Historically, rosy candidate performance predictions tend to produce calculations projecting that the potential convention benefits will outweigh the costs. Looking ahead to 2016, it appears unlikely that either party would favor cutting back the 2016 conventions to a single day unless networks promise gavel-to-gavel coverage or costs of the event become prohibitive. Both parties have potential candidates—and speakers—that could greatly impact the subsequent direction of the campaign. Some have already speculated that Republicans may have the deeper, more diverse "bench" ready to go in 2016. Names like Marco Rubio, Susan Martinez, Bobby Jindal, Nikki Haley, and Ted Cruz are frequently mentioned in such discussions. However, the Democratic speaker list might include formidable and experienced husband-and-wife teams like the Clintons, Bidens, and Obamas, as well as rising stars like Julian Castro or Tammy Baldwin.

### The Presidential and Vice Presidential Debates

In 1987, the nonpartisan Commission on Presidential Debates (CPD) was established. It has sponsored and produced all the presidential and vice presidential debates ever since. On July 25, 2012, the CPD announced the date, location, topic, rules and format of the three presidential and one vice presidential debate to be held in the fall; the debate moderators were selected in August. The CPD debate announcement was as follows:[24]

> *First presidential debate (October 3, 2012, University of Denver, Denver, CO); Moderator Jim Lehrer, Executive Editor PBS NewsHour.* The debate will focus on domestic policy and be divided into six time segments of approximately 15 minutes each on topics to be selected by the moderator and announced several weeks before the debate. The moderator will open each segment with a question, after which each candidate will have two minutes to respond. The moderator will use the balance of the time in the segment for a discussion of the topic.

> *Vice presidential debate (October 11, 2012, Centre College, Danville, KY); Moderator: Martha Raddatz, ABC News Senior Foreign Correspondent.* The debate will cover both foreign and domestic topics and be divided into nine time segments of approximately 10 minutes each. The moderator will ask an opening question, after which each candidate will have two minutes to respond. The moderator will use the balance of the time in the segment for a discussion of the question.

*Second presidential debate (October 16, 2012, Hofstra University, Hempstead, NY) Moderator: Candy Crowley, Chief Political Correspondent for CNN.* The second presidential debate will take the form of a town meeting, in which citizens will ask questions of the candidates on foreign and domestic issues. Candidates each will have two minutes to respond, and an additional minute for the moderator to facilitate a discussion. The town meeting participants will be undecided voters selected by the Gallup Organization.

*Third presidential debate (October 22, Lynn University, Boca Raton, FL); Moderator: Bob Schieffer, CBS News' Chief Washington Correspondent; moderator of Face the Nation.* The format for the debate will be identical to the first presidential debate and will focus on foreign policy.

In the month between the ends of the conventions and the first debate, the general feeling was that the debates would have little impact on the race, which at the time Obama was leading handily. In fact, polls showed that a majority of Americans believed President Obama would easily best his opponent in the debates.[25] Nothing could have been further from the truth. President Obama did poorly in the first debate, as virtually every post-debate survey showed. Some debate experts had warned of the possibility of a less-than-stellar performance by Obama, noting that incumbent presidents "almost invariably lose their first debate" for a number of reasons—difficulty in scheduling time to prepare due to competing needs, being "out of practice at verbal jousting," or simply arrogance.[26]

The magnitude of Governor Romney's surprisingly strong performance in the first debate stunned even the most seasoned political observers and changed the momentum of the race almost overnight. Suddenly Republicans' enthusiasm returned after having been deflated considerably after Obama's convention bounce. The gender gap closed somewhat, independents leaned more toward Romney, and polls in the swing states narrowed. Although Obama rebounded in the second and third debates, nearly every post-election analysis identified the first debate as a "momentum changer" that kept the contest close right up until Election Day.[27] Prior to that debate, many in the Romney camp were rightfully convinced that the debates were the only way for him to catch up with Obama.

Peggy Noonan of the *Wall Street Journal* summarized the 2012 debate season best:

> The presidential debates this year have been more consequential than such debates have ever been. They've been historic, shifting the mood

and trajectory of the race. They've been revealing of the personalities and approaches of the candidates. And they've produced a new way in which winners and losers are judged. It's a two-part wave now, the debate and the post-debate, and you have to win both.[28]

There were other unique aspects of the debates that generated considerable controversy: (1) the moderators—the news outlets they represented, their objectivity, and/or their management of the debate; (2) the exclusion of third-party candidates; (3) candidate decorum, or lack thereof; and (4) the rise of fact and fairness checkers.

*Moderators.* Jim Lehrer, moderator of the first debate, was roundly criticized by some for being too deferential to the candidates, repeatedly failing to enforce time limits, and consistently allowing the candidates to ignore his instructions to answer key questions.[29] Those on the political left were particularly harsh in their criticism, arguing that Romney was the worst offender in ignoring the moderator's instructions. Candy Crowley, moderator of the second debate, caught a lot of flak for appearing to overstep her bounds by "improperly inserting herself into the conversation with questionable facts" and siding "with the President over whether he had deemed the Libya attack an act of terror, when the reality was not so clear cut."[30] Even Martha Raddatz, moderator of the vice presidential debate, came under attack for having had Obama as a guest at her wedding in 1991[31] and for appearing to intentionally give Joe Biden more time than Paul Ryan.[32] CBS News' Bob Schieffer, who came under the least criticism, still was attacked for allowing the third debate to stray far from the intended focus on foreign policy.[33]

There was also considerable criticism from conservatives who charged that *all* the moderators chosen by the CPD represented liberal news outlets.[34] If the 2012 debate cycle tells us anything, it is that "In this polarized political age, a debate moderator has little chance to escape a harsh critique."[35]

*The CPD.* Even the CPD itself was criticized for its lack of ideological diversity[36] as well as for its bias against inclusion of third-party candidates in the debates. Libertarian Party presidential nominee Gary Johnson sent a letter to the CPD arguing in favor of including any contending candidate (a candidate who has the mathematical chance to win, being on all fifty states' ballots) in the debates, but to no avail. Since the CPD adopted the 15 percent requirement after Ross Perot's participation in the debates in 1992, no third-party candidate has participated. Johnson's letter read: "In all due respect, it is not the proper role of an nonelected, private and tax-exempt organization to narrow the voters' choices to only the two major party candidates—which is the net effect of your arbitrary polling requirement."[37]

*Candidate decorum, or lack thereof.* All the candidates (presidential and vice presidential) got bad marks for some of their debate antics, whether intentional or not. Television brings such antics up close and personal, especially split-screen shots that enable viewers to see how a candidate interacts with the opponent. The 2012 debates laid bare the worst sorts of traits. For Obama, it was most evident in the first debate—his scribbling, looks of disdain for Romney, and seeming disinterest in the whole process.[38] For Romney, it was his constant interruptions of Obama and the moderator and a "forced smile" tendency in awkward situations.[39] For Biden, it was his bizarre facial expressions, propensity to laugh at even the most serious topics, and repeated accusations that Paul Ryan was full of malarkey (lying).[40] And for Ryan, it was his smirking at Biden (again, visible via split-screen) and constantly grabbing a glass of water, then taking a sip.[41]

*Fact and Fairness Checking.* The 2012 campaign saw the proliferation of fact and fairness checkers. With regard to the debates, journalists and partisans alike parsed nearly every statement made and statistic cited, then judged each as true, partially true, or totally false (Politifact's "pants-on-fire" rating). There were also tallies of the total time given to each candidate by the moderator in the course of a debate (down to the second), the relative number of positive or negative questions posed to each candidate, and the number of softball questions tossed to each candidate (judged relative to the perceived ideological bent of the moderator). By the end of the debates . . . and the campaign . . . "fact-checkers were checking fact-checkers."[42] The exercise became increasingly partisan and ended up frustrating some voters who genuinely just wanted to know who was telling the truth. Some have attributed the lower turnout rate in the 2012 election to voter frustration with blatantly false information given to them, whether in the debates or via thirty-second TV spots or web-based ads.

Each of these controversies, along with others, will undoubtedly raise debate-centered questions related to the CPD's role and composition, moderator selection, inclusion of third-party candidates, candidate decorum (and nonverbal behavior), and fact checking before, during, and after the 2016 election cycle. The questions we can expect in 2016 will likely be:

*What is the role of the presidential debate commission? Who is on it? Is it outmoded?* The major question raised about this nine-member commission in 2012 is whether it is truly nonpartisan or biased toward the two-party system. There is also a question about the degree to which its members represent the changing face of the electorate (demographics).

*Should there be more ideological balance to the moderators selected to avoid claims of media bias?* This question took on added meaning as media bias concerns escalated significantly in 2012. A widely cited Gallup Poll conducted in September 2012 found that a record-high 60 percent of those surveyed had little or no trust in the mass media to report the news fully, accurately, and fairly.[43] Such sentiments are bound to keep pressure on the CPD to pay more attention to ideological balance of the moderators in 2016.

*How many debates should be held, and which formats work best?* Opinions varied considerably in 2012 on such debate dimensions as the following: Should the format pit the candidates against each other or take place in a town hall setting? Should the candidates stand at a podium, be free to wander, or sit at a table? Should questions come from a single moderator or a panel of journalists?

*Where should the debates be held? Private universities or public universities? In safe or swing states or a mixture?* All four 2012 presidential/vice presidential debates were held at private universities. Critics say it is because the private institutions can raise more money for the debates. Supporters say these institutions are smaller and easier to secure. In 2012, two were held in swing states (Colorado, Florida), one in a red state (Kentucky), and one in a blue state (New York).

*Should the debates include third-party candidates? If so, should the 15 percent rule be revised and, if so, how?* Interest in third-party candidates was high enough to prompt the Free and Equal Elections Foundation to sponsor a televised third-party debate moderated by former CNN anchor Larry King the day after the CPD debates concluded. The debate featured Libertarian Party candidate Gary Johnson, Green Party candidate Jill Stein, Constitution Party candidate Virgil Goode, and Justice Party candidate Rocky Anderson.[44] While not widely carried on major broadcast and cable networks, the debate was broadcast on C-SPAN and streamed via the Internet to interested viewers.

*Does interest naturally wane (smaller audiences) as the debate season winds on, or is viewership more determined by the subject or the candidates involved?* The first presidential debate (domestic policy) drew 67.2 million viewers, the second (town hall), 65.6 million, and the third (foreign policy), 59.2 million. In fairness, the third debate was pitted against two major sporting events (Monday Night Football on ESPN and Major League Baseball playoffs on Fox). The vice presidential debate drew 51.4 million—down considerably from the Joe Biden–Sarah Palin debate in 2008—69.9 million—the highest of all debates in 2008.

*How much can debates **really** change the trajectory of a campaign? The outcome?* The underlying question is whether the most recent election was the beginning of a new trend where televised debates may give a candidate a bigger bounce than the party convention, or was 2012 rather unique in that regard? Romney's first debate performance did permanently tighten the race in swing states. But in the end, the outcome was Obama's reelection, which was not at all surprising to many Americans. Polls had consistently shown that a large majority *expected* the president to be reelected, underscoring longstanding conventional wisdom: It's tough to defeat an incumbent.

## MAJOR VOTER MOBILIZATION EFFORTS: KEY QUESTIONS RAISED

### Goal: Getting Supporters to Actually Vote

The last part of this summary chapter focuses on voter mobilization efforts, particularly those designed to get voters to vote early—absentee or in person (where permitted)—or on Election Day. "Beyond the presidential debates, one final factor matters more than all the rest in a close race—ground game. It's the ability to get your voters to the polls—a way of moving soft support into actual votes."[45] While the ground game picked up speed after the debates, a lot of the groundwork had been laid much earlier to enable the heavy GOTV push at the campaign's end.

As part of the efforts to organize staff and volunteers at the grassroots level, both campaigns worked to construct and constantly update extensive databases that were created with one goal in mind: to effectively target key blocs of voters and get them to actually vote. Targeting tactics included personal contact by local-level campaign activists, ads on TV or the web, social media, and/or candidate and surrogate visits in key swing states. Each of these major efforts cost millions; the overall cost of the 2012 election is estimated to have cost more than $6 billion.

In the end, the Obama campaign was more effective at reaching the late deciders—mostly young (many minorities, especially Hispanics and Asians) and female voters—just in time to pull the president across the finish line in all the swing states. Whether it was a better message, last-minute candidate visits, persuasive ads, or personal contacts by the Obama campaign's "embedded community organizers," turnout among the traditional late decider groups (9 percent of all voters, according to exit polls) went up in 2012—and broke for the president. (See table 13.1.) One conservative columnist poignantly described the significance of the superiority of the Democrats' "end game":

> If there's a well-recognized "enthusiasm gap," and you need that few extra points at the margin, an extremely organized well-oiled machine of millions of passionate volunteers, expertly trained in what to do, equipped with the very most advanced tools, and intrinsically prone to creativity and initiative might just be your margin of victory. And

**Table 13.1. Young, Minority, and Single Women Shares of the Electorate Expanded in 2012**

| | % of Voters | | 2008 | | 2012 | |
|---|---|---|---|---|---|---|
| | 2008 | 2012 | Obama | McCain | Obama | Romney |
| | % | % | % | % | % | % |
| **Are you:** | | | | | | |
| Male | 47 | 47 | **49** | 48 | 45 | **52** |
| Female | 53 | 53 | **56** | 43 | **55** | 44 |
| | | | | | | |
| **In which age group are you?** | | | | | | |
| 18–29 | 18 | 19 | **66** | 32 | **60** | 37 |
| 30–44 | 29 | 27 | **52** | 46 | **52** | 45 |
| 45–64 | 37 | 38 | **50** | 49 | 47 | **51** |
| 65 or over | 16 | 16 | 45 | **53** | 44 | **56** |
| | | | | | | |
| **In which age group are you?** | | | | | | |
| 18–24 | 10 | 11 | **66** | 32 | **60** | 36 |
| 25–29 | 8 | 8 | **66** | 31 | **60** | 38 |
| 30–39 | 18 | 17 | **54** | 44 | **55** | 42 |
| 40–49 | 21 | 20 | 49 | 49 | 48 | **50** |
| 50–64 | 27 | 28 | **50** | 49 | 47 | **52** |
| 65 or over | 16 | 16 | 45 | **53** | 44 | 56 |
| | | | | | | |
| **Are you:** | | | | | | |
| White | 74 | 72 | 43 | **55** | 39 | **59** |
| Black | 13 | 13 | **95** | 4 | **93** | 6 |
| Hispanic/Latino | 9 | 10 | **67** | 31 | **71** | 27 |
| Asian | 2 | 3 | **62** | 35 | **73** | 26 |
| Other | 3 | 2 | **66** | 31 | **58** | 38 |
| | | | | | | |
| **Age by race** | | | | | | |
| White 18–29 | 11 | 11 | **54** | 44 | 44 | **51** |
| White 30–44 | 20 | 18 | 41 | **57** | 38 | **59** |
| White 45–64 | 30 | 29 | 42 | **56** | 38 | **61** |
| White 65+ | 13 | 14 | 40 | **58** | 39 | **61** |
| Black 18–29 | 3 | 3 | **95** | 4 | **91** | 8 |
| Black 30–44 | 4 | 4 | **96** | 4 | **94** | 5 |
| Black 45–64 | 4 | 4 | **96** | 3 | **93** | 7 |
| Black 65+ | 1 | 1 | **94** | 6 | **93** | 6 |
| Latino 18–29 | 3 | 4 | **76** | 19 | **74** | 23 |
| Latino 30–44 | 3 | 3 | **63** | 36 | **71** | 28 |
| Latino 45–64 | 2 | 3 | **58** | 40 | **68** | 31 |
| Latino 65+ | 1 | 1 | **68** | 30 | **65** | 35 |
| All other | 5 | 5 | **64** | 33 | **67** | 31 |

(*Continued*)

**Table 13.1.    Continued.**

| | % of Voters | | 2008 | | 2012 | |
|---|---|---|---|---|---|---|
| | 2008 | 2012 | Obama | McCain | Obama | Romney |
| | % | % | % | % | % | % |
| **Sex by race** | | | | | | |
| White men | 36 | 34 | 41 | **57** | 35 | **62** |
| White women | 39 | 38 | 46 | **53** | 42 | **56** |
| Black men | 5 | 5 | **95** | 5 | **87** | 11 |
| Black women | 7 | 8 | **96** | 3 | **96** | 3 |
| Latino men | 4 | 5 | **64** | 33 | **65** | 33 |
| Latino women | 5 | 6 | **68** | 30 | **76** | 23 |
| All other races | 5 | 5 | **64** | 32 | **66** | 31 |
| **Are you currently married?** | | | | | | |
| Yes | 66 | 60 | 47 | **52** | 42 | **56** |
| No | 34 | 40 | **65** | 33 | **62** | 35 |
| **Gender by marital status** | | | | | | |
| Married men | | 29 | | | 38 | **60** |
| Married women | | 31 | | | 46 | **53** |
| Non-married men | | 18 | | | **56** | 40 |
| Non-married women | | 23 | | | **67** | 31 |

*Source*: National Election Exit Poll, Edison Research.
*Note*: All figures from www.foxnews.com/politics/elections/2008-exit-poll; www.foxnews.com/politics/
elections/2012-exit-poll/US/President.

moreover, at some point, if you keep ignoring a development of such magnitude while the other side keeps using it against you, your outdated tactics start making you look like the Polish Cavalry being mowed down by German tanks. We [the GOP] have reached that point.[46]

### Identifying and Targeting Key Blocs of Voters: Database Construction and Updating

The same conservative columnist that scolded his party for not keeping up with technological change took Republican officials to task for underutilizing the Internet and failing to generate its own sophisticated GOTV database for use throughout the campaign:

The Internet is about mass communities, networking, conversation, organizing. . . . The Internet is also about Big Data, and therefore microtargeting. But the GOP is largely lacking this political atomic bomb because they continue to ignore Silicon Valley or anyone else outside the Beltway consultancy class. By contrast, a Facebook co-founder was drafted to run Obama's Internet campaign in 2007; and in 2012, media reports indicate that 34 Facebook executives and staff took leadership roles on the campaign.[47]

Actually, the Obama campaign created a "futuristic analytics department" headed by a private sector database guru and employing hundreds of engineers and technologists. The extensiveness of the personal information generated enabled "the campaign's analysts to test the effectiveness of messages aimed at narrow demographic slices. Although it was often described as 'micro-targeting,' the most important element was 'micro-listening.' If people tell us they're interested in cats, we probably took that down," said one campaign official.[48] And that person likely got some e-mail or pop-up ad from the campaign featuring a cat.

The closest thing the Romney camp had to the Obama database (nicknamed Narwhal) was Project Orca—a new software program designed to keep track of who had already voted on Election Day, leaving volunteers to target those who had not yet gone to the polls. It never worked as planned,[49] and even got tagged as "Failed Whale" by the popular website Politico.com. Even if it had been operating up to speed, it is not clear whether it would have been as effective as the Democrats' database in convincing the late deciders or unenthusiastic voters to go to the polls. They were more Obama's natural base than Romney's. Also, the Obama campaign relied more on in-person contacts with these young "low propensity" voters who needed "extra nudges and last-minute reminders"[50] to get them to vote, while the Romney campaign relied on less effective phone calls. The Obama campaign reveled in pointing out the difference:

[On Election Day], our volunteers are not driving to some large office miles from their homes and handed a phone and a call sheet. Instead, Canvass Captains, Phone Bank Captains and scores of local volunteers will be knocking on the doors of the very voters they registered, have been talking to for months and know personally. And they will be directing them to polling locations in their communities—the schools their kids go to, the places of worship they attend each week and community centers they know well.[51]

*Organizing Staff and Volunteers at the Grassroots Level*

The difficulties of competing against an incumbent president were crystal clear when it came to organizing at the grassroots level. As the

Romney campaign learned, the 2008 Obama organization never really shut down. A number of field offices and staff were kept in place, especially those in neighborhoods housing supportive, but low–turnout, voters and in key swing states like Iowa, Ohio, Florida, and Virginia.[52] The organizational structure was simply transferred to the newly formed Obama For America (OFA) campaign. Early on, the Obama campaign took the 2010 Census numbers and rushed to register new voters, especially Latinos, in swing states like Florida and North Carolina.

The Romney campaign tried to play catch–up, but was never quite able to do so because of money and time constraints. By one count, in mid–October, the Obama campaign had 755 local offices across the country compared to just 283 for Romney.[53] (See figure 13.4.)

These organizational dynamics will be different in 2016 when there is no incumbent president in the race for the White House. Key questions that are bound to be raised are the following:

*How will the Obama team keep the organization and database together? How will it be funded? Who will be in charge? Is the Obama coalition primarily loyal to him (to an individual personality) or to the Democratic Party?*

*Will the Republicans finally start building a twenty-first-century state-of-the-art database now? Or will they continue to fight over whether their 2012 turnout deficit was largely due to flawed software that had not been adequately tested or to the candidate's own failure to excite millions of would-be GOP voters?*

*When and where should organizational structures be put in place? Who should have the most control over the campaign office site selection—the national party or the candidate?*

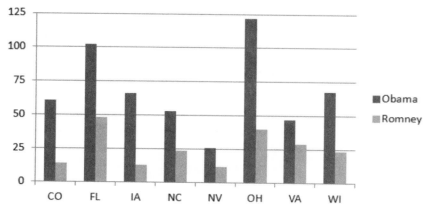

**Figure 13.4.   Obama and Romney Campaign Headquarters by State**

Some judged the major problem in making such decisions was a lack of coordination between the national Republican Party and the Romney campaign. Too much control over such decisions in Washington meant bad decisions at the grassroots level in key swing states.[54]

*Ads and Social Media versus Personal Contact with Sporadic Voters*

One well-known political strategist for a conservative PAC took Republican donors, party committees, and third-party groups to task for putting too much effort into "raising tens of millions of dollars to spend on massive ad campaigns that most voters tuned out" rather than "beefing up the GOP ground game to match the Obama machine."[55] In the future, he argues, these groups must spend less on TV ads and invest equally or more on "micro-targeted voter mobilization campaigns and support organizations that execute those campaigns" (like unions do for Democratic candidates).

The highly negative tone of most TV ads (85 percent of them, by some estimates) certainly made it more difficult to get any message through to late deciders in heavily ad-saturated swing states. (See figure 13.5 for the amount of money each campaign spent on TV ads in swing states.) The same was true for robo calls and mailers. This is not to say that ads were not effective. They were, particularly in mobilizing each candidate's base supporters. But to the casual, less-informed voter, the economic-oriented ads seemed to conflict with each other, leaving these already unenthusiastic voters to conclude that neither candidate had a good plan for how to fix the floundering economy and fix it fast. They simply did not vote. This appears

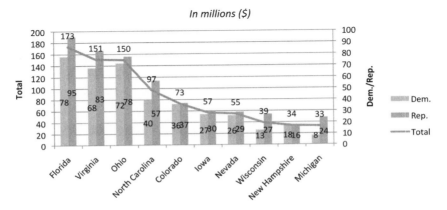

**Figure 13.5.   Highest TV Ad Spending by State**

to have been particularly damaging to Governor Romney because many of these stay-at-home voters were white suburbanites—a key demographic the Republicans had counted on for victory.

Use of social media had its own shortcomings in rallying sporadic voters at the campaign's end. In the words of one digital scholar: "[The Internet] is still much better for rallying committed supporters rather than for persuading new ones."[56] She says it is getting harder to do something catchy on the web: "Online tools have gone from novel to fashionable to completely unexceptional." Plus, younger voters often regard unwanted politically oriented invasions into their social media (their entertainment world) as unacceptable and intrusive.[57]

Every election cycle, advertising strategies are reexamined, taking into account new communication technology and new voter media habits. Such will be the case in 2016:

*When should the bulk of TV ads be aired? Early or later in the campaign?* In 2012, the Obama campaign intentionally spent a lot of ad money early when the airwaves were less congested. Romney saved more to spend nearer the end of the campaign, which some have branded a big mistake.

*Is spending on TV ads still more effective than spending on online ads?* This issue was not totally resolved in 2012 and will certainly be revisited in 2016 when new figures will be available on where Americans are getting most of their campaign news.

*How much does over-saturation of TV ads tamp down turnout among key demographic bases? How does over-saturation make it difficult to reach late deciders who might hold the key to victory?* The lower voter turnout rate in 2012 on the heels of the most massive ever TV ad campaign will undoubtedly raise this question. So, too, will studies concluding that the vast sums of money spent on TV ads in 2012 mostly canceled out each other.[58]

*How much social media communication with potential supporters should be focused on fund-raising? By contrast, how much of that communication should be focused on informing potential supporters about candidate issue positions or upcoming events, or requesting input on voter priorities?* In 2012, young voters were turned off by the candidates' fixation on using social media to "dial for dollars" rather than to inform the voters about issue stances and exciting upcoming events or volunteer opportunities.

### Reaching Voters via Candidate and Surrogate Visits

It is commonly believed that you can tell how important a state is to a candidate by how much money is spent there on ads *and* the number of visits or campaign stops the candidate makes there.[59] These are most likely to be the swing states, although some visits are made to one-party states to raise money (California and New York for Democrats and Texas for Republicans). As shown in figure 13.6, the Obama-Biden team had far fewer total visits to fewer swing states after the Democratic National Convention than the Romney-Ryan team (101 versus 152).

There were two major reasons for the post-convention visit differential. First, Romney had a much tougher road to the White House than Obama because the president could count on support from more solidly blue states than Romney on solidly red states since there are fewer of the latter. In other words, the Electoral College map worked in Obama's favor. That meant that Romney needed to carry almost all the swing states to win—a daunting task.

A second reason was that the Obama campaign staff was more confident in their projections about winning key swing states like Ohio, Virginia, Iowa, Colorado, and Florida even as polls were showing these states up for grabs or even leaning toward Romney near the end of the campaign. The Obama campaign remained confident that their database was far superior to Romney's and was generating much more accurate polls (internal) and turn-out projections. In their opinion, each of these numbers helped the campaign to more effectively pinpoint locations where strategic last-minute visits by Obama, Bill Clinton, and Michelle Obama could turn out traditionally late-deciding young, minority, and women voters (college campuses, urban core areas with large concentrations of minorities, union-dominated midwestern states). In a *Time* magazine interview, a member of the Obama analytics team (the data crunchers) was quoted as saying:

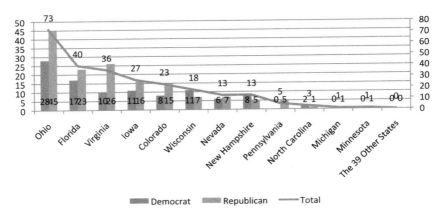

**Figure 13.6.   Most Candidate Visits in Fall 2012**

We were much calmer than others. The polling and voter contact data were processed and reprocessed nightly to account for every imaginable scenario. We ran the election 66,000 times every night [describing the computer simulations the campaign ran to figure out Obama's odds of winning each swing state]. And every morning we got the spit-out—here are your chances of winning these states. And that is how we allocated resources [including candidate visits].[60]

In 2016, questions about candidate visit strategies are likely to be the following:

*Can the Republicans catch up with the Democrats in the micro-targeting game to more accurately plan and gauge candidate visits?* Some analysts wonder whether ineffective last-minute visits and ad buys by the Romney campaign in blue states like Pennsylvania and Michigan were intentional bluffs by the GOP or simply decisions made with bad data—namely, poor polling.

*Will the GOP get better at calculating voter support and turnout?* On this there is a high level of consensus among Republicans: "We have to."

*Was the GOP loss in 2012 simply a matter of a failure to turn out some key elements of the party's base, or does the base need to be expanded?* The overwhelming majority of post-election analyses concluded that "demographics is destiny"—that a failure to figure out ways to attract younger voters (a higher proportion of whom are minorities) will make it impossible for Republicans to win in 2016. (See figure 13.7, racial/ethnic population projections.)

Others aren't so sure. Andrew Kohut, president of the Pew Research Center (one of the most reputable and accurate polling operations), cautions that "the current American electorate is hardly stacked against the Republican Party." He noted that "Republicans increased their share of the presidential vote among many major demographic groups [men, whites, younger voters, white Catholics, and Jews, independent voters]." Kohut, as others, attributed more of the GOP loss to Romney himself, whom Kohut identified as a rather weak candidate. He identified the GOP's bigger future challenge as more ideological in nature: "Republicans should realize that, on balance, Americans remain moderate—holding a mix of liberal and conservative views. . . . Threading the ideological needle with this electorate is vital for the Republicans in the future." But, he predicts, it will be vital for the Democrats, too.[61]

## WHERE DO WE GO FROM HERE?

Presidential campaigns are complex, and no two are alike. Candid political consultants warn their candidates against trying to replicate successful

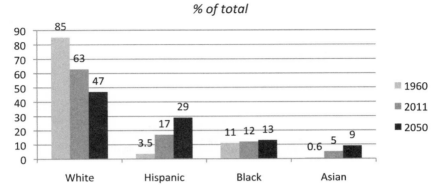

**Figure 13.7.  Population by Race and Ethnicity, Actual and Projected, 1960, 2011, and 2050**

practices in one year's election to win the next. Obama's campaign manager, Jim Messina, quickly warned candidates of the potential pitfalls of purchasing another candidate's data set "because that candidate wouldn't have the same connection to voters, rendering the data potentially useless."[62] Messina, like others, knows the importance of the messenger (the candidate) and the message, as well as unexpected events (including Mother Nature).

Looking back to the 2012 race, it is clear that the Obama campaign's superior database and attentiveness to the nation's changing demographics were both important factors leading to victory. But just as some have warned about the potential pitfalls in transferring a database from one candidate to another, others have cautioned against relying too heavily on the demographics of the electorate. Two well-known scholars, Ruy Teixeira and John Halpin, have pointed out: "Demographics are important but not determinative of election outcomes. *Politics and campaigns matter in putting together viable electoral majorities.*" After all, the 2012 election was a "complex mix of demographics, economics, and ideology" (author's emphasis).[63]

Howard Kurtz, the *Daily Beast* and *Newsweek*'s Washington bureau chief, turned to history to warn against the demise of the GOP:

> For all the talk of a new Democratic majority—by 2016, Obama's party will have held the White House for 16 of 24 years—the pendulum can swing in unexpected ways. Voters rarely give one party three consecutive terms in the executive mansion. What's more, second-term presidencies often run out of gas, and the Democrats could be viewed as having exhausted their agenda. If that happens, then four years from

now we could be talking about a Republican ascendancy—and an ideological war among Democrats for the soul of their party.[64]

Democrats, having just won the big prize (the White House) in a down economy, just aren't buying it!

## NOTES

1. Kelley Beaucar Vlahos, "Analysis: Slivers of Hope in Economic Recovery Helped Boost Obama," FoxNews.com, November 7, 2012, www.foxnews.com/politics/2012/11/07/analysis-slivers-hope-in-economic-recovery-helped-boost-obama/.

2. Anita Kumar and Lesley Clark, "Obama Win Signals New Democratic Coalition," *Miami Herald*, November 7, 2012, www.miamiherald.com/2012/11/07/3086832/obama-win-signals-new-democratic.html.

3. Janet Hook, "Republicans Differ on Why Party Fell Short," *Wall Street Journal*, November 8, 2012, http://online.wsj.com/article/SB10001424127887324894104578113412715240772.html.

4. Associated Press, "Obama Election Speech: President Makes 2012 Victory Address," *Huffington Post*, November 7, 2012, www.huffingtonpost.com/2012/11/07/obama-election-speech_n_2086418.html.

5. Craig Timberg, "Campaigns 'Use of Supporters' Data Worriers Privacy Advocates," *Washington Post*, November 21, 2012, www.washingtonpost.com/business/technology/campaigns-use-of-supporters-data-worries-privacy-advocates/2012/11/20/12510a0c-3356-11e2-9cfa-e41bac906cc9_story.html.

6. Jon Ward and Mark Blumenthal, "Mitt Romney Needs Early 2012 Knockout to Avoid Extended GOP Primary," *Huffington Post*, November 27, 2011, www.huffingtonpost.com/2011/11/27/mitt-romney-2012-gop-primary-calendar_n_1114117.html.

7. John Avlon, "The GOP's Chaotic Primary Calendar Makes Early Nomination Clinch Tough," *Daily Beast*, February 17, 2012, www.thedailybeast.com/articles/2012/02/17/the-gop-s-chaotic-primary-calendar-makes-early-nomination-clinch-tough.html.

8. The RNC rule for 2012 allowed New Hampshire, Iowa, South Carolina, and Nevada to hold contests a month ahead of all other states, but no earlier than February 1. Following Florida's actions, South Carolina Republicans moved their primary up to January 21. In turn, New Hampshire secretary of state Bill Gardner, following a state law that requires the Granite State to hold its primary seven days ahead of any "similar election," set New Hampshire's primary for January 10. As a result, the RNC punished New Hampshire, South Carolina, and Florida by allowing them to bring only half their delegates to the Republican National Convention. Tim Buckland, "RNC Could Adopt Rules at Convention to Keep NH's

First-in-the-Nation Primary Status Intact," *Union Leader,* August 24, 2012, www
.unionleader.com/article/20120824/NEWS0605/708249952/0/news06.

9. Election Central, "2012 Primary Debate Schedule," 2012presidentialelection
news.com, accessed November 21, 2012, www.2012presidentialelectionnews.com/
2012-debate-schedule.

10. Scott Conroy, "Florida GOP More Likely to Play by Rules in 2016," RealClear-
Politics, November 21, 2012, www.realclearpolitics.com/articles/2012/11/21/
florida_gop_more_likely_to_play_by_rules_in_2016_116218.html.

11. Heather Higgins and Alex Cortes, "The Phrase That Lost Romney the
Election," RealClearPolitics, November 23, 2012, www.realclearpolitics.com/
articles/2012/11/23/the_phrase_that_lost_romney_the_election_116235.html.

12. Michael D. Shear, "Demographic Shift Brings New Worry for Republicans,"
*New York Times,* November 7 2012, www.nytimes.com/2012/11/08/us/politics/
obamas-victory-presents-gop-with-demographic-test.html?pagewanted=all;  Jonathan Martin, "Election Aftermath: GOP Soul-Searching: 'Too Old, Too White,
Too Male'?" *Politico,* November 7, 2012, www.politico.com/news/stories/1112/
83472.html.

13. Michael Grunwald, "Why the GOP Will Double Down on a Losing Strategy," *Time Swampland,* November 7, 2012, http://swampland.time
.com/2012/11/07/why-the-gop-will-double-down-on-a-losing-strategy/.

14. Scott Conroy, "Branstad Opens Gates for Iowa Straw Poll Criticism,"
RealClearPolitics, November 22, 2012, www.realclearpolitics.com/articles/
2012/11/22/branstad_opens_gates_for_iowa_straw_poll_criticism_116225.html.

15. Charlie Cook, "The Cook Report: There's No Question, Romney
Changed the Game," *National Journal,* October 11, 2012, www.nationaljournal
.com/columns/cook-report/the-cook-report-there-s-no-question-romney
-changed-the-game-20121011.

16. Grunwald, "Why the GOP Will Double Down."

17. Charlie Cook, "Romney's Defeat Exposes Inconvenient Truths of the
Republican Party," *National Journal,* November 12, 2012, www.nationaljournal
.com/columns/off-to-the-races/romney-s-defeat-exposes-inconvenient-truths-of
-the-republican-party-20121112.

18. Amanda Terkel, "Jeb Bush Goes After Alan Grayson: Stay Out of Florida GOP Primary," *Huff Post Politics,* August 10, 2012, www.huffingtonpost
.com/2012/08/10/jeb-bush-alan-grayson-florida-gop_n_1765312.html.

19. Molly Ball, "The Incredible Shrinking Political Convention," *Atlantic,*
August 28, 2012, www.theatlantic.com/politics/archive/2012/08/the-incredible
-shrinking-political-convention/261664/.

20. Doug Mataconis, "Time of Get Rid of Political Conventions?," *Outside the
Beltway* (blog), August 28, 2012, www.outsidethebeltway.com/time-of-get-rid
-of-political-conventions/; Mike Murphy, "Potemkin Conventions: Why Are We
Doing This Again?" *Time Swampland,* August 27, 2012, http://swampland.time
.com/2012/08/27/potemkin-conventions-why-are-we-doing-this-again/.

21. Paul Begala, "From Newsweek: How the GOP Helped Obama Win," *Daily Beast*, November 9, 2012, ww.thedailybeast.com/newsweek/2012/11/09/how-the-gop-helped-obama-win.html.

22. CNN Political Research Unit, "What You May Not Know about Conventions Past and Present," CNN Politics, August 29, 2012, www.cnn.com/2012/08/29/politics/convention-trivia-2/index.html.

23. Begala, "How the GOP Helped."

24. Commission on Presidential Debates, "CPD Announces 2012 Debates Format," Debates.org, July 25, 2012, www.debates.org/index.php?mact=News,cntnt 01,detail,0&cntnt01articleid=38&cntnt01origid=15&cntnt01detailtemplate=news page&cntnt01returnid=80.

25. American Enterprise Institute, "Election 2012 Face-off: Domestic Policy Debate," AEI.org, October 3, 2012, www.aei.org/article/politics-and-public-opinion/elections/election-2012-face-off-domestic-policy-debate/?gclid=CION6_PH6rMCFQWnnQody08AuA.

26. Adam Nagourney, Ashley Parker, Jim Rutenberg, and Jeff Zeleny, "How a Race in the Balance Went to Obama," *New York Times*, November 7, 2012, www.nytimes.com/2012/11/08/us/politics/obama-campaign-clawed-back-after-a-dismal-debate.html?ref=jimrutenberg&_r=0.

27. Cf. Alexander Burns and Maggie Haberman, "If Obama Loses . . . ," *Politico*, November 5, 2012, www.politico.com/news/stories/1112/83301.html.

28. Peggy Noonan, "The Year the Debates Mattered," *Wall Street Journal*, October 18, 2012, http://online.wsj.com/article/SB10000872396390444734804578065023315500416.html.

29. Brian Stelter, "After a New-Look Debate, a Harsh Light Falls on the Moderator," *New York Times*, October 4, 2012, www.nytimes.com/2012/10/05/us/politics/after-debate-a-harsh-light-falls-on-jim-lehrer.html?_r=0; Jason Linkins, "Jim Lehrer Loses Control during Presidential Debate in Denver," *Huffington Post*, October 3, 2012, www.huffingtonpost.com/2012/10/03/jim-lehrer-presidential-debate_n_1937855.html.

30. Brian Montopoli, "Conservatives Assail Debate Moderator Candy Crowley," CBS News, October 17, 2012, www.cbsnews.com/8301-250_162-57534438/conservatives-assail-debate-moderator-candy-crowley/.

31. Josh Peterson, "ABC News Scrambles to Downplay Obama's Attendance at VP Debate Moderator's Wedding," *Daily Caller*, October 10, 2012, http://dailycaller.com/2012/10/10/abc-news-scrambles-to-cover-up-barack-obamas-attendance-at-vp-debate-moderators-wedding/.

32. Stelter, "Harsh Light."

33. "Bob Schieffer Responds to Criticism of Debate Moderating," *Huffington Post*, October 23, 2012, www.huffingtonpost.com/2012/10/23/bob-schieffer-debate-foreign-policy_n_2004934.html.

34. Bobby Eberle, "Where Are the Conservative Presidential Debate Moderators?," GOPUSA.com, August 15, 2012, www.gopusa.com/theloft/2012/08/15/where-are-the-conservative-presidential-debate-moderators/.

35. Stelter, "Harsh Light."

36. Jeanne Zaino, "Zaino: Does the Commission on Presidential Debates Need a Shake-up?," *Newsday*, October 3, 2012, http://newyork.newsday.com/opinion/zaino-does-the-commission-on-presidental-debates-need-a-shake-up-1.4070789.

37. Kevin Reilly Jensen, "Gary Johnson Fights Commission on Presidential Debates for Third Party Inclusion," *Rocky Mountain Collegian*, October 3, 2012, www.collegian.com/2012/10/03/gary-johnson-fights-commission-on-presidential-debates-for-third-party-inclusion/.

38. Nagourney, "How a Race."

39. Karen Tumulty, "Debate Winner: Interruptions," *Washington Post*, October 5, 2012, www.washingtonpost.com/blogs/election-2012/wp/2012/10/05/its-official-wednesdays-debate-was-full-of-interruptions/; Carol Kinsey Goman, "Body Language Advice for the Second Presidential Debate," *Body Talk* (blog), October 8, 2012, www.nonverbaladvantage.com/blog/?p=486.

40. Peter Hamby, Mark Preston and Paul Steinhauser, "Five Things We Learned from Thursday's Vice Presidential Debate," CNN.com, October 13, 2012, www.cnn.com/2012/10/12/politics/debate-five-things-learned/index.html.

41. Dan Merica, "First Two Debates Couldn't Be More Different," CNN.com, October 12, 2012, www.cnn.com/2012/10/12/politics/debate-tone/index.html.

42. L. Gordon Crovitz, "Double-Checking the Journalist 'Fact Checkers,'" *Wall Street Journal*, September 9, 2012, http://professional.wsj.com/article/SB1000087239639044368600457763974392340620.html?mg=reno64-wsj; Cathy Young, "Who Fact-Checks the Fact-Checkers?" *Minneapolis Star Tribune*, September 17, 2012, www.startribune.com/opinion/commentaries/169840236.html?refer=y.

43. Lymari Morales, "U.S. Distrust in Media Hits New High," Gallup, September 21, 2012, www.gallup.com/poll/157589/distrust-media-hits-new-high.aspx.

44. Nicola Menzie, "Presidential Debate Tonight with Third-Party Candidates Moderated by Larry King," *Christian Post*, October 23, 2012, http://global.christianpost.com/news/presidential-debate-tonight-with-third-party-candidates-moderated-by-larry-king-83805/.

45. John Avlon and Michael Keller, "Ground Game: Obama Campaign Opens Up a Big Lead in Field Offices," *Daily Beast*, October 19, 2012, www.thedailybeast.com/articles/2012/10/19/ground-game-obama-campaign-opens-up-a-big-lead-in-field-offices.html.

46. Rod D. Martin, "Seven Things That Mattered in the 2012 Election," FoxNews.com, November 9, 2012, www.foxnews.com/opinion/2012/11/09/seven-things-that-mattered-in-2012-election/.

47. Martin, "Seven Things."

48. "After the Election: A Transcript of the Weekend's Program on Fox News Channel," *Wall Street Journal*, November 11, 2012, http://online.wsj.com/article/SB10001424127887324894104578113412715240772.html.

49. Adi Robertson, "Killer Fail: How Romney's Broken Orca App Cost Him Thousands of Votes," The Verge, November 9, 2012, www.theverge.com/2012/11/9/3624636/killer-fail-how-romneys-broken-orca-app-cost-him-thousands-of-votes.

50. Travis Pillow, "Obama's Florida Election Edge," *Tallahassee Democrat*, November 11, 2012, www.tallahassee.com/article/20121111/POLITICSPOLICY/311110026/Obama-s-Florida-election-edge.

51. Sam Stein, "Obama Campaign: We've Contacted One Out of Every 2.5 People in the Country," *Huffington Post*, November 3, 2012, www.huffingtonpost.com/2012/11/03/obama-voter-contact_n_2069289.html.

52. Craig Timberg and Amy Gardner, "Democrats Push to Redeploy Obama's Voter Database," *Washington Post*, November 20, 2012, www.washingtonpost.com/business/economy/democrats-push-to-redeploy-obamas-voter-database/2012/11/20/d14793a4-2e83-11e2-89d4-040c9330702a_story.html.

53. Avlon and Keller, "Ground Game."

54. Molly Ball, "Obama's Edge: The Ground Game That Could Put Him Over the Top," *Atlantic*, October 24, 2012, www.theatlantic.com/politics/archive/2012/10/obamas-edge-the-ground-game-that-could-put-him-over-the-top/264031.

55. Brian J. Wise, "Republicans Lost the Ground Game," *Washington Times*, November 11, 2012, www.washingtontimes.com/news/2012/nov/11/republicans-lost-the-ground-game/.

56. Dorie Clark, "How Presidential Elections Made Social Media Marketing Banal," *Harvard Business Review* (blog), November 1, 2012, http://blogs.hbr.org/cs/2012/11/how_presidential_elections_made_social_media_marketing_banal.html.

57. Lee Rainie, "Social Media and the 2012 U.S. Presidential Election," Pew Research Center's Internet and American Life Project, briefing to the Foreign Press Center, U.S. Department of State, June 20, 2012, http://fpc.state.gov/193458.htm.

58. "Daily Chart: Money, Votes, and Imponderables," *Economist*, November 6, 2012, www.economist.com/blogs/graphicdetail/2012/11/daily-chart-1.

59. Andie Levien, "Tracking Presidential Campaign Field Operations," FairVote.org, November 14, 2012, www.fairvote.org/tracking-presidential-campaign-field-operations.

60. Michael Scherer, "Inside the Secret World of the Data Crunchers Who Helped Obama Win," *Time Swampland*, November 7, 2012, http://swampland.time.com/2012/11/07/inside-the-secret-world-of-quants-and-data-crunchers-who-helped-obama-win/.

61. Andrew Kohut, "Misreading Election 2012," *Wall Street Journal*, November 13, 2012, http://online.wsj.com/article/SB100014241278873238947045781133231375465160.html.

62. Reid Wilson, "Election Exposes Looming Challenges for Both Parties," *National Journal*, November 7, 2012, www.nationaljournal.com/columns/on-the-trail/election-exposes-looming-challenges-for-both-parties-20121107.

63. Ruy Teixeira and John Halpin, "Opinion: Demographic Fundamentals Remain Critical to 2012 Presidential Outcome," *National Journal*, October 9, 2012, www.nationaljournal.com/thenextamerica/demographics/opinion-demographic -fundamentals-remain-critical-to-2012-presidential-outcome-20121009.

64. Howard Kurtz, "From Newsweek: Hillary in 2016!" *Daily Beast*, November 9, 2012, www.thedailybeast.com/newsweek/2012/11/09/looking-ahead-to -2016-presidential-run.html.

# INDEX

# ABOUT THE CONTRIBUTORS

**Alan Abramowitz** is the Alben Barkley Professor of Political Science at Emory University, a nationally renowned expert on American elections and voting behavior and a regular contributor to the University of Virginia Center for Politics' *Crystal Ball* newsletter. His latest book, *The Polarized Public: Why American Government Is So Dysfunctional*, was published in 2012 by Pearson Longman.

**Jamelle Bouie** is a staff writer at *The American Prospect* and a Knobler Fellow at The Nation Institute. In addition to *The Prospect*, his work has appeared in *The Nation*, *The Atlantic*, CNN, the *Washington Independent*, and the *Washington Post*. He is based in Washington, DC, where he covers campaigns and elections.

**James E. Campbell** is a UB Distinguished Professor of Political Science at the University at Buffalo, SUNY. As the author of three books and over eighty journal articles and book chapters, his research focuses on American elections and campaigns.

**Nate Cohn** is a staff writer at *The New Republic*, where he writes about electoral politics, demographics, and public opinion. Previously, he was a researcher at the Stimson Center, a nonprofit organization focused on international security in Washington, DC.

**Rhodes Cook**, a veteran political reporter and analyst, publishes his own political newsletter, the *Rhodes Cook Letter*, and is a contributor to the University of Virginia Center for Politics' *Crystal Ball* newsletter

**Robert Costa** is Washington editor for *National Review*. Over the course of the 2012 campaign, he interviewed Mitt Romney and Paul Ryan on numerous occasions. He is also a contributor to CNBC, where he frequently appears on *The Kudlow Report*.

**Kyle Kondik** is the house editor at the University of Virginia Center for Politics. Kondik previously worked in newspapers and state government in Ohio.

**Susan MacManus** is the Distinguished University Professor in the Department of Government and International Affairs at the University of South Florida and the long-time political analyst for WFLA-TV (Tampa's NBC affiliate). She is the author of multiple books and articles focusing on electoral politics and demographic trends nationally and in Florida. **David J. Bonanza** is a research associate who routinely works with Susan MacManus on election analyses. He is the president of a math tutoring firm and an honor graduate of the University of South Florida. **Ashleigh Powers** is a research assistant to Susan MacManus. She is an undergraduate student at the University of South Florida majoring in communication and broadcast journalism.

**Diana Owen** is associate professor of political science and director of American studies at Georgetown University. She is the author, with Richard Davis, of *New Media and American Politics* (Oxford, 1998) and *Media Messages in American Presidential Elections* (Greenwood, 1991), and editor of *The Internet and Politics: Citizens, Voters, and Activists*, with Sarah Oates and Rachel Gibson (Routledge, 2006).

**Larry J. Sabato** is the Robert Kent Gooch Professor of Politics at the University of Virginia, and director of its Center for Politics. He is the author or editor of more than twenty books on American politics and elections.

**Geoffrey Skelley** is a political analyst at the University of Virginia Center for Politics. He is a graduate of the University of Virginia and has a master's in political science from James Madison University.

**Michael E. Toner** is a former chairman of the Federal Election Commission and is currently co-chair of the Election Law and Government

Ethics Practice Group at Wiley Rein LLP in Washington, DC. Mr. Toner previously served as general counsel of the 2000 Bush-Cheney presidential campaign, general counsel of the Bush-Cheney Transition Team, and chief counsel of the Republican National Committee. Mr. Toner received a BA with distinction from the University of Virginia, an MA in political science from Johns Hopkins University, and a JD *cum laude* from the Cornell Law School.

**Karen E. Trainer** is a senior reporting specialist at Wiley Rein LLP and previously served as a senior campaign finance analyst at the Federal Election Commission. She holds a BA *cum laude* from Muhlenberg College and an MPP from the George Washington University.

**Sean Trende** is the senior elections analyst for RealClearPolitics. He is the author of *The Lost Majority: Why the Future of Government Is Up for Grabs and Who Will Take It*, and will coauthor the forthcoming *Almanac of American Politics 2014*.